Pathway to Change

Pathway to Change

Culture, Economics, Human Progress, and Prosperity

Naci Mocan

The MIT Press
Cambridge, Massachusetts
London, England

The MIT Press
Massachusetts Institute of Technology
77 Massachusetts Avenue
Cambridge, MA 02139
mitpress.mit.edu

The MIT Press would like to thank the anonymous peer reviewers who provided comments on drafts of this book. The generous work of academic experts is essential for establishing the authority and quality of our publications. We acknowledge with gratitude the contributions of these otherwise uncredited readers.

This book was set in Stone Serif and Stone Sans by Westchester Publishing Services. Printed and bound in the United States of America.

Library of Congress Cataloging-in-Publication Data

Names: Mocan, Naci author
Title: Pathway to change : culture, economics, human progress, and prosperity / Naci Mocan.
Description: Cambridge : The MIT Press, 2026. | Includes bibliographical references and index.
Identifiers: LCCN 2025024945 (print) | LCCN 2025024946 (ebook) | ISBN 9780262053044 paperback | ISBN 9780262053051 pdf | ISBN 9780262053068 epub
Subjects: LCSH: Economics | Organizational change
Classification: LCC HB171 .M5565 2025 (print) | LCC HB171 (ebook)
LC record available at https://lccn.loc.gov/2025024945
LC ebook record available at https://lccn.loc.gov/2025024946

10 9 8 7 6 5 4 3 2 1

EU Authorised Representative: Easy Access System Europe, Mustamäe tee 50, 10621 Tallinn, Estonia | Email: gpsr.requests@easproject.com

To Madeline Mocan, and to the memories
of Leman Mocan and Abidin Mocan

Contents

1 Introduction

I grew up in Istanbul and attended a school that was jointly established by the Turkish and German governments. Students were admitted to this school after completing primary education and received their middle school and high school educations there. The curriculum featured science, mathematics, and German literature classes taught in German by German teachers using German textbooks; other subjects were taught by Turkish teachers in Turkish.

Our German teachers lived in Istanbul for five or six years, sometimes longer, before returning to Germany, and they were succeeded by new teachers. But it was evident that even those who spent more time in Turkey behaved quite differently in certain situations compared to Turks. In particular, we perceived our German teachers as rigid rule followers. For instance, I recall an episode from our first year when the entire class skipped school to attend a basketball game in another part of the city between our school's team and a rival school. The following day, we found ourselves in serious trouble with our German teachers, whereas the Turkish school administration was inclined to overlook the incident. I also remember some of my classmates trying to negotiate with one of our German teachers to round up their grades, only to be told, "There has to be a cutoff somewhere. If your grade is 69.5, it does not mean that it is 70."[1] As eye-opening as it was to hear such a perspective, we found the rigidity of Germans hard to understand in certain situations—like stopping at a red traffic light in the middle of the night when no other cars or pedestrians were in sight.[2] Such behavior was normal practice in Germany, whereas for a Turk it demonstrated lack of judgment and automated rule following with no creativity. (A few decades later, stopping at a red light when nobody is around became normal behavior in Turkey, which I will discuss later in the book.)

Who Trusts Others?

Differences in beliefs and behavioral patterns across societies are striking in some cases, and they can be bewildering. A Turkish friend told me about a scene that surprised her on a recent visit to New York City. During lunch hour, she was on the ground floor of a skyscraper that housed several fast-food restaurants and cafes. Many of these places had shelves filled with brown bags, containing food already prepared and awaiting pickup. Each bag had a ticket, displaying the name of the customer who had ordered the food, as well as the details of the order. She observed people inspecting the tickets, grabbing a bag, and leaving.

What my friend saw was a system adopted by some restaurants in commercial buildings in America. Customers order online, make the payment, wait for ten to fifteen minutes, and then go to the restaurant and retrieve their order by selecting the bag with their name from the many bags waiting. My friend was astounded by the feasibility of this payment system as it relies on trusting people to act honestly. After all, anyone could simply pretend to have placed an order, grab a bag, and walk away without arousing suspicion. Despite this inherent vulnerability, the system's existence indicates that at least some businesses have confidence in the trustworthiness of most individuals, believing that they will not take a bag that does not belong to them. Of course, not everyone behaves honestly, and theft would increase the production costs for restaurants. However, this is factored into the pricing, and whatever the extent of theft, it is clearly not substantial enough to warrant abandoning this trust-based method. But this particular system would not be viable in a setting where distrust is widespread.

The propensity to trust others varies tremendously across countries. A scientific survey, designed to measure trust, selects random groups of individuals from each country to form representative samples, and asks them the following question: "Generally speaking, would you say that most people can be trusted, or that you can't be too careful when dealing with others?"[3]

While more than 65 percent of residents in Scandinavian countries believe that most people are trustworthy, the rate is around 50 percent in Switzerland, Iceland, and New Zealand, and 40 percent in the US. It drops to the 20–25 percent range in Argentina, South Africa, Iran, Israel, and France, and to about 15 percent in Mexico, Tunisia, and Nigeria.

At the low end is Turkey: Only about 10 percent of Turks believe that people are trustworthy. An even smaller percentage of individuals (7 percent or less) in Nicaragua, Brazil, Zimbabwe, and the Philippines believe that others can be trusted.

Lack of trust in a society is undesirable because trust plays a key role in economic activity. Nobel laureate economist Kenneth Arrow argued that "virtually every commercial transaction has within itself an element of trust, certainly any transaction conducted over a period of time. It can be plausibly argued that much of the economic backwardness in the world can be explained by the lack of mutual confidence."[4]

The intuition behind this statement is not difficult to understand. When individuals trust one another, economic transactions can be conducted smoothly and efficiently, resulting in reduced costs. Consider the simplicity of a handshake agreement built on mutual trust. In contrast, when trust is absent, protective measures become necessary, such as strict supervision, random inspections, or drafting detailed contracts covering various contingencies. A lack of trust can impede economic transactions, even with detailed contracts in place, especially when distrust in individuals is coupled with distrust in institutions. For example, if people do not trust their country's judicial system and the courts, then contractual agreements will not necessarily motivate them to participate in economic transactions because they will perceive contract enforcement as uncertain.

Meanwhile, an environment in which people trust others will lead to less waste of resources on self-protection, monitoring others, and legal action. If employers trust that employees will carry out their work diligently without oversight, then no resources will need to be allocated to the surveillance of employees' activities on the job through methods such as rigorous supervision, tracking computer activity, and so on. Labor markets would work more efficiently if people trusted each other. Employers would hire strangers based on their qualifications rather than relying on personal relationships with less qualified individuals they deem trustworthy, like friends or relatives. If customers trust producers and sellers, they will not be reluctant to purchase goods and services from them. If citizens trust politicians and policymakers, then economic and social policies announced by political leaders and laws passed by legislators will have credibility, allowing for reliable long-term private economic planning by firms and households.

Trust between employers and employees, between buyers and sellers, and between citizens and the government therefore would cultivate an economic environment conducive to long-term planning and investment, which would enhance efficiency and economic activity.

An example of the impact of trust on economic transactions is provided by an influential study investigating how bilateral trust between countries affects international trade.[5] The economists who conducted the study analyzed European countries and first demonstrated the existence of substantial differences in trust levels between nations.[6] Among the fifteen countries analyzed, Italians and Greeks are the least trusted populations, while Greeks and Portuguese have the lowest levels of trust in others. Swedes and Norwegians are both the most trusted and the most trusting.[7] The study showed that even after accounting for other factors that affect trade between countries, exports from country A to country B are reduced when citizens of country A have lower trust in the people of country B. Likewise, bilateral trust significantly affects foreign direct investment and portfolio investment between countries.

This is one of many studies showing that people are less willing to engage in economic transactions when they perceive the other party as untrustworthy. Research based on data from various nations has revealed that people who do not trust others are less likely to invest in the stock market and that venture capital firms are less likely to invest in start-ups in countries they trust less. It has been shown that distrust leads to advocacy for extensive government controls over the economy. Countries with high levels of trust impose minimal regulations on starting new businesses. Conversely, in countries where trust levels are low, governments implement stringent regulations and controls. Research has also revealed that the economic growth of countries is positively related to the extent of interpersonal trust.[8] All of this means that economic activity in a society is hindered by a lack of trust among its members—yet the degree of distrust varies greatly between nations.

Who Likes Leisure More?

Similar to the differences in trust levels across nations, preferences for leisure also differ significantly among countries. Unless they are complete workaholics, people enjoy leisure time, during which they do not work but instead engage in recreational activities, spend time with their family and friends, or just relax. However, people in some countries place a greater emphasis on leisure compared to those in other countries. For example, the minimum statutory annual paid leave is twenty-five days in countries such as Austria, Sweden, France, and Denmark. It drops to fifteen days in South Korea, Chile, and Colombia, and to zero in the US. In other words, while the Swedes, Danes, Austrians, and French are entitled to twenty-five days of paid vacation each year, no law in America grants workers the right to any paid vacation.

In the United States, Christmas is observed as a one-day holiday on December 25. In contrast, in Italy, the Christmas holiday is extended, with many nongovernmental institutions closing for a week. In Turkey, when a religious holiday spans from Monday to Wednesday, it's customary for the government to include Thursday and Friday of that week in the holiday, resulting in a shutdown of businesses for the entire week and effectively creating a nine-day vacation period for workers, starting from the previous Saturday and extending to the following Sunday.

The average number of hours worked per year also differs substantially between countries. In a typical year, the average American worker spends 1,800 hours at work, whereas the annual hours worked per worker are 1,700 in Italy, 1,500 in France, and 1,400 in Sweden. Considering a typical workweek of forty hours, this means that an American works almost two months more per year than a typical French worker, and 2.5 months more than a Swedish worker.[9]

Some of the variation in hours worked between countries is related to differences in the economic environment, such as the tax rates, the strength of the labor unions, government regulation of the workplace, and so on. For example, both labor and income tax rates differ among countries, and high income taxes discourage people from supplying extra hours of labor.[10] Similarly, if workers receive unemployment payments from the government for a very long period of time when they lose their jobs, then the average annual number of hours worked in that economy will generally be lower.[11] People's own circumstances are also important determinants of how much they are willing to work in the labor market. Examples include their level of wealth, wage rate, and marital status. But even after accounting for all these economic factors, nontrivial differences remain among countries in the extent to which their residents are willing to spend time working for pay.

Capitalizing on this fact, a TV advertisement for Cadillac automobiles from about ten years ago highlighted the perceived American desire for work and the drive for success, contrasting it with the more laid-back attitude found in some other countries. In the commercial, a middle-aged man stands in front of the swimming pool of his luxury home and asks: "Why do we work so hard?" He points at the pool of his fancy house and asks again: "For what? For this? For stuff?" He then continues: "Other countries. They work, they stroll home. They stop by the café. They take August off. Off!! Why aren't you like that? Why aren't we like that?"

In the next scene, he is walking briskly inside the house, where everyone is busy. Two children seem to be doing their homework. He then answers his own question: "Because we are crazy, driven, hardworking believers. That's why. Those other countries think we are nuts. Whatever! Were the Wright brothers insane? Bill Gates, Les Paul, [Muhammad] Ali?"

In the following scene, he continues his fast-paced walk through the house and encounters his wife, who also seems to be in a hurry, walking quickly toward him. He continues his speech by asking: "Were we nuts when we pointed to the moon? That's right. We went up there. You know what we got? Bored. So we left. Got a car up there. Left the keys in. You know why? Because we are the only ones going back up there. That's why!"

At the end of the clip, he gets into his shiny Cadillac, and declares: "It's pretty simple. You work hard, you create your own luck, and you got to believe anything is possible." While he is driving away, he says: "As for all the stuff: That is the upside of only taking two weeks off in August. *N'est-ce pas*?"

The obvious suggestion of this advertisement is that Americans are fundamentally different from others in their drive for work and success and that they exhibit a stronger preference for work over leisure, compared to residents of other countries.

To quantify the differences in tastes for leisure, I analyzed thousands of individuals from various countries who were asked the following question: "Please tell me if generous holidays are important in a job." Respondents rated their answers on a scale from 0 (not important) to 100 (very important). The average response in each country represents the significance placed on generous holidays as a job attribute by the residents of that country, with higher values indicating stronger importance. The mean value among the forty-four countries analyzed is 30, but there is substantial variation between countries. The average value in the US, Estonia, and Indonesia is about 30–31 out of a maximum of 100. Germany and the Czech Republic have values in the range of 23–25, indicating a lesser emphasis on holidays as a job benefit. In contrast, Russians, Ukrainians, and Belarusians place more emphasis on holidays, with values of 38 to 40. Vietnam has a value of 42, Portugal and Turkey are in the range of 50–51, and Moroccans value generous holiday benefits very highly, with an average response of 77.

So, there are notable differences between countries in the extent to which their citizens would like to take time off from work, participate in leisure activities, and go on vacations. Unsurprisingly, a stronger preference for leisure in a country is associated with fewer hours worked by its residents, which, of course, results in lower levels of production and reduced gross domestic product. As I will discuss later, even if people migrate to and live in a different country, the emphasis on leisure in their country of origin influences how much they work in their new environment.[12]

The main takeaway is that there are substantial differences between nations in how much their residents value leisure time. This variation in preferences for leisure plays a significant role in explaining the differences in economic activity and per capita income between these nations.[13]

Culture and Its Transmission

There are a multitude of other beliefs, attitudes, and behavioral patterns that remain rather stable over time but differ dramatically between countries and sometimes between regions of the same country. These are the *cultural characteristics* of countries.

Various disciplines, ranging from sociology to anthropology, from ethnography to cultural psychology, have defined culture in slightly different ways. The culture of a society can be defined as the collection of values, beliefs, preferences, and behavioral patterns that are common in that society, which are related to customs and norms and which are passed down from generation to generation.

The *values* of a group are the shared beliefs about what is desirable in the group. *Norms* prescribe certain behaviors and prohibit others. These norms, which are commonly shared by the group, lead to cultural practices. Violation of the norms is associated with costs, such as disapproval from the members of the group, being shunned, or more severe social sanctions.

Commonly held values lead to the formation of norms. For example, if a society places a value on personal hygiene and cleanliness, this can lead to the creation of the norm of washing hands before meals. This norm, enforced by society, can become a cultural practice. If the cultural norm of a society dictates that women spend most of their time in the home, this can shape individuals' behaviors, which may lead to outcomes such as lower participation of women in the formal labor market, in politics, and in other spheres of public life.[14]

Culture is passed down from generation to generation but it is also transmitted among the members of the same generation. Friends and peers can influence each other's behaviors, values, and preferences, leading to cultural change within the same generation. In other words, though culture is transmitted vertically across generations, it is also transmitted horizontally via interactions between individuals or groups through socialization processes that lead to imitation and learning, as described in economic models of cultural transmission.[15] For example, a conservative set of parents might instill their conservative values and preferences in their children (vertically), but the children also interact with peers and teachers who may have more liberal perspectives. These interactions may lead to the transmission of these liberal values from peers or teachers (horizontally).

The end result of horizontal and vertical cultural transmissions can be uncertain as it depends on the relative strength of these influences. Furthermore, altruistic parents may consciously choose to either reinforce or limit the transmission of their cultural values and beliefs to their children, based on their assessment of how this will contribute to their children's overall well-being and success in that society.

A similar framework for cultural transmission can be found in theoretical models of cultural evolution developed by evolutionary biologists. In these models, to enhance their well-being, individuals can learn for themselves, but they can also engage in what is termed *social learning*, which refers to imitating someone from the previous generation and copying their behavior.[16] Individual learning is error-prone and costly. The decision to rely on social learning by imitating the behavior of previous generations versus to adopt new behaviors based on individual learning depends on the stability of the environment. In stable environments, social learning may be optimal, while in rapidly changing environments, it may pay off to experiment and rely on individual learning.

As an example, imagine that you're a fisherman, and your father, also a fisherman, passed down all his fishing knowledge to you. He taught you everything, including the types of equipment to use and the best spots to fish based on weather conditions. He might have told you, for instance, "You should fish at Blue Bay when the winds are northerly, but head to Cape Cat when the winds come from the south and the currents are strong." If these conditions remain the same, it makes sense to follow his methods and imitate his behavior, relying on social learning. Straying from these time-tested cultural behavioral patterns might lead to poor results. If the winds are northerly and you decide to fish elsewhere instead of Blue Bay, you might return empty-handed, when fishing in Blue Bay would have guaranteed at least some catch under those conditions.

But imagine the weather patterns have changed: The winds now blow from the east half the time, and the currents have shifted in strength. In this case, it might be worth taking a risk and experimenting in a new spot, relying on individual learning. The changed environment (with new wind and current conditions) could favor a different fishing location or technique, indicating that adapting your father's traditional methods to these new conditions might yield better results.

Similarly, individual learning can take the form of observing and learning from the behavior of others and imitating peers and role models who demonstrate success in areas such as the dating market, wealth accumulation, or social influence. This horizontal transmission of culture between individuals of the same generation plays a significant role in shaping societal norms, and we will explore it in depth later in the book.

The Thesis of the Book

I am an economist, and the central thesis of this book is grounded in academic research in economics, primarily from the past two decades. It also draws on insights from a variety of other fields, including political science, philosophy, social psychology, linguistics, and neuroscience.

Compared to other disciplines, economists have been late to focus on culture and formally incorporate it into their theoretical frameworks for analyzing decision-making. The importance of the context in which decisions are made, as well as the heterogeneity of preferences across decision-makers, has long been acknowledged. However, the challenge of defining and measuring the concept of culture in theoretically coherent ways, which can be used in economic models to create testable implications, and the paucity of real-world data with which to empirically test these models were arguably the main reasons for the delay in focusing on culture.

As its title suggests, this book is about the interplay between culture, human progress, and prosperity. The term *prosperity* might imply a focus on how culture impacts *economic growth*, defined as the increase in a nation's per capita income over time. However, this is a book about prosperity, not about economic growth. Although prosperity is related to economic growth, it includes dimensions of human and societal development not captured by growth. These involve various aspects of a society, such as health, education, freedom of speech, safety, security and the absence of violence, respect for human rights, and quality of life more generally.

Higher income is undoubtedly preferable to lower income, and a higher rate of economic growth is better than economic stagnation. However, prosperity is a broader concept that extends beyond income to include various factors affecting human well-being. Two countries may experience the same economic growth, but if one exhibits higher corruption and greater infringements on individual freedoms and property rights, then its overall prosperity is lower than that of the other.

Over the past two decades, China has achieved remarkable economic growth. Yet according to the United Nations Human Development Index—which considers life expectancy at birth, expected years of schooling, and per capita income—China ranks seventy-fourth globally. It has the highest number of imprisoned journalists worldwide, with forty-four behind bars, accounting for one in five imprisoned journalists globally. More than a quarter of Chinese men believe that it is sometimes or always justified for a man to beat his wife. Despite its economic growth, it is therefore difficult to claim that China is a country where individual well-being is thriving and prosperity is at a high level.

Of course, there cannot be prosperity alongside poverty and lack of economic growth. Although economic growth is not sufficient to achieve prosperity, it is necessary. Certain cultural traits, such as trust, discussed earlier, play a significant role in influencing a country's economic growth. Throughout the book, we will explore other examples of cultural attributes that directly impact economic growth by affecting its key determinants, such as investment and innovation.

The book will provide examples of numerous cultural differences between countries and explore the economic, geographical, and historical factors that have given rise to these cultural differences. It will show that cultural preferences, norms, and behaviors have a direct impact on individuals' well-being. Consequently, cultural differences between nations help explain the variations in people's well-being and prosperity across these nations.

An obvious implication of the previous paragraph is that some cultural preferences, norms, and behaviors are beneficial to human well-being, while others are not so useful or even harmful. Therefore, if we are concerned with human well-being and prosperity, we should find ways to promote beneficial cultural practices and discourage those that are detrimental. The scientific evidence forming the foundation of this book compels us to firmly reject any version of the *cultural relativism* argument, which asserts that all cultural practices are equally beneficial, serve a purpose, and contribute to the well-being of the society that practices them.

However, the goal of the book is not to categorize societies as having "better" or "worse" cultures, but rather to identify cultural norms and practices that have adverse effects or positive impacts on human welfare.

I will also demonstrate how culture changes in response to various factors, sometimes quite rapidly. Finally, using this insight, I will show how policy tools can be effectively leveraged to foster positive cultural change, enhancing individual well-being and prosperity.

Institutions and Culture

Nobel laureate Douglass North defines *institutions* as "the rules of the game in a society" and "humanly devised constraints that shape human interaction."[17] Because culture puts constraints on human behavior and shapes human interactions, culture can be thought of as part of the institutional structure of a society.

However, in this book, I will keep culture outside of institutions and define institutions instead as the rules that determine the political, legal, and economic structure of the society. Political institutions involve types of political systems and governments (democracy vs. dictatorship, parliamentary vs. presidential system, etc.). Legal institutions include constitutions, laws, regulations, and the judicial system. Economic institutions are those that determine the broad parameters of economic transactions—for example, whether they are based on a market economy versus a communist system, whether the property rights of individuals are protected, and so on.

A lot of ink has been spilled over the past three and a half decades discussing the role of institutions in economic growth. A well-known example is England's Bill of Rights of 1689, which established an independent judiciary, granted fundamental rights to citizens, and significantly strengthened the power of Parliament. These institutional reforms are widely believed to have paved the way for England's economic growth.[18]

This book, instead, will demonstrate how formal institutions shape the beliefs, behaviors, and preferences of individuals in a society. In other words, a society's political, legal, and economic structures influence its culture. Culture, in turn, affects individual well-being, economic growth, and prosperity. This does not suggest that the direct impact of institutions on economic growth can be overlooked. In fact, the 2024 Nobel Prize in Economics was awarded to scholars who have demonstrated the significant role institutions play in driving economic growth.[19]

It is important to note that institutional differences between societies do not arise randomly. A society with specific preferences and beliefs will establish and accept institutions that align with those preferences and beliefs. Is it a coincidence that one country has a system of illiberal democracy where elected leaders can act like dictators, while another country operates under a liberal democratic system where elected leaders' power is constrained? Is it by chance that a nation adopts a particular economic system, while a different system is selected by another nation? Is it by chance that workers who lose their jobs receive very generous financial support for long periods of time in some countries, whereas unemployment benefits are very limited in others?[20]

Institutions and culture thus are intertwined, with institutions affecting culture and culture, in turn, influencing institutions. For instance, two nations may have identical laws aimed at safeguarding the judiciary's independence from the executive branch. This means that in both nations, laws may exist to prevent a president or prime minister from influencing the actions and decisions of prosecutors and judges. In practice, however, this legal institutional framework may function very differently in two different societies with different cultural makeups. The intended independence of the judiciary may not work in practice in a society where obedience to authority is a cultural norm, but it may work well in a different society where individualistic culture is dominant.

The impact of culture on the functioning of institutions presents a challenge, especially when proposing institutional reforms. As an example, central bank independence is a desirable institutional characteristic for a country. Economists have long argued that a nation's monetary policy should be determined separately from its fiscal policy, meaning that a central bank should operate independently, free from the influence of government spending decisions. The central bank needs to assess economic conditions independently when making monetary policy decisions, such as adjusting interest rates. The reasoning is straightforward: Without such independence, governments might exert pressure on central banks to adopt policies that, given the current state of the economy, serve short-term political goals but could harm the economy in the long run. For instance, ahead of national elections, a government might push the central bank to lower interest rates to spur borrowing and spending, aiming to stimulate the economy. However, such a move could backfire by driving up inflation later.

To address this issue, the International Monetary Fund (IMF) often requires countries seeking loans during severe economic crises to implement institutional safeguards that ensure central bank independence from the executive branch. In some cases, securing an IMF loan is contingent upon the country enacting reforms that protect this independence. These reforms might include legislation that establishes checks and balances, such as appointing a central bank president to an extended term, and restricting the ability of the prime minister or president to fire the central bank president.

The central bank of the United States (the Federal Reserve, a.k.a. the Fed) has this type of independence. The chair of the Federal Reserve is appointed for a four-year term by the president of the US, but the president does not have the authority to fire the chair of the Fed unless there is evidence of serious misconduct or inability to perform the duties of the office. In US history, no Federal Reserve chair has ever been removed from office before the end of their term.

During his first term in office, President Trump frequently exerted pressure on Federal Reserve Chairman Jerome Powell to maintain low interest rates, especially throughout 2019. Trump repeatedly called for rate cuts, arguing that they were necessary to stimulate economic growth and keep the US competitive on the global stage. Despite these demands, Chairman

Powell remained steadfast in his approach, basing monetary policy decisions on economic data rather than political influence. Trump's efforts to sway the Fed were ultimately unsuccessful, as Powell continued to act independently, adhering to the Federal Reserve's mandate.

In contrast, there are numerous examples from other countries where similar pressures from the president or prime minister resulted in the central bank president complying with government demands, despite legal safeguards meant to ensure the bank's independence. In other cases, if the central bank head resisted, they were dismissed and replaced with someone more amenable to implementing the government's desired monetary policy.

This stark difference can be attributed to various cultural factors, including attitudes toward hierarchy and power, as well as tendencies toward corruption. These cultural differences determine how the central bank's institutional independence is maintained or undermined in practice.

Consider another example, though unrelated to institutional reform, that highlights how the success of a policy can vary depending on the cultural context in which it is implemented. The cultural attribute here is the practice of handwashing. There are marked differences between countries in how frequently people wash their hands at critical times, such as before preparing food, before eating, after cleaning a child, and after using the bathroom. In developing nations, the rate of handwashing is approximately 30 percent, and it can be as low as zero in some regions.[21] Although economic development plays a role in access to water and sanitation, which in turn affects handwashing practices, substantial variation exists between countries with similar economic development levels and access to sanitation. This suggests that the lack of handwashing and its persistence over time, as recognized by the World Bank, the United Nations, and the World Health Organization (WHO), has a strong habitual and cultural component.

A recent joint report by WHO and UNICEF highlights the variation in handwashing before eating and after using the toilet in schools across Latin American and Caribbean countries, stating that "the availability of handwashing facilities at schools does not ensure students always wash their hands at critical times."[22]

Now, imagine you work for a charitable organization that raises funds to build and equip healthcare facilities worldwide—specifically, facilities to treat infectious diseases. You build hospitals in various countries, install beds and equipment, provide funds to hire doctors and nurses, and begin operations. After some time, you review the data and notice significant differences in the hospitals' effectiveness in treating infections and in the rates of infections occurring in these hospitals. The same type of hospital, treating similar patients, yields different health outcomes in different countries.

One key reason for the variation in hospital effectiveness is the difference in handwashing practices across healthcare facilities in various countries. Medical research reveals that healthcare-associated infections affect hundreds of millions of patients annually. Hand hygiene is acknowledged as the most effective and cost-efficient method to prevent these infections. Numerous studies have shown that contaminated hands of healthcare workers are the primary mechanism through which pathogens are transmitted in hospitals and other healthcare settings, and a recent survey conducted in ninety countries highlights significant disparities across nations in the handwashing practices of healthcare workers.[23]

Furthermore, there are other cultural differences related to religious practices that affect hand hygiene in health care. The report *WHO Guidelines on Hand Hygiene* contains a chapter titled "Religious and Cultural Aspects of Hand Hygiene," in which it is written: "In some populations, both inherent and elective hand hygiene practices are deeply influenced by cultural and religious factors. . . . As an example, in the Hindu culture, hands are rubbed vigorously with ash or mud and then rinsed with water. The belief behind this practice is that soap should not be used as it contains animal fat."[24] It goes on to add the following:

> In some religions, alcohol use is prohibited or considered an offence requiring a penance (Sikhism) because it is considered to cause mental impairment (Hinduism, Islam). As a result, the adoption of alcohol-based formulations as the gold standard for hand hygiene may be unsuitable or inappropriate for some HCWs [health care workers], either because of their reluctance to have contact with alcohol, or because of their concern about alcohol ingestion or absorption via the skin. Even the simple denomination of the product as an "alcohol-based formulation" could become a real obstacle in the implementation of WHO recommendations.

This means that the effectiveness of hospitals will vary significantly based on culturally ingrained handwashing habits among both patients and medical staff. Therefore, the investment (outlays for the hospital) will provide differential returns (patient health outcomes) based on the cultural attributes of the location of the hospital. We will discuss in chapter 6 a more concrete example of a failed attempt to change the institutional design, implemented in hospitals in India. But the key takeaway here is that the effectiveness of institutions depends on the cultural context of the society in which they operate. More generally, we will examine in this book how institutions, political and economic conditions, and culture all influence one another.

A final thought on institutions pertains to religion. Religion influences the behavior of its followers by establishing guidelines on what is acceptable or unacceptable in different areas of life. In this way, religion functions as an institution, shaping norms that govern actions ranging from dietary rules (e.g., no alcohol for Muslims, no shellfish for Jews, no beef for Hindus) to sexual conduct to obligations for charity. Some religions also regulate economic practices, with usury laws in Islam and Catholicism serving as notable examples.[25] Any comprehensive definition of religion acknowledges its institutional aspect, as in the following description: "Religion, or what societies hold sacred, comprises an institutionalized system of symbols, beliefs, values, and practices focused on questions of ultimate meaning."[26]

So religion can be classified as an informal or social institution, distinguishing it from formal institutions like legal, political, and economic systems.[27] At the same time, religion is woven into the cultural fabric of society, passed down through generations, with differing religious doctrines leading to tangible differences across societies.

The Rest of the Book

In the next chapter, I will present various examples of cultural attitudes, beliefs, and behaviors that differ significantly across societies. These will include honesty, perceptions of economic fairness, women's participation in the workforce, the prevalence of individualistic attitudes, and domestic violence against women. The chapter will also discuss the persistence of cultural norms, even when they harm human well-being or lack a scientific foundation, and will provide insights into how these beliefs and norms have developed over time.

Chapter 3 will discuss the origins of culture, focusing on ancient agricultural production technologies. It will explore how the suitability of land for different types of farming has led to the emergence of long-lasting cultural differences among societies, including variations in women's participation in the labor market, and tendencies toward violence, such as homicide and female genital mutilation. Chapter 4 continues the discussion of how ecology and historical production methods have shaped cultural norms, beliefs, and practices. It provides examples such as societal preferences for sons over daughters, tendencies toward individualism, and varying levels of patience.

Although a country's geographical location plays a significant role in shaping its cultural attributes, it is not the sole factor influencing culture. Chapter 5 demonstrates that geography alone does not determine a society's destiny. This chapter highlights how exposure to violence serves as a critical factor in shaping key cultural attributes, such as trust and tendencies toward further violence, using examples that span a wide range of contexts—from the Crimean Tatars to the African Slave Trade, and from soccer players in Europe to Black jockeys in America.

Chapter 6 describes the impact of institutions on cultural beliefs and attitudes through various examples, such as the effects of communism, the influence of corruption in Ottoman, Russian, and Habsburg bureaucracies, and the role of the Protestant Reformation in shaping Jewish lending practices and the subsequent rise of anti-Semitism. This chapter also examines the interplay between culture and institutions, emphasizing that the success of institutional reforms depends on the cultural composition of the society in which they are implemented.

Chapter 7 presents the connection between language and culture, illustrating how language serves as a cultural marker and shapes the way individuals perceive and think about concepts such as the present versus the future, influencing their decisions and behaviors. Drawing on evidence from neuroscience, the chapter highlights how learning new skills—particularly language—affects cognition and demonstrates how the complexity or simplicity of a language can impact culture.

Chapter 8 examines morality as a cultural attribute, explains why ethics and moral standards vary across societies, and investigates how these differences are linked to disparities in economic outcomes. It discusses cultural differences in moral behavior, such as the propensity to cheat or exploit others, the tendency to offer preferential treatment to in-group members, and the inclination to discriminate against outsiders.

Chapter 9 is focused on cultural persistence and the mechanisms of cultural transmission, including vertical transmission from parents to children and horizontal transmission through social interactions. It provides examples of persistent cultural beliefs and attitudes, such as the belief in the power of the Dragon in the Chinese zodiac, anti-Semitism, and witch killings. The chapter also examines how economic conditions and exposure to "others" can influence and alter cultural norms.

Chapter 10 discusses cultural contagion and spillovers, highlighting how dishonesty and lawbreaking can spread within a society, ultimately altering cultural norms. It illustrates how the enforcement of laws and the deterrence of illicit and dishonest acts can create positive spillover effects, making them powerful tools for fostering positive cultural change. The chapter also explores how the actions of political and religious leaders shape individual behavior by signaling prevailing or desired social norms.

Chapter 11 provides examples of how the media, the education system, and institutional changes act as powerful tools for shaping and transforming culture.

Finally, chapter 12 offers a summary and concluding thoughts, emphasizing that achieving greater human well-being and prosperity may require cultural change. It underscores the idea that a vast body of scientific research across disciplines such as economics, neuroscience, and social psychology has provided valuable tools that can be leveraged to facilitate cultural transformation.

2 Cultural Differences Between Societies

This chapter will present examples of cultural differences between societies, including norms of economic fairness and the desire to take revenge when those norms are violated, women's participation in paid employment outside of the home, tendencies toward violence, individualistic versus collectivist attitudes, the practice of marrying blood relatives, and intrinsic honesty.

This is not an exhaustive list of cultural differences between societies; others will be provided in later chapters. Nevertheless, these examples demonstrate the remarkable variation in cultural norms and behaviors across countries. In the second part of this chapter, I will discuss the purpose of cultural norms, as well as their persistence, and provide examples of how they emerge.

Economic Fairness

The notion of economic fairness differs between societies. Consider a scenario in a checkout line at a supermarket. The line is long, and everyone in line has a few items. Suddenly, a customer arrives at the end of the line, observes how long the line is, and mentions that she has only one item to purchase and that she is in a hurry. Hearing this, the person at the front of the line offers to swap places with her for ten dollars. The offer is accepted, and these two individuals swap places. Is this transaction between these two customers fair and acceptable?

Right before the collapse of the Soviet Union, economists conducted a survey in Moscow and asked people for their opinions on the scenario just described.[1] Seventy percent of Russians objected to this transaction. This strong negative reaction is surprising for economists because the transaction is just between two customers, with no negative impact on anybody else.[2]

But the customer who was at the end of the line is better off because she accepted the offer made to her. We can infer that she is better off because even though she gave up ten dollars, she did this voluntarily to save time and leave the store quickly. Although the customer at the front of the line moved to the end, we know this move made him better off because the transaction (receiving ten dollars in exchange for moving) was his idea.

In other words, this exchange made two people better off without making anyone else worse off—so this was a good move for the "society" consisting of the people waiting in line. Yet because the majority evidently viewed this voluntary exchange between two people as akin to cutting the line and gaining an unfair advantage, they likely would have stopped this transaction if they had the authority, considering it unjust.

When provided with the same scenario, only 44 percent of New Yorkers indicated their annoyance with this transaction under the same circumstance. The difference between Russians and Americans was likely the reflection of the communist mindset that was prevailing in Russia, underlining different concepts of fairness in economic transactions between societies with different economic structures.[3] The influence of economic and political institutions on people's beliefs and behaviors will be discussed in detail in chapter 6.

Fairness and Revenge

Consider a second fairness example. Imagine that you hit the lottery jackpot and suddenly received a large sum of money. Would you share part of your fortune with a complete stranger? A related question is whether you would be pleased if one of your friends received a large, unexpected sum of money and shared a small portion with you as a gift, or would you feel disappointed and upset by the modest amount she deems appropriate to give, given her newfound wealth?

To make these hypothetical questions more concrete, imagine a game between two people. The rules are as follows. A coin flip determines who will be Player A and who will be Player B. Once this is determined, Player A is given a sum of money and asked to decide how much of it to share with Player B. The game is played anonymously, meaning that the players don't know each other's identity, but they are aware of the amount of money involved in the game.

Player A can offer any amount to Player B, from zero to the entire amount given to him. At that point, Player B has two options: to accept or to reject the offer. If Player B accepts the offer, he keeps the money offered to him, Player A retains the rest, and the game ends. If Player B rejects the offer, nobody gets anything, and the game is over.

In this so-called ultimatum game, the rational decision for Player A is to offer the smallest possible amount of the money given to him. This is because Player B, who receives the offer, has no money to start off with, and even the lowest offer from Player A is better than nothing. If Player B rejects the offer, he will leave the game with no money. So, rationality dictates that Player B should accept any offer so long as it is greater than zero. Knowing this, Player A should offer as little as possible. Therefore, the expected rational outcome of this game is for Player A to offer the smallest amount possible to Player B, and for Player B to accept the offer.

This experiment has been conducted by economists many times in many different countries. Two striking results emerged. First, those in the role of Player A don't offer the smallest amount possible to the opposing players. In fact, the average offer in these ultimatum games is around 40 percent of the money given to Players A. That Players A offer a substantial portion of the money to Players B (instead of offering, say, 4 or 5 percent) indicates that they consider some notion of "fairness" in the division of the money and that they probably also think about what kind of offer Player B would consider a fair proposal.

Second, although it is in the interest of Player B to accept any offer greater than zero, people in the Player B position do not always behave that way. Instead, they frequently reject the offers made to them. As a result, they end up with nothing, but by doing so they also reduce Player A's payoff to nothing. In other words, Player B punishes Player A for proposing a division of money that Player B evidently deems unfair, and he willingly makes himself worse off in the process by rejecting the offer.

Of course, very small offers are easy to reject, but the stakes in these games are not too small. The money given to player A is typically equivalent to the income a typical worker can earn in a day or two. Therefore, even a small offer, such as 10 percent of the available money, is not insignificant. Nevertheless, people in Player B positions frequently reject small percentage offers made to them.

Perhaps the more interesting aspect of this game is that people's behaviors are quite different based on the country in which they live. The rejection rate of offers is less than 5 percent in Paraguay, Peru, Bolivia, Mongolia, and Kenya. This means that almost all Players B in these countries accept any offer made to them by Players A. The rejection rates go up to about 10 percent in Germany, Zimbabwe, the Netherlands, and in the Western states of the US. The rejection rates are in the range of 20–30 percent in Tanzania, Japan, Spain, the UK, Israel, Romania, and the Eastern states of the US. About one in three offers is rejected in France and Papua New Guinea.[4] So the inclination to inflict punishment on someone due to the perception of being treated unfairly, and harming yourself in the process, varies from country to country.

These cross-country differences suggest that people in different societies vary in their assessment of what is fair and what is unfair, and that they differ in their proclivity to punish those whom they consider to be violators of the norm of fairness.[5]

Are You an Honest Person?

In addition to beliefs about economic fairness, trust, and preferences for leisure, discussed already, there are a host of other beliefs and behaviors that differ between nations. For example, in some countries people cheat more on their taxes; they steal more; they are more likely to conceal the defects of merchandise they are selling; and they are more likely to buy something they know or suspect is stolen. They also are more tolerant of dishonesty. In other words, intrinsic honesty differs across societies.

In a research project focusing on the determinants of honesty, my colleagues and I used data from European countries.[6] I will discuss this research later in the book, but one key finding is the existence of substantial differences across nations in people's proclivity for lawbreaking and dishonesty. When asked the question: "Over the last five years, have you bought something you thought might be stolen?", less than 2 percent of the Portuguese answered in the affirmative. About 5 percent of people in Bulgaria and Poland said they bought stolen goods. The rate is about 8 percent in Spain, and 13 percent in Slovakia. Fifteen percent of people in the Czech Republic reported that they bought something they thought was stolen.

When asked about their bribery experience, almost no one (less than 1 percent of residents) in Iceland, Finland, and Norway stated that they offered a bribe to a public official in return for their services during the last five years. The proportion of people who offered a bribe was 5 percent in Poland, and 9 percent in the Czech Republic and Slovakia.[7]

Importantly, the data also revealed significant differences between countries in the *tolerance for* and *acceptance of* illegal and dishonest behaviors. In the same survey, people were asked, "How wrong is a public official asking someone for a favor or bribe in return for their services?" In answering this question, if the respondent stated that the public official was "Not wrong at all" or "A bit wrong," this indicated that the respondent found bribery acceptable. The proportion of such responses, declaring bribery as appropriate behavior, was 2 percent or less in Germany, Denmark, and Iceland. It was 4 percent in Poland, and more than 6 percent in Spain.

The proportion of people who indicated that it was "Not wrong at all" or only "A bit wrong" to the question of "How wrong is it to buy something you thought might be stolen?" ranged from 3 percent in Denmark to 15 percent in Croatia to 22 percent in France to 30 percent in Russia. Finally, consider the following statement: "If you want to make money, you can't always act honestly." The proportion of individuals who agreed with this statement varied widely across nations. Only 31 percent of the Portuguese agreed that you cannot always act honestly if you want to make money, whereas the rate was 42 percent in Sweden, almost 60 percent in Turkey, 65 percent in Hungary, and 70 percent in Italy.

In another project, I analyzed data from around the world to investigate the determinants of exposure to bribery across countries.[8] Large groups of randomly selected people from many countries were asked: "During the past year has any government official—for instance, a customs officer, police officer, or inspector in your own country—asked you or expected you to pay a bribe for his services?" Fewer than 1 percent of the respondents answered this question affirmatively in high-income countries such as the US, Japan, Switzerland, Canada, and the Scandinavian countries. But there is wide variation between countries that are in the same income category and in the same geography. For example, among Latin American countries, the proportion of people who were asked to give a bribe range from 14 percent in Paraguay to 29 percent in Argentina. The rate is 5 percent in Mongolia and 21 percent in the Kyrgyz Republic, both of which are situated in the same geographical region and have similar per capita incomes. The corruption rate is 7 percent in Zimbabwe and 24 percent in Uganda. It is

5 percent in Poland, but 11 percent in Romania and 19 percent in Ukraine and Russia.

In the same vein, a group of researchers conducted the following experiment in various countries.[9] They pretended to have found wallets on the street, which contained the equivalent of thirteen dollars in the local currency, adjusted for the purchasing power level in each country. For example, the wallets contained 20.75 Swiss francs in Switzerland, 9 euros in Greece, 11 euros in France, 49 yuan in China, 51,300 rupiah in Indonesia, and 16 Turkish liras in Turkey when the experiments were conducted between 2013 and 2016. The wallets had the name, phone number, and email address of the fictional owner inside. The researchers handed the wallets to random persons to see if they would contact the owners of the wallets. The phone numbers and the email addresses of "lost wallets" were linked to the research group. This lost wallet experiment has been conducted seventeen thousand times (handing out wallets to seventeen thousand people), in 355 cities of forty countries.

The results revealed significant differences between countries in the likelihood of returning the wallet to its owner, as opposed to keeping the wallet and its contents. The return rates were low in China, Morocco, Peru, Kazakhstan, Ghana, Kenya, Mexico, and Malaysia, ranging from 10 to 15 percent. They were in the range of 55–65 percent in the US, the UK, Romania, Canada, France, Russia, Germany, and Spain. Meanwhile, more than 80 percent of wallets were returned in Denmark, Sweden, and New Zealand.

The rate of wallet returns is positively correlated with the per capita income of countries. This is not surprising because a randomly selected person from a high-income country is less likely to be unemployed or living in poverty, compared to a person from a low-income country. Therefore, on average, people from wealthier countries have less financial incentive to keep the wallet compared to people from poor countries. However, return rates vary significantly between countries that are more or less in the same income level. For example, the World Bank classifies Peru, Mexico, China, Malaysia, Turkey, Thailand, and Brazil as upper-middle-income countries. In Peru and Mexico, only 15 percent of people chose to return the wallets to their owner. In China and Malaysia, 20 percent of people opted to return the wallets. The rate of returned wallets was 40 percent in Turkey and Thailand, and 50 percent in Brazil.

United Arab Emirates, Italy, the US, Australia, and Denmark are high-income countries, but only 35 percent of people returned the wallets they found in the United Arab Emirates. The rate of returned wallets ranged from 50 percent in Italy to 60 percent in the US, 70 percent in Australia, and 80 percent in Denmark.

These examples illustrate that societies exhibit differences in the extent of their honesty, the propensity for illicit behavior, and tolerance toward dishonest and criminal acts. These differences cannot be fully explained by variations in economic development levels between these nations.

Other Differences Between Countries

There are other, well-known, persistent differences across countries. In some countries, people are more individualistic, whereas they are more collectivist in others. *Individualistic countries* are those where ties between individuals are loose; people are expected to look after themselves and their immediate family. In contrast, in *collectivist societies*, people are integrated from birth onward into strong, cohesive groups, such as extended families, which continue protecting them in exchange for unquestioning loyalty.[10] Autonomy and personal initiative are important in individualistic societies, with individuals seeing themselves as masters of their own destiny. In contrast, collectivist societies prioritize duties and obligations, and conformity to the group is expected.

The widely used *individualism index*, created by Dutch sociologist Geert Hofstede, evaluates and ranks countries, with lower values of the index representing more collectivist societies and higher values indicating more individualism.[11] In this rating, the Unites States, Australia, and the UK are the most individualistic countries, with scores of 91, 90, and 89, respectively. The most collectivist countries are Indonesia, Pakistan, Colombia, Venezuela, Panama, Ecuador, and Guatemala, with scores below 15. China, Thailand, and Nigeria are also collectivist countries, with scores of 20. Turkey, Greece, and Uruguay have somewhat higher individualism scores in the range of 35–37. Spain, Israel, Hungary, and Austria range from 51 to 55. Belgium, Italy, New Zealand, and the Netherlands have high individualism scores: between 75 and 80.

Collectivist societies differ from individualistic ones in many ways. Geographic mobility is lower in collectivist societies; people tend to live close to their communities and families instead of moving to other cities for jobs or other reasons. It has been shown that more individualistic societies produce more innovation and achieve higher rates of economic growth in the long term because they reward personal achievement more than collectivist ones. Studies indicate that collectivist countries embrace democracy later than individualistic countries, and they are more likely to switch to autocracy. Also, economic growth takes place at a slower pace in collectivist countries.[12]

Another notable difference between countries is the rate at which women work outside the home for pay. In some countries, women participate in the labor force at high rates, while in others, their involvement in work outside the home is very limited. In Algeria, Iran, and Egypt, fewer than twenty of every one hundred women aged fifteen to sixty-four participate in the labor market. The rate is around 40 percent in Turkey, Sri Lanka, and Guatemala. It is around 55 percent in Mongolia, Romania, and Chile. Meanwhile, seventy out of every one hundred women in the same age bracket work for pay in the US, China, Russia, and Azerbaijan; and female labor force participation rate is 80 percent or higher in Switzerland, Iceland, and Madagascar.[13] Economic conditions of countries; human capital levels, measured by the quantity and quality of education; and religion-related factors partly explain these differences. However, even after adjusting for these determinants, large and persistent differences in female labor force participation rates remain between countries.

A low rate of female labor force participation does not imply that women do not engage in work, nor does it mean that women do not contribute to the economy. Housework, childcare, and work in the informal economy, where work for pay is not recorded, all contribute to economic activity. Nevertheless, the observed differences across countries in women's propensity to work for pay suggest that gender roles regarding working outside the home are quite different between nations.

In some countries, people do not marry their blood relatives. In other countries, as high as 50 percent of all marriages take place between first or second cousins. As I will discuss in chapter 11, though the offspring of blood-related parents face significant health risks, these marriages can offer economic and other benefits to the families involved, which may explain their continued practice. Although specific types of religion may shape individuals' inclination to marry blood relatives, the prevalence of consanguineous marriages varies significantly across countries that share the same religious tradition. Take Morocco, Turkey, Qatar, and Saudi Arabia, for example, which are all Muslim-majority countries. Although only 10 percent of all marriages take place between people who are first or second cousins in Morocco, the rate is 20 percent in Turkey. It goes up to 30 percent in Qatar, and 40 percent in Saudi Arabia.[14] This variation indicates that other differences between countries beyond religion determine the acceptability of marrying a blood relative.

The extent and tolerance of violence against women is another societal attribute exhibiting tremendous variation between countries. When asked, "Please tell me whether you think it can always be justified, never be justified, or something in between for a man to beat his wife," a small percentage of men in some countries believe that this act can be justified. In some other countries, a significant percentage find wife-beating acceptable.[15] Specifically, global responses to this question reveal that though only 6 percent of German men and 13 percent of American men consider such domestic violence acceptable, more than a quarter of Chinese and Turkish men think that this act might be justifiable. The rate goes up to 35 percent in Mexico and to 45 percent in Russia. At least half of men in South Korea, Egypt, Malaysia, Philippines, and Kenya think that domestic violence may be justified, and the rate is a staggering 63 percent in Vietnam, 66 percent in Mongolia, and 73 percent in Tajikistan.[16]

The Purpose of Cultural Norms and Cultural Persistence

Cultural customs and norms, which are passed down from generation to generation, have emerged in the first place because they served a purpose. Examples are not difficult to find. I live in Louisiana, the cuisine of which is primarily based on seafood. Louisiana, located on the Gulf of Mexico, offers ideal conditions for oyster farming at the delta where the Mississippi River meets the gulf, and oysters are a significant element in the state's cuisine. Louisianians observe a custom of eating oysters only in months that include the letter *r* in their name—namely, September to April. That is, local people avoid eating oysters during the months of May, June, July, and August. These are summer months with warm ocean waters and hot air temperatures, where the likelihood of bacterial infection in oysters rises. Eating raw oysters during these months can result in illness.

The tradition of refraining from eating oysters during months without the letter *r* likely originated from previous generations discovering the detrimental health effects associated with consuming oysters in those months. With the advancement of refrigeration technology, the consumption of oysters is now safer even in the summer months. As a result, the practice of avoiding oyster consumption during the summer is fading, although it has not disappeared. In chapter 9, I will discuss the topic of why certain cultural behaviors change, while others persist—even if they are detrimental to human well-being.

Some cultural behaviors are clearly harmful. In ancient Aztec society, a cultural norm required the sacrifice of some citizens on certain days of the year; their hearts were taken out of their chests to appease the gods and prevent natural disasters. The loss of life in the Aztec ritual may have brought comfort and a sense of safety to society. Anthropologists suggest that some members of the Aztec society may have even voluntarily offered themselves to be sacrificed, perceiving it as a source of honor and a gateway to a blessed afterlife. The practice may have also served as a vehicle to demonstrate the power of the ruling class and to intimidate adversaries.[17] So this gory cultural practice served a purpose. But seven hundred years later, with our current understanding of science and with a goal of improving human well-being and respecting human dignity, this practice is not tolerated in any society today.

Although human sacrifice, as practiced by the Aztecs, no longer occurs anywhere on the planet, other violent cultural practices continue to exist. Examples include honor killings, which are prevalent in parts of the Middle East, witch killings in certain regions of Africa, and female genital mutilation, which will be discussed in later chapters.

Certain behaviors that are rooted in culture, although not as violent as killing or mutilating a person, continue despite being unambiguously detrimental to human well-being. One example is the practice of open defecation in India, where a substantial portion of the population goes to the bathroom not inside of a dwelling, but in outdoor locations such as behind bushes, in fields, in rivers, and at roadside areas. WHO and UNICEF reported in 2015 that nine hundred million people in the world practiced open defecation, and about 524 million of them resided in India.[18]

This widespread unsanitary practice causes serious health issues. Exposure to fecal contamination leads to the spread of disease and death. About three hundred thousand children die each year from diarrhea in India, and about 3 percent of children die before their fifth birthday.[19] In addition, *stunting* in children, which refers to a child being too short for his/her age, is a major problem.[20] Mental and physical development is hindered in stunted children because their bodies are continuously fighting exposure to bacteria, chronic infections, and parasites. These children do not develop well physically—and, more importantly, their brain development is hindered.

One of every three children under the age of five are stunted in India. More than one-third of the 150 million stunted children in the world live in India.[21] Given that stunting is irreversible and that it permanently damages brain development and cognition (in addition to impeding physical development), this is a problem of epic proportions that impacts the economic development of the country because millions of children, cohort after cohort, do not fulfill the potential that they could have achieved had they not been stunted. These children are destined to have less education, lower productivity, worse health outcomes, and lower earning power as an adult in comparison to what they could have accomplished in the absence of stunting.[22]

Although poverty-related malnutrition and inadequate access to running water are also factors that impact child stunting, they are not the primary causes of the extreme stunting rate in Indian children. Rather, open defecation is the culprit. We know this because the prevalence of stunting is also high among the wealthiest Indian families: One-third of stunted children are from the country's richest families.[23]

The root of this behavior of open defecation is attributed to the concept of *purity*. The ancient Hindu notion of cleanliness dictated that people defecate at a safe distance from their residence because it was believed that having latrines inside or near the house was spiritually polluting. A few centuries ago, when population density was low, the practice of people relieving themselves away from home may have constituted less of a problem. However, in today's India, with 1.4 billion people and a population density of 464 people per square kilometer (which is one of the highest population densities in the world, and more than twelve times higher than that of the US), this cultural practice has become a catastrophic health hazard.[24]

Acknowledging the magnitude of the problem, the Indian government initiated its ambitious *Swachh Bharat Mission* (Clean India Mission) in 2014 with a goal of building one hundred million toilets. In October 2019, Prime Minister Narendra Mondi declared India "open defecation free." Despite this Herculean effort of the Indian government, which cost $31 billion, the practice of open defecation does not seem to have changed drastically. Although the program created access to toilets for 94 percent of the population,

15 percent of the population, and 30–40 percent of those who live in rural areas, still defecate in the open.

A key barrier to the elimination of open defecation is the cultural concept of what constitutes purity and dirtiness, and the resultant persistence in attitudes and behaviors. Many Indians consider relieving themselves outside to be part of a wholesome, healthy, virtuous life.[25] This is acknowledged by Sue Coates, chief of water, sanitation, and hygiene (WASH) at UNICEF, who stated, "Just building toilets is not going to solve the problem, because open defection is a practice acquired from the time you learn how to walk. When you grow up in an environment where everyone does it, even if later in life you have access to proper sanitation, you will revert back to it."[26] The *New York Times* quoted Jairam Ramesh, a former sanitation minister of India, who noted, "We need a cultural revolution in this country to completely change people's attitudes towards sanitation and hygiene."[27]

This problem in India is an uncomfortable example of how certain cultural behaviors can persist for centuries and still exist today even though they are detrimental to human well-being.

Persistence and Malleability

Another example of a cultural belief that has persisted for hundreds of years and that continues to exist today is the belief in the power of the zodiac in the Chinese culture.[28] The traditional Chinese zodiac has twelve animal signs, which supposedly represent different characteristics of the people born in different Chinese lunar years. The order of the zodiac animals is Rat, Ox, Tiger, Rabbit, Dragon, Snake, Horse, Sheep, Monkey, Rooster, Dog, and Pig. Of these twelve signs, the Dragon is considered special because of its place in legends and myths. The Dragon is a symbol of power and greatness in Chinese culture, and Chinese people believe that babies born in a Dragon year will have better fortunes than babies born in other years. Chinese parents try to time their pregnancies for their offspring to be born in a Dragon year.[29] This belief in the power of being born in a Dragon year has persisted for hundreds of years.

The zodiac follows the Chinese lunar calendar; therefore, each sign appears approximately every twelve years. For example, the period between February 10, 2024, and January 28, 2025, was a Dragon year. The Year of the Rabbit, which precedes the Dragon year, started on January 22, 2023, and ended on February 9, 2024. Thus, according to this cultural belief, a child born on February 10, 2024, is destined for greatness because she was born on the first day of a Dragon year, but a child born the previous day, on February 9, 2024, will not be as fortunate because she was born in a Rabbit year.

Of course, absent extraordinary circumstances such as prenatal exposure to some shock induced by war, chemical pollutants, or the like, having been born on a particular day cannot influence a person's life in comparison to someone born a few days, weeks, or months before or after. So how could such a belief, without a scientific basis, become embedded in the culture of a society for centuries? I will provide the answer in chapter 9.

Although some cultural beliefs and behavioral patterns seem to be very stable, as in the example of the Chinese belief in the power of the Dragon sign, others change rather quickly despite having persisted for generations. During my childhood in Istanbul, a cultural behavioral norm, which was applied to adults but not children, was to refrain from eating in public. Defying this norm, such as by eating a sandwich on the street, was considered crass, and it was frowned upon.

This custom also manifested in other forms. For example, society expected that food purchased from grocers, bakeries, butchers and other vendors would be carried in paper bags or in cloth bags to conceal the contents. The overarching aspect of this custom, which was part of a broader cultural attribute, was modesty.

Part of the reason for this custom was likely a desire to prevent envy. It is difficult to pin down when and how this behavioral pattern emerged in the distant past, but it is not difficult to imagine that it served a purpose in ancient societies with low average income and high income inequality. In such societies, conspicuous consumption could create resentment, which could lead to social unrest. Yet this particular tradition, which persisted for many generations, has been completely abandoned in a span of a couple of decades. In Turkey, eating a hamburger on the street would not evoke envy or malice because everyone can afford a hamburger. But income inequality is significant, and not everyone can afford to eat filet mignon, drive a luxury sports car, or vacation at a five-star resort. Nonetheless, conspicuous consumption of luxury goods and services is no longer frowned upon. Revealing to the world, through various means—including social media—what is being consumed at any given instant, ranging from an exotic dish to champagne, has become the new behavioral pattern in a society in which such behavior would have been unthinkable only thirty years ago.

Cultural preferences, beliefs, and attitudes are malleable. They change through interactions with and learning from the environment, including peers, society members, social networks, media, and role models. Cultural behaviors and norms also change in response to education, and they adjust to modifications in external constraints, such as laws and sanctions. The ways in which culture can be altered are a key focus of this book and will be discussed in chapter 11.

Emergence of Beliefs and Norms

Some cultural beliefs have emerged from a combination of random events and fears. For example, ethnographer and anthropologist Adolph Bastian described an outbreak of bubonic plague in the nineteenth century in the Malembo municipality of Angola. It was believed that the plague was caused by the death of a white Portuguese person in the area. This belief prompted the residents of Malembo to take precautions to prevent further deaths of white people in their community. It is unclear whether the Portuguese individual brought the disease to the town or contracted it there, but his death appears to have sparked the belief that any white person who died in Malembo would generate an outbreak of disease.[30]

Eating out at Chinese restaurants has become a custom for Jewish people who migrated to New York City from Eastern Europe at the end of the nineteenth century. It has even been said that Chinese cuisine is so beloved among New York Jews that it is their secondary cuisine. Chinese food does not contain milk and milk products. Thus, it satisfies one of the requirements of a Jewish kosher diet, which prohibits the consumption of milk and meat together. Although some Chinese dishes contain pork and shellfish, which are nonkosher foods, ethnographers pointed out that this may have been overlooked because Chinese eateries were inexpensive and did not discriminate against any customers, including Jews.[31] As a result, it has been argued that Chinese food, which is outside of the traditional Jewish culture and tradition, has become part of it in New York City.

The ecological environment also influences the emergence of rituals and superstition. As described by economist Nathan Nunn, Trobriand Islanders of Melanesia engage in fishing either in lagoons or out in the open sea. The tranquil waters of the lagoon provide a safe environment for fishing, whereas deep sea fishing presents uncertainties and dangers due to the open sea conditions, such as high waves and strong currents. Consequently, distinct rituals emerged within these two fishing communities. To address the risks involved in open sea fishing, deep-sea fishermen developed highly intricate and tightly practiced magical rituals, whereas lagoon fishermen did not.[32]

Cultural beliefs and practices also can be deliberately created for a specific purpose. One example is a tradition among the Mursi, an indigenous ethnic group from southwestern Ethiopia. Mursi women traditionally wear large clay or wooden lip plates, a practice that involves piercing the lower lip and gradually stretching it over time. This process alters the shape of the lips and often requires the removal of some front teeth. This practice, which continues to this day, is believed to have originally developed as a way to make women less appealing to slave traders.[33]

Another example of a deliberately created cultural belief is the superstition that emerged in the Democratic Republic of the Congo in 2012, in which it was believed that a person could become bulletproof by following a series of rituals.[34] Specifically, a village elder claimed to have had a dream that showed him how to make people bulletproof through the performance of specific rituals, such as abstaining from sex, not drinking rainwater, and avoiding specific vegetables. The goal of this village elder was to instill confidence in the villagers so that they could confront armed bandits who had been raiding and terrorizing the village, by making the villagers believe that the ritual would protect them from the bandits' gunfire.

The belief that the performance of these rituals could confer bulletproof status motivated the villagers to attack the bandits. These attacks were successful, and the bandits were defeated. Some villagers died in the process because the ritual, of course, did not make them bulletproof. However, the loss of life among the villagers could easily be rationalized as a result of their own failure to properly follow the rituals. The widespread belief in this superstition led to a large-scale, organized, and successful defense against the perpetrators, which in turn strengthened people's conviction in this superstition.

Although the subject of the emergence of religion is beyond the scope of this book, it is worth mentioning research demonstrating that the intensity of religiosity, as a cultural trait, is influenced by negative life shocks. Economist Jeanet Bentzen analyzed religious beliefs of over four hundred thousand individuals from ninety-six countries. Their religiosity is measured by responses to questions such as "Do you believe in God?", "Are you a religious person?", "How often do you attend religious services?", and "Do you believe in life after death?" The findings showed that people who live in countries with a higher risk of earthquakes tend to be more religious. Furthermore, residents within the same country are shown to exhibit higher levels of religiosity if they live in more earthquake-prone regions of that country, even after accounting for personal attributes. The author also found that average religiosity in a district went up following a recent earthquake, with this effect being more pronounced in areas with lower income and education levels.[35]

Another study demonstrated that the intensity of prayer increased significantly during the COVID-19 pandemic. An analysis of Google searches for prayer texts from 107 countries revealed that prayer intensity in 2020 was higher compared to the previous year, with prayer-related searches remaining 10 percent above prepandemic levels. This increase was more pronounced in countries with lower education levels. A Pew Research Center survey of fourteen high-income countries similarly revealed that 10 percent of respondents reported their religious faith had strengthened as a result of the pandemic.[36]

The connection between life-threatening experiences and increased religiosity has also been observed in a study of US Army servicemen deployed to Iraq and Afghanistan after the September 11, 2001, attacks in the US.[37] Some soldiers were randomly assigned to combat zones, while others were placed in noncombat areas. Furthermore, some experienced direct combat, where their units "received incoming fire from small arms, artillery, rockets, or mortars . . . or fired on the enemy." The study found that those exposed to combat were more likely to pray and attend religious services more frequently afterward. Similarly, suffering a combat injury had a comparable effect on boosting religiosity.

These findings indicate that religiosity, as a cultural attribute, tends to strengthen during periods of unpredictable crises, and societies that regularly face unexpected hardships tend to be more religious, as religion serves as a coping mechanism during stressful life events.

In summary, there are significant differences between countries across various cultural dimensions. Examples include the inclination toward violence and its acceptance; the prevalence of corruption and dishonesty, as well as tolerance for them; the extent of individualism versus collectivism; women's participation in the labor market; the tendency for cousin marriage; and the norms of fairness. These beliefs, preferences, and their resulting behaviors emerged for various reasons. Some were created deliberately, while others emerged in response to natural events. Some cultural practices and beliefs have persisted for centuries, even though they are harmful to human well-being. Open defecation is one such example; others will be discussed later in the book.

Although cultural beliefs and behaviors tend to be long-lasting, in some cases they can change in relatively short periods. In chapter 11, we will examine specific examples of how culture can change within a single generation, shedding light on how cultural norms and practices can be altered to promote human well-being.

3 Origins of Culture: Geography, Ancient Farming Technology, and Herding

The previous chapter highlighted differences in cultural beliefs, norms, and behaviors between societies, along with examples of how they emerged in specific cases. One key determinant of these differences is geography and the ancient farming technologies associated with it. The suitability of land for specific types of agriculture and the characteristics of the terrain have historically influenced whether herding or farming was the appropriate method of sustenance, as well as whether the plough could be used as a production technology in agriculture. These factors shaped various cultural attributes and practices, such as the extent to which women work outside the home, men's inclination toward violence, and the practice of female genital mutilation. Ecological factors and agricultural legacies have influenced other important cultural traits as well, including preferences for sons over daughters, present-oriented versus future-oriented thinking, and individualism versus collectivism. This chapter and the next will provide specific examples of how geography influenced cultural attributes.

Labor Force Participation of Women

Consider people who are between the ages of fifteen and sixty-four. Take the number of people who are currently employed in this group and add the number of people who are jobless but looking for work. Then, divide this sum by the population in the fifteen- to sixty-four-year age group. This provides the labor force participation rate, which tells us the proportion of working-age people who are employed or looking for work.

Labor force participation rates vary across nations, but differences are relatively small in the case of men. Between seventy and seventy-five out of every one hundred men in Ghana, Belgium, Egypt, Turkey, Greece, and Chile are in the labor force. The rate is close to 80 percent in Argentina, South Korea, Norway, and the US. On the high end, around 90 percent of working-age men are in the labor force in such countries as Japan, the Netherlands, and Paraguay.[1]

In contrast to men, women's labor force participation rates vary greatly across countries. In some nations like Egypt, Morocco, and Pakistan, only 20–25 percent of women participate in the labor market, but the rate is around 80 percent in various countries including Switzerland, Madagascar, Iceland, Tanzania, and the Netherlands. Nations from every continent fall along the spectrum between these low and high female labor force participation rates. On the lower end, nations like Turkey, Bangladesh, Sri Lanka, and Guatemala have approximately 40 percent of working-age women engaged in the labor market. The female labor force participation rate is around 55 percent in South Africa, Indonesia, Italy, and Romania. It goes up to 70 percent in the US, France, Uruguay, and Israel.[2]

Economic reasons are, of course, important in explaining individuals' propensity to participate in the labor force. A primary factor is the wage rate one can command in the labor market, as higher wages motivate people to work. Wages depend on education, job experience, and skill. Education is particularly important. Individuals with higher levels of education are more productive, and this increased productivity translates into higher wages. For example, American workers with a high school education earn 25 percent more than those who have no high school diploma. College-educated workers earn more than 60 percent in comparison to those with a high school degree. More generally, economists have shown that an additional year of schooling increases wages by an average of 6–12 percent, depending on the country.[3]

Because the less educated command lower wages and therefore have less incentive to work outside of the home, existing differences in female education between countries are partly responsible for the differences in their female labor force participation rates. The educational attainment of women differs dramatically across nations. For women aged twenty-five and older, the average number of years of education is four in Morocco and Pakistan and about five in Bangladesh. It is seven years in Turkey and eight years in Indonesia. Average female education goes up to nine years in Uruguay, ten years in South Africa, and eleven in France, Romania, and Italy. It is twelve years in the Switzerland and Russia, thirteen years in Israel, and fourteen years in the US.[4]

The positive correlation between average female education and female labor force participation rates across countries is shown in figure 3.1, where each point represents one country. The straight line on the graph depicts the best fit through the data points and shows the average relationship between these two variables across countries.

Nations located on the lower-left segment of the graph are those with low levels of female education and low female labor force participation. Most of these are Muslim-majority countries.

The influence of religion on female education is widely recognized as religious beliefs and traditions shape preferences, behaviors, and norms. Nevertheless, significant variations in female education are observed among countries that adhere to the same religion. For instance, as shown in the graph, the average amount of female education in countries such as Tajikistan, Kyrgyzstan, and Kazakhstan is in the range of eleven to twelve years, but these are also Muslim-majority countries, indicating that religion alone does not determine female education in society.[5]

It is also important to underline the significant variation in female labor force participation rates among countries with similar levels of female education. This is true even among nations that adhere to the same religion. For example, Egypt and Bangladesh are both Muslim-majority countries with low female education (around five to six years), but 20 percent of women participate in the labor market in Egypt, while the rate is 40 percent in Bangladesh. Average years of female schooling is ten to eleven in both Malaysia and Jordan, but female labor force participation rate is less than 20 percent in Jordan, while more than half of the women in Malaysia are in the labor force. Similarly, although the Philippines, Bolivia, and Peru are all Catholic-majority countries with about nine years of female education on average, the female labor force participation rate is 50 percent in the Philippines, 60 percent in Bolivia, and 70 percent in Peru. The same variation exists within Protestant-majority countries as well.

There are, of course, additional factors, ranging from marital status to number of children, from spouse's education to the level of household wealth, all of which influence whether or not women work outside the home. The economic conditions of the country also impact labor force participation propensity. When job opportunities are limited and the unemployment rate

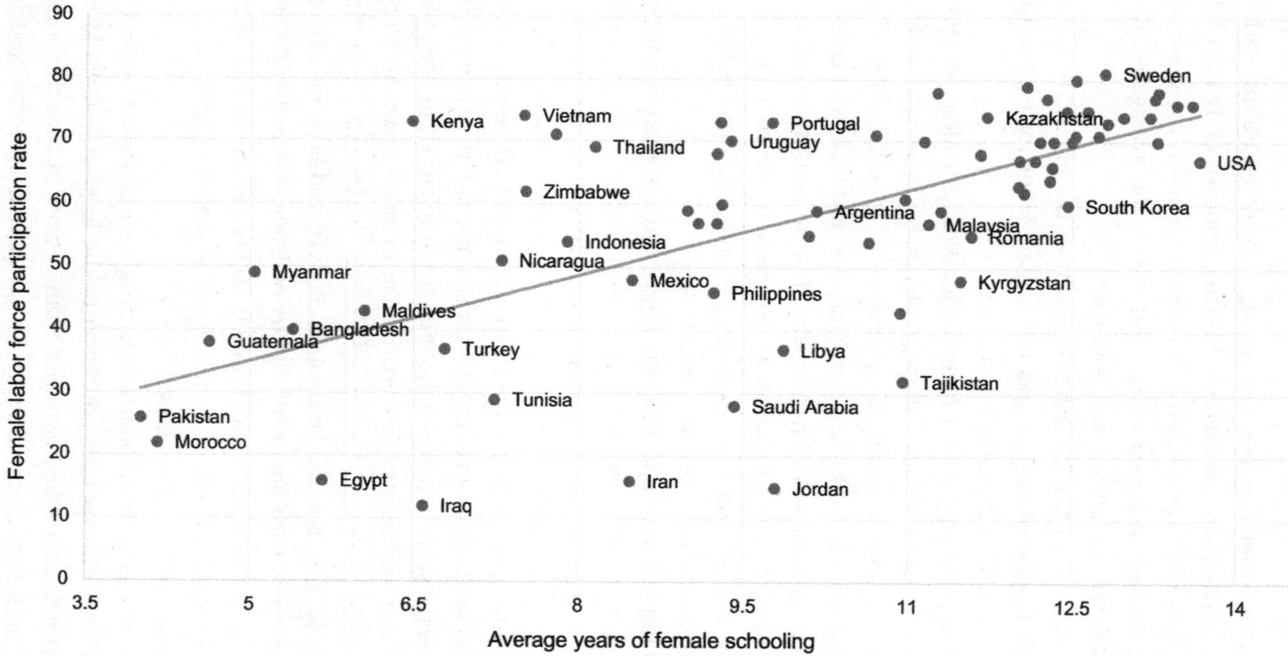

Figure 3.1

Relationship between female education and labor force participation

remains persistently high, individuals seeking employment may become discouraged, lose motivation in their job search, and ultimately withdraw from the labor market. However, differences in these economic attributes of countries do not fully explain the differences in female labor participation rates between countries.[6]

These observations indicate the presence of a more fundamental and overarching factor influencing women's involvement in the labor market in a country. One key factor is the general attitudes toward gender roles.

An effective method for assessing attitudes toward gender roles involves evaluating individuals' perspectives on employment opportunities for women versus men. This can be done by measuring people's agreement with statements like, "When jobs are scarce, men should have more right to a job than women." This question elicits widely varying levels of agreement among countries, as illustrated in figure 3.2. Ninety percent of Egyptians concur with this statement, but only 3 percent of the Dutch agree. Reflecting this significant difference in attitudes toward men's job priority over women's, the female labor force participation rate in Egypt is only 20 percent, whereas over 75 percent of women work outside the home in the Netherlands.

This connection between people's beliefs about whether men should have priority in job opportunities and the extent to which women participate in the labor market is not confined to specific countries or particular religions; it is a global phenomenon.[7] In general, the higher the proportion of residents in a country who believe that jobs should be reserved for men, the lower that country's female labor force participation rate. As shown in figure 3.2, only 7 percent of Australians believe that men should have priority in employment, resulting in a high female labor force participation rate of 75 percent. In contrast, approximately one in three Bolivians support the idea that jobs should belong to men, leading to a lower female labor force participation rate of 60 percent in Bolivia. In Jordan, where more than 80 percent of people believe that men should have priority over women in job opportunities, the female labor participation rate is only 15 percent.[8]

These statistics reveal that the extent to which a society agrees with the notion that men should have priority over women in job opportunities reflects its societal norms and attitudes toward women's roles. These cultural differences in gender norms across nations are manifested in the rates at which women in these nations engage in employment outside the home.

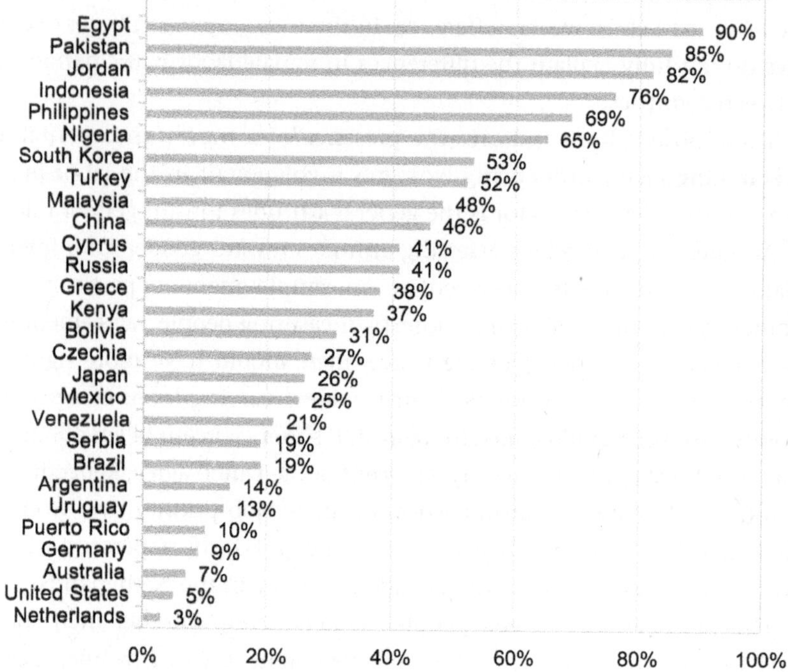

Figure 3.2
Percentage agreeing that men deserve priority in employment over women when jobs are scarce

It is worth highlighting that beyond the factors mentioned earlier, such as education and job experience, there are additional determinants of women's inclination to engage in the labor market in a given society, including the availability and affordability (or lack thereof) of day care services for small children, and discrimination in employment and wages against women. Nevertheless, the core idea is that all these factors, ranging from restricted educational opportunities for women to the lack of market-based formal day care arrangements, from the availability of birth control to employment discrimination, are grounded in attitudes toward women's perceived role in society. The question then is: Why do attitudes regarding the perceived role of women in society differ dramatically across countries?

Ancient Production Methods and Current Beliefs About Women's Role in Society

What is the root cause for the cultural belief that men are entitled to have jobs, rather than women? To answer this question, economists Alberto Alesina, Paola Giuliano, and Nathan Nunn measured attitudes toward women's work outside the home in each country by using the extent of agreement with the statement mentioned earlier: "When jobs are scarce, men should have more right to a job than women." In addition, they used the proportion of people who concur with the statement, "On the whole, men make better political leaders than women do," as another indicator of opinions regarding women's role in society. The study showed that these two indicators of attitudes toward gender roles, as well as the female labor force participation rate itself, are strongly associated with the agricultural legacies of societies.[9]

The hypothesis, originally put forth by economist Ester Boserup, is that the suitability of land for agriculture many centuries ago determined the mode of agricultural production.[10] More specifically, it has been argued that the distinction between shifting cultivation and plough cultivation has led to different forms of production technology and different gender specializations. This difference in agricultural production technology subsequently resulted in the emergence of different cultural attitudes about gender norms.

Shifting cultivation relies on hand tools, such as the hoe and the digging stick, and it is labor-intensive. In this system of production, men and women work together in the fields to cultivate and grow crops. In contrast, *plough cultivation* is less labor-intensive. A plough is used to till the soil, and either a person pulls the plough or an animal, such as an ox or a horse, is used for this purpose and somebody controls both the plough and the animal. Farming with the plough therefore requires upper body strength and muscle power. Consequently, men have an advantage in handling the plough in comparison to women. As a result, in societies with ancestral plough cultivation, men specialized in fieldwork using the plough, while women specialized in other production tasks such as cooking, caring for domesticated animals, and producing secondary products—for example, churning milk to butter and processing wheat grain into bulgur, among other activities.

These differences in ancient production technologies among societies, and the resultant division of labor between men and women, is conjectured to have generated vastly divergent attitudes and norms in these societies regarding women's role in the workforce. This, in turn, has led to significantly different tendencies of women to work outside of the home, which still persist as cultural behaviors centuries later.

This hypothesis has been supported by detailed statistical analyses. An investigation of data from countries across the globe by the same authors revealed that even after accounting for a large number of socioeconomic attributes that vary between nations (including contemporary country attributes and historical ethnographic characteristics), women are less likely to participate in the labor market if they reside in countries where agriculture has been done using the plough over centuries. Women are also less likely to participate in national politics and are less likely to own firms if their country has ancestral origins in plough-based agriculture.

The same impact of the traditional use of the plough is detected when comparing regions within the same country. By analyzing data on more than eighty thousand individuals who live in six hundred regions of seventy-four countries, and adjusting for the impact of these individuals' characteristics such as age, marital status, sex, and education, as well as a number of attributes of the countries in which they live, it has been shown that people who reside in different regions of the same country have different attitudes about female employment and female leadership, depending on whether or not their ancestors were engaged in traditional plough use in those regions. Individuals residing in regions of their country with a history of plow-based agriculture are more likely to harbor the belief that men make better political leaders and men should be given priority in job opportunities. Furthermore, women in these regions are less inclined to engage in the labor market compared to their counterparts residing in other regions of the same country without a tradition of plow use.

These findings indicate that in locations where ancient agricultural production technology motivated men to work on the fields using the plough, cultural norms have emerged that assigned women's place as the home. And these norms, transmitted from generation to generation, impact behaviors and economic outcomes still today.

But you might worry that some alternative factors might be at play in contemporary societies, generating disparities between these societies regarding attitudes toward women, and also influencing women's economic behavior we observe today. An insightful experiment to gain a deeper understanding of this issue could be conducted as follows: Suppose we moved individuals from a diverse group of nations worldwide to a single country and then observed their behaviors in this new environment. In conducting such an experiment, it would be crucial to ensure that the countries of origin vary in terms of their ancient agricultural production heritage. This would involve relocating individuals from nations where agriculture was historically plough-based and from countries that traditionally did not rely on plough-based production. Once all participants settled in the same destination country, they would be free to live and behave as they wished, and we would observe whether people from plough-based agricultural traditions exhibit different behaviors compared to those whose countries of origin did not rely on the ancient plough technology.

Of course, such an experiment cannot be conducted, but there is an alternative approach to carry out an analysis with the same intent. Studying immigrants who have relocated to a particular destination country from various parts of the world provides valuable insights into the influence of diverse ancestral agricultural production heritages on their behaviors and attitudes.

One example of this approach is the study of second-generation Americans. These individuals are considered "second generation" because their parents moved to the US from other countries, but they themselves were born and raised in the US. As a result, they all encounter the same legal environment and the same economic incentives, such as identical tax structure, and so on. But if parents transmitted the cultural norms of their countries of origin to their children, then these cultural norms would be reflected in the behaviors of their children when they become adults.

Comparisons of second-generation immigrants have, in fact, revealed differences in their labor market activity based on their parents' country of origin. Even after adjusting for various factors influencing labor force participation, such as age, education, marital status, rural and urban residence, and attributes of the husband (if present), second-generation immigrant women's likelihood of working outside the home varies depending on their parents' country of origin. Specifically, second-generation American women have a lower tendency to participate in the labor force if their ancestors are from a country where plough-based agriculture was historically prevalent.[11]

The plough is not the only example of ancient production technology in agriculture that has influenced gender norms. The introduction of irrigation in farming represents another technological innovation that contributed to the division of labor between men and women. Constructing and maintaining irrigation canals, safeguarding them, managing water allocation, and resolving water disputes all demanded physical strength. Consequently, men held a physical advantage in these tasks, leading them to engage in these activities, while women concentrated on other responsibilities centered around the home.

A study has shown that ancestral irrigation has a negative influence on contemporary female labor force participation. The authors of the study conducted detailed analyses using a variety of datasets. By comparing 156 countries around the world and analyzing more than fifty-three thousand individuals who reside in 515 subnational regions around the world (i.e., including multiple regions of a given nation), and also investigating more than one hundred thousand second-generation American women, they consistently detected a negative relationship between female labor participation today and ancestral irrigation agriculture.[12] Everything else being the same, the greater the historical involvement of their country in irrigation agriculture, the lower is women's inclination to engage in the labor force today.

The takeaway is that historical variations in farming production technology resulted in two distinct outcomes: one involving joint work by men and women in the fields, and another where men predominantly worked in the fields while women concentrated on domestic tasks. This dichotomy gave rise to the formation of differential norms concerning women's role outside the home, which have persisted over time and continue to influence women's engagement in the labor market.

Geography, Herding, Warfare, and Culture of Violence

An increase or a decrease in the price of meat will not impact the meat consumption of a vegetarian. In contrast, if someone loves meat, and has a big enough budget, that person may not care about the fluctuations in the price of meat and may not alter his meat consumption in response to a price change. In other words, neither a vegetarian nor a rich meat lover would react to any change in the price of meat—but this is not true for everyone. Most people are not strict vegetarians or strict carnivores. So most people would react, in different degrees, to the variation in the price of meat. More generally, most people adjust their behavior (be it the purchase of meat or cars, the consumption of alcohol or drugs, the decision to work for pay, etc.) in reaction to changes in prices and incentives.

Some people would never commit a crime. They would never steal even if they starved to death. Some people would never hurt anyone under any circumstance; they would never cheat or lie. Others commit these acts quite easily. But most people are probably somewhere in the middle, and their proclivity to engage in crime reacts, in different degrees, to variations in incentives.

What are the incentives that make people more or less likely to engage in criminal acts? Since the seminal work of Nobel laureate Gary Becker, economists have shown that people respond to the costs and benefits of committing crime.[13] These include such items as economic opportunities (unemployment rates, wage rates, etc.), as well as deterrence factors, including the size of the police force, the apprehension probability of offenders, and the harshness of punishment (sentence lengths). Dozens of research findings reveal that people tend to commit more crime when their economic conditions worsen. They commit less crime when the likelihood of arrest goes up and when punishment for crime gets stiffer.[14] This means that cross-national differences in criminal activity, including homicide, in part, reflect differences in economic conditions, joblessness, and poverty, as well as the extent of law enforcement and criminal deterrence across countries.

The rate of intentional homicide varies substantially between countries. Over the last decade, the average number of intentional homicides per one hundred thousand residents was one in Australia, three in India, five in the US, and seven in Russia. The number of homicides was as high as twenty-five in Brazil, thirty in Colombia, and thirty-five in South Africa.[15]

However, any discussion of violence as a cultural attribute should not refer to the raw magnitude of violence, such as the prevailing homicide rate in a country at a point in time. Rather, it should focus on the persistent pattern of violent behavior after filtering out all possible determinants of violence, including demographic factors, economic circumstances, and sanctions and punishment severity. In other words, the proclivity for violence as an attribute of a society is determined by the persistent violent behavior of its members, which cannot be explained by variations in economic conditions, deterrence, and other socioeconomic and demographic factors.

One such example is the persistently high homicide rate in the Southern United States. In the early 1920s, the homicide rate in the South was 2.5 times higher than the rest of the country, and in 1935 the Southern homicide rate was 200 percent higher than the corresponding rate in other regions of America.[16] Similarly, the average homicide rate in the Southern

US during the mid-1960s was more than twice as high as the homicide rate of the rest of the country.[17] The same pattern has continued to this day. In the 1990s, the average homicide rate in Southern states was 9.7 homicides per one hundred thousand residents, while the homicide rate in other states was 5.7. Between 2000 and 2020, there were 6.6 homicides per year for each one hundred thousand residents in the South, which was 60 percent higher than the homicide rate in the rest of country.[18]

It has long been observed that a multitude of factors, including socioeconomic and demographic influences (ranging from joblessness to racial composition of the population) as well as criminal deterrence indicators, do not possess sufficient explanatory power to fully account for the disparity between Southern and non-Southern homicide rates in the US. Historians and sociologists, starting in the early twentieth century, emphasized that an explanation of the high and persistent homicide rate in the South must be based on an understanding of the influence of Southern regional culture.[19] Social psychologists Richard Nisbett and Dov Cohen argued that Southerners differ from the rest of the United States in an important dimension, which is how they perceive an insult and how they react to it. These researchers attributed this persistent proclivity for violence to the "culture of honor" in the South, referring to customs, attitudes, and beliefs that lead to violence if someone's reputation or property is challenged or threatened.[20]

The root cause of this violent culture of honor is ascribed to the way of life Southerners inherited from their Scots-Irish ancestors. The idea stems from the fact that Scots-Irish immigrants were settled in large numbers in the Southern United States between the early eighteenth and the early nineteenth centuries. It is hypothesized that these immigrants brought with them their culture of resolving disputes with violence, which was then transmitted through generations and became the culture of violence of the American South.

Scots, regardless of whether they lived in the lowlands or highlands of Scotland, were not farmers because the land was not suitable for productive agriculture. As a result, Lowland Scots never engaged in significant agriculture but instead practiced animal husbandry and kept cattle and pigs. Highland Scots lived in the mountains, and they were herders.

Scots were engaged for centuries in constant warfare against England, which caused both lawlessness and the destruction of resources in Scotland. In the absence of a strong state and institutional authority, as was the case in Scotland for many centuries, people were exposed to raids and theft of animals. In herding societies, the loss of animals meant losing one's entire livelihood, and in the absence of any meaningful system of law and order, herders had to resort to violence to protect themselves. To signal strength, to protect their property, and to deter potential perpetrators, behavioral norms developed for survival that emphasized toughness and an eagerness to fight to protect one's honor. Thus, Scots developed a culture that involved the demonstration of strength and power when one's honor is questioned or challenged. This meant a heightened sensitivity to insults, strong reactions to perceived threats, and resolving disputes with violence.

The name Scots-Irish is given to those Scots who were relocated from Scotland to the Ulster region in the north of Ireland by King James I of England in the early seventeenth century.[21] The king's idea was to subdue the Irish and their rebellion by using the culturally aggression-prone Scots against the Irish. King James implemented this so-called plantation of Ulster plan by seizing the land in Ulster from the Irish and giving it to the Scots who relocated there. This, of course, created hostility between the Irish and the Scots, and after generations of conflict, Scots started migrating from Ireland to America in large numbers in the early to mid-1700s. The Ulster Scots, who are also known as the Scots-Irish, settled heavily in southern US states.

The link between the high homicide rate in the Southern US and the inherited Scots-Irish culture of violence has been investigated by economist Pauline Grosjean via statistical methods, utilizing county-level US data from the years 2000 to 2007. She accounted for traditional determinants of crime, such as poverty, inequality, racial composition, population density, education, and historical prevalence of slavery.

Adjusting for these local socioeconomic and historical attributes that are related to crime, she showed that counties in which Scots-Irish immigrants were settled more heavily in the eighteenth century (based on information obtained in the US census of 1790, which identifies local populations and their ancestry) have higher homicide rates today. She also showed that this impact of the herding-based culture of violence, related to Scots-Irish origin, persists until today only in those areas that lacked strong law enforcement in the eighteenth and nineteenth centuries (a shortage of sheriffs and constables) and in areas that had limited newspaper presence. Put differently, the transmission of culture of violence took place in locations with weak governance and poor institutional quality, emphasizing the influence of institutions on culture—a theme that will be exposed further in subsequent chapters of the book.[22]

When discussing homicide, it is inevitable to think about the extent of gun ownership in America, especially in the South. The proportion of adults who live in a household with a firearm varies greatly across America. In Massachusetts, New Jersey, Hawaii, and Rhode Island, only 15 percent of individuals live in households with a firearm, whereas the highest rate, reaching approximately 66 percent, is observed in Wyoming and Montana. In the ranking based on this measure of gun ownership, Southern states are notably overrepresented in the top tier. Four of them—Arkansas, Alabama, Mississippi, and West Virginia—appear in the top ten, and nine Southern states are included in the top twenty.[23]

But the elevated gun ownership rate in the South is not the root cause of Southern violence. This is because, in addition to other researchers who identified the Scots-Irish cultural heritage as the main culprit of violence, the aforementioned study by Grosjean establishes a significant impact of the Scots-Irish heritage on violence through the examined counties *in the same state*. Considering that the attitudes toward gun ownership are more or less uniform within a given state, the extent of the sentiment for guns—whether high or low—cannot account for the variation in violence observed among counties within that state. On the other hand, significant variation exists in the magnitude of the early Scots-Irish migration and their settlement across counties of the Southern states, and this variation explains the difference in the prevalence of violence across counties of the same state.

Culture of honor and its associated violence is not restricted to the Scots-Irish. Other societies around the world, ones that were historically dependent on animal herding as their primary economic activity, also developed violent attitudes and behavioral patterns, which are reflected in the behaviors of their descendants today. A recent study used ethnographic data to identify thousands of ethnic groups around the world. These data allow researchers to categorize the historical reliance of each group on animal herding as its primary economic activity. Analyses of these data have similarly revealed that traditional herding is related to the prevalence of violence and retaliation.[24]

It should be emphasized that when we make the claim that ancient herding, as an economic activity, resulted in permanent violent tendencies as a cultural attribute, we need to make sure that we account for the possibility that the causality might instead flow the other way around: from violent tendencies to herding.[25] In other words, it is conceivable that certain groups, predisposed to violence to begin with, might have chosen herding over agriculture as an economic activity centuries ago. If this is the case, the story could be the following: The observed positive association between violence and the herding tradition is not because herding causes violence, but because people who were inherently prone to violence had chosen herding as an economic activity in the distant past, and subsequent generations inherited both the herding tradition and a proclivity for violence from their ancestors.

To minimize this concern, the same study has demonstrated that the reliance of an ethnic group on herding, as opposed to agriculture, is significantly influenced by ecological factors. The conditions of the land in a particular location play a crucial role in determining whether agriculture, pastoralism, or both have been viable means of survival. Consequently, the historical involvement of an ethnic group in herding activity can be traced back to the suitability of the land for agriculture versus pastoralism in the location in which that ethnic group has existed. In other words, research indicates that the choice of the most suitable type of economic activity is dictated by the conditions of the land and terrain. This decision, in turn, has influenced the proclivity for violence among those who chose herding as an economic activity.

More nuanced analyses can be carried out by focusing on people who live in the same country. Indeed, analyses of thousands of ethnic groups that live in more than two hundred nations have revealed that different ethnic groups who live in the same country differ in their propensity to engage in armed conflict. If an ethnic group's ancestors were pastoralists, then the frequency and severity of armed conflict are higher today for that ethic group. The same is true for the willingness to take revenge and punish others for unfair behavior. Preindustrial societies that relied on animal herding have contemporary descendants who are more likely to engage in armed conflict and who are more willing to inflict punishment on others for perceived unfair behavior.[26]

This line of research indicates that populations that picked up pastoralism instead of agriculture because of the conditions of the land on which they lived (terrain, climate, temperature) developed behavioral patterns and cultural norms involving violence and revenge-taking because "a stance of aggressiveness and willingness to kill . . . is useful in announcing a herder's determination to defend his animals."[27] This attribute of aggression has been transferred through generations as a cultural trait to the descendants of these populations.

This link between pastoralism and aggression has also been reported by anthropologists and ethnographers. Describing his research among the Sebei tribe of Uganda, anthropologist Walter Goldschmidt wrote: "At that time [around 1954] anthropologists were unquestionably speaking of tribes as social entities, assuming the homogeneity of tribal cultures. . . . It was clear that homogeneity did not characterize the Sebei [tribe]. . . . It was the recognition of this situation that led to the central idea [that] a shift from pastoralism to farming, or vice versa, had profound effects of the patterned behavior of people."[28]

Following on this observation, an ambitious field study of anthropologists and ethnographers sixty years ago focused on four tribes that live in Tanzania, Uganda, and Kenya. Each of these tribes (the Sebei, the Hehe, the Kamba, and the Pokot) had populations that were engaged in either farming or in pastoralism. Studying these populations and analyzing a wealth of data collected, researchers uncovered stark differences between farmers and pastoralists *within each tribe* regarding their aggression, concern with death, and military prowess.[29] People who were farmers had different beliefs, values, attitudes, and behavioral patterns than those who were pastoralist, even when both of these groups were members of the same tribe. Researchers wrote: "Compared to farmers, pastoralists strongly value independent and direct action. They make decisions as individuals, openly pursue goals, and typically say and do what they wish directly. They even aggress openly, abusing or assaulting an adversary . . . The farmers avoid direct conflict; the pastoralists accept it, sometimes even seek it."[30]

Female Genital Mutilation

Many countries around the world have customs and norms designed to control and regulate women's behaviors. Well-known examples of these norms include dress codes requiring women to conceal their bodies in public, restrictions on the places they can visit and the people they can interact with, and rules dictating which family members have the authority to grant women permission for specific activities outside their homes, such as driving a car or embarking on a journey.

Anthropologists and evolutionary psychologists argue that these norms are designed to prevent women from engaging in promiscuous behavior or interacting with men who are not immediate family members. Central to these norms are the concepts of chastity and maintaining "purity." It has been hypothesized that the main driver of these norms is the biological uncertainty surrounding paternity, and that men evolved to be jealous because they can never be certain of women's fidelity. This instinct is argued to be the driving force behind the adoption of strategies aimed at deterring female promiscuity, which, in turn, gave rise to the emergence of norms that impose constraints on and oversee women's behavior.[31]

One such strategy is the violent practice of *female genital mutilation*, which refers to procedures involving the partial or total removal of the external female genitalia to suppress women's sexual desires and to signal a woman's "purity" for her future husband.[32] Female genital mutilation is a form of violence against women and girls, and it is considered a human rights violation by both the United Nations and the WHO.[33] There are 230 million women alive worldwide who have been subjected to female genital mutilation typically performed on girls between infancy and adolescence.[34]

Scholars have noted that, underscoring the power of cultural norms, this violent practice is sometimes defended, supported, and transmitted by women.[35] Female genital mutilation is notably widespread in sub-Saharan African countries such as Sudan, Ethiopia, Eritrea, Somalia, Kenya, Burkina Faso, Mali, Mauritania, Senegal, Guinea, and Nigeria. It is also prevalent in Egypt. Although Islam is the dominant religion in the majority of these countries, female genital mutilation is not practiced in most Islamic nations. The origin of this cultural custom is elusive, but it is known to predate the rise of Islam and Christianity.

If a primary purpose of female genital mutilation is to provide insurance for men against the possibility of their spouses engaging in extramarital affairs, then the practice would be more prevalent in societies where husbands experience prolonged absences from home. In pastoral societies, men often spend a considerable amount of time away from their homes in search of grazing areas for herding livestock such as cattle, sheep, or camels. During these periods, it is difficult for men to monitor women's behavior. Thus, the prevalence of female genital mutilation is expected to be higher in pastoral societies compared to agricultural ones, where men do not experience extended periods of absence from home.

Economist Anke Becker tested this hypothesis utilizing data from more than ninety-six thousand women who reside in thirteen sub-Saharan nations where female genital mutilation is prevalent. These women's ethnicity and the language they speak facilitate the assessment of their ethnic heritage. An anthropological database, containing information on historical details of 1,200 ethnic groups worldwide, allowed for the determination of each ethnic group's historical dependence on pastoralism. Through careful statistical analyses, it was uncovered that women who are of the same age and who reside in the same country display differences in their likelihood of undergoing female genital mutilation depending on their ancestors' pastoral history. Women from ethnic groups that historically relied on pastoralism are more prone to having experienced mutilation compared to those from the same country but belonging to ethnic groups with a lesser historical dependency on pastoralism.[36]

The same conclusion is reached when analyzing women's freedom of movement outside their homes. The responses of approximately seven hundred thousand women from forty-one countries to inquiries regarding conditions such as their husbands' sole authority in deciding visits to relatives, the husbands' insistence on knowing their wives' whereabouts, and the perceived justification for a husband to beat his wife for going out without informing him, were analyzed. The results revealed, once again, that the extent to which a woman's ancestors relied on pastoralism was a strong predictor of that woman's freedom of mobility. That is, women who reside in the same country exhibit variations in their freedom of mobility, with those from ethic groups historically reliant on pastoralism having less autonomy.

In summary, the ecological environment, terrain, and soil conditions historically determined the most suitable forms of production in a given location. The viability of agriculture or pastoralism in these areas influenced the behaviors of those engaged in these practices, which eventually became cultural traits of their societies. Similarly, soil conditions determined the appropriate agricultural methods—such as plough cultivation or shifting cultivation—leading to the formation of societal behavioral patterns. In other words, geography influenced ancient production methods, which, in turn, shaped behaviors and preferences that have persisted as cultural attributes, including tendencies toward violence, women's participation in the workforce, and the prevalence of female genital mutilation.

4 Origins of Culture: Ecology, Soil Conditions, and Farming

This chapter presents additional examples of cultural preferences and attitudes rooted in the ecological conditions of the land where the society is located. These include preferences for sons over daughters, time orientation and patience, preferences for work versus leisure, and individualistic versus collectivist attitudes.

Preference for Sons

Some societies display a cultural preference for sons over daughters. This preference has basis in economic reasons. For instance, in the absence of effective law enforcement, physical strength serves as a means for self-protection and deterrence. In societies characterized by weak governance and inadequate and unreliable criminal justice and legal systems, disputes between parties may remain unresolved through peaceful discussions, mediations, or court proceedings, leading people to resort to physical force for contract enforcement and conflict resolution. In such a setting, having a son, who presumably has more physical strength than a daughter, might be viewed as advantageous.

Parents may also view sons as a more valuable investment in economic environments where reliable social protection, sufficient social security, and retirement pensions for older ages are lacking. This perception may arise from the belief that sons are better equipped to provide old-age care and protection than daughters. This belief, in turn, may be based on the presumption that sons are more likely to possess the financial resources necessary to support their parents. Such a belief could be particularly widespread in countries where women have less education and limited participation in the labor market, leading to a lack of independent economic power and financial autonomy for them (I will return to this topic in chapter 11).

In some societies, religious values can also lead to a preference for a male offspring. For example, according to Hindu tradition, only a son has the responsibility of lighting a man's funeral pyre. Similarly, in certain customs, like those observed in China, lineage is exclusively traced through the male members of the family. In these traditions, the absence of a son is considered equivalent to the discontinuation of the family lineage. In Turkey, about a quarter of women and more than one out of every three men agree with the statement, "Only a son can ensure the continuation of the family blood line."[1]

A good indicator of the societal bias favoring boys is the male-to-female ratio in the population. Biologically, more male babies are born than female babies, with an average of approximately 105 boys born for every 100 girls. However, higher early life mortality among boys tends to equalize the male-to-female ratio in teenage and adult populations. Nonetheless, there are many countries around the world where the ratio of males to females (multiplied by 100) exceeds 100, highlighting the prevalence of this gender bias.

China is a well-known example, where the male-to-female ratio is 115 in the zero to fourteen age group of children, indicating that there are 115 boys for every 100 girls. This is largely attributed to China's *one-child policy*, which was in effect until recently. Chinese parents who desire a boy as their only child would resort to various methods to ensure that their surviving child is a boy rather than a girl. But China is not the only country with an imbalanced male-to-female ratio. Many nations across every continent exhibit sex ratios greater than 100. In the zero to fourteen age group of children, the boys-to-girls ratio is 115 in Kuwait. There are 110 boys for every 100 girls in India and Albania. The ratio is 109 in Georgia, 108 in Lebanon, and 107 in Pakistan. There are 106 Greek boys for every 100 Greek girls, and there are 105 Turkish boys for every 100 Turkish girls.[2]

Among the US-born children of Chinese, Korean, and Indian parents, significant son-biased sex ratios have been observed, especially for third children. If these parents have two daughters, their third child is 50 percent more likely to be male.[3] The same pattern is observed among immigrants to Canada from East Asian countries.[4] Immigrant families in the US have higher fertility if their first-born child is female, and this effect is more pronounced among both first-generation and second-generation immigrants if their parents originated from countries with gender inequality.[5]

Sex-selective abortion and infanticide result in a larger number of boys compared to girls. Also, if family resources are allocated more favorably toward boys than girls during childhood, this can lead to higher mortality rates among girls and would result in more boys than girls in that society. This kind of family resource allocation decision in favor of boys can take many forms, such as unequal food allocation between boys and girls, differences in immunization practices, disparities in medical care provisions, and general neglect of girls.[6] In India, where there are 110 boys for every 100 girls, boys are breastfed for longer periods than girls, and girls with congenital heart disease are less likely to receive surgery compared to boys with the same condition.[7]

In 1990, Nobel laureate Amartya Sen estimated that globally there were one hundred million *missing women*—women who would have been alive if gender ratios were equal in each country. A 2020 United Nations report indicated a higher estimate, placing the number of missing women worldwide at 143 million.[8] The overwhelming majority of these women are missing in China and India, because these countries have large populations and their sex ratios are highly skewed.

Does the contemporary preference for male offspring observed in some societies, reflected by skewed sex ratios favoring men, have its origins in historical agricultural production methods? The answer is yes. Ancient production technology in farming has an influence on a society's present-day ratio of boys to girls. As discussed in the previous chapter, in some ancient societies, women and men worked together in the fields. In other societies, which relied on the use of the plough for agricultural production, men specialized in the field as their physical strength was needed to control the plough and handle the animal that pulled it. This latter type of production technology created higher demand for boys compared to girls because the physical strength of men was needed in plough-using societies.

A comprehensive analysis of data from 152 countries around the world uncovered a strong positive association between ancestral plough use in a country and its current male-to-female ratio. This association holds true even after adjusting for country-specific factors such as per capita income, fertility, and infant mortality. In other words, the descendants of societies that historically engaged in plough agriculture have male-to-female ratios today that are greater than the level dictated by biology. This suggests that ancient plough use has shaped the preferences of societies in favor of boys, which has been transmitted across generations to this day.[9]

Along the same lines, it has been shown that soil type in a location impacts the son preference of people who reside in that location. A study focusing on India, where more than 70 percent of the population resides in rural areas, made use of the fact that soil type determines the form of agriculture that can be practiced.[10] Loamy soil allows for deep tillage, making it possible to carry out a range of agricultural tasks such as seeding, weeding, transplanting, and fertilizing with less labor compared to soil which has a clayey texture. Clayey soil, characterized by its dense and hardened texture, poses challenges for ploughs and tillers to effectively penetrate. Consequently, agricultural activities in clayey soil tend to be more labor-intensive, resulting in increased demand for women's labor in regions with such soil composition. Because the formation of soil is a very slow geological process, the type and texture of soil in a particular location remain constant. This implies that successive generations have encountered the same soil conditions in a given locality.

A detailed analysis of more than 360 districts of India reveals substantial differences in the sex ratios across districts, even within the same states. The percentage of households owning land, the average land size, and the per capita household expenditures (a proxy for income) are unaffected by whether households reside in areas with clayey or loamy soil. However, areas with a larger share of loamy soil have more tillage equipment and more buffaloes owned by farmers—the animals that tow the tillers—providing evidence that loamy soil encourages deep tillage practices. Consistent with these findings, areas with higher proportion of loamy soil have lower rates of female participation in agriculture. Importantly, populations of these areas exhibit higher male-to-female ratios.

This means that historically, the labor intensity in agriculture has been shaped by soil conditions. Soft and loamy soil textures in some regions have facilitated deep tillage using ploughs or tillers, reducing the need for female labor in agriculture in those areas. Consequently, in these areas, the sex ratios are skewed toward boys today.

The lives of the 143 million missing women, mentioned earlier, were ended directly because they were killed as infants; through selective abortion; or through neglect, maltreatment, lack of medical care and similar circumstances. The resultant sex imbalance has additional economic and social consequences for women.

It is a challenging task to figure out the ramifications for women of an increased male-to-female ratio in their society. This is because the cultural factors responsible for the male-biased sex ratio may also directly influence women's well-being. However, clever scientific analyses provide insights. For example, two researchers capitalized on a historical phenomenon in the late eighteenth and nineteenth centuries, in which a large number of convicts, predominantly male, were transported by the British to Australia.[11] This event led to an unforeseen and substantial increase in the male-to-female ratio. In the mid-nineteenth century, the sex ratio in Australia jumped to approximately two men for every woman. Although this ratio declined over time, it remained above one in the early twentieth century.

Researchers analyzed data from all counties in Australia, based on population censuses conducted since the mid-nineteenth century. They found that the surge in the male-female ratio in a county, resulting from the influx of British convicts, increased the probability of women getting married in that county. Higher sex ratios were also associated with a decrease in women's likelihood of engaging in the labor market, as well as a decline in their chances of being employed in high-ranking occupations at the end of the nineteenth century. The findings also revealed that counties with elevated male to female ratios in the mid-nineteenth century exhibit more conservative attitudes today toward women working, and women in these regions are less involved in the labor market. A high or low female labor force participation rate does not imply that women's well-being is higher or lower, but it is clear that male-skewed sex ratios lead to changes in societal attitudes toward women's work.

Another consequence of a male-biased sex ratio is its impact on interactions between men and on societal perceptions of masculinity. Biologists and psychologists have long demonstrated that an increase in the male-to-female ratio in the population of most species leads to intensified competition among males, which is associated with increased aggression and violence.[12]

A group of researchers utilized the same increase in male-to-female ratios in Australia generated by the arrival of British convicts to investigate its impact on masculinity norms.[13] Detailed analyses revealed that areas that experienced larger increases in the male-to-female ratio in the eighteenth and nineteenth centuries had more men volunteer to join the Commonwealth Army during World War I. These areas are characterized by higher levels of violence today, including a greater prevalence of bullying among boys in schools and a higher incidence of male suicide.

Another study along these lines focused on the impact of the slave trade. It has been estimated that about twelve million individuals were enslaved in the Transatlantic Slave trade between the fifteenth and nineteenth centuries, with roughly two-thirds of these slaves being men. This led to a decline in male-to-female ratios in regions of Africa that were targeted by slave traders, but there were significant differences across areas. The regions that were more intensively affected by the slave trade experienced more pronounced losses of men, resulting in sex ratios as low as one man for every two women.

Research has shown that the unexpected changes in male-female ratios centuries ago, the magnitude of which varies across regions, continue to influence women's behavior in those regions today. Women whose ancestors were more heavily exposed to the slave trade and who therefore experienced a more significant "missing men" phenomenon are more inclined to be in the labor force today and have fewer children. Women in these regions are also more likely to participate in household decisions and are more likely to state that women should have the same rights as men.[14]

The preceding discussion highlights that son preference, as a cultural attribute, directly impacts women's well-being. A strong preference for sons over daughters leads to the phenomenon of women going "missing." Furthermore, in societies where the male-to-female ratio is above the level dictated by biology, attitudes toward women's work tend to be more conservative, women participate in the labor market at a lower rate, and they are less likely to perceive themselves as equals to men. The preference for sons, which creates a male-biased sex ratio in society, has its roots in ancient production technologies.

Ancestral Farming and Impatience as a Cultural Attribute

In this section, I will discuss the connection between the ancestral farming traditions of a society and how they impact the time preferences of individuals in that society. However, before diving into this, we need to define the term *time preference* and explore whether it varies across different groups of people.

Imagine that somebody offered you $500 today, or $800 six months from today. Which option would you prefer? Your answer, no doubt, will depend on several factors. If you have unpaid bills and credit card debt, you may prefer to have $500 now instead of waiting for six months to receive $800. The economic conditions of your country could also influence your decision. For example, the inflation rate in the country may be high. This means that prices are rising rapidly, and the goods and services you would like to buy will be more expensive in six months. If this is the case, it may make sense to get $500 now and purchase those goods today.

However, even if people face the same economic circumstances, some of them may be more patient, and they would like to wait and receive $800 in six months rather than receiving $500 right now. In contrast, some others may not put as much value on future income or future consumption as they do on current income and consumption. These individuals would rather receive a smaller amount now instead of getting a larger amount six months later. So, time preference differs between people.

Research has shown that individuals with higher cognitive ability are more patient. Women tend to be less patient than men, although not in every country. Middle-aged people are more patient in comparison to the young and the elderly. But even if we compare people who have the same personal attributes—the same income, age, education, gender, and so on—we find that some of them are more impatient than others. These individuals have an inherently stronger preference for immediate gratification over delayed rewards. They discount more heavily the benefits of waiting for the future. Put differently, they have a time preference for today over tomorrow.[15]

The capacity to be patient and to delay gratification is a key determinant of many economic and social outcomes, because the extent to which people care about the future as opposed to the present impacts all kinds of behaviors. It has been shown, for instance, that people who are more patient acquire more education. Long-term oriented individuals save more, and they have less credit card debt.[16] Several studies have also documented that individuals who demonstrate patience and who can defer current rewards in exchange for larger future gains tend to avoid risky health behaviors such as smoking and using drugs. They also invest more in their health, engaging in physical exercise and maintaining a lower body mass index.[17]

As we can measure the time preferences of individuals, we can also quantify the time preferences of nations. This is done by randomly sampling a large group of individuals from each country. Such a sample includes all kinds of people: men and women, young and old, poor and rich, some less educated, some highly educated, those who live in urban areas and those who live in rural areas, and so on. These samples of individuals are then surveyed to gauge their patience and their preference for future rewards as opposed to current gratification with questions such as "Would you rather receive fifty dollars today or seventy dollars next month?" The mean value of these responses, adjusted using statistical methods to reflect the average (or typical) person of that country, represents the average time preference of the country.

Regardless of how we measure the patience and time preference of individuals across various countries, the results consistently indicate that people in some countries exhibit higher levels of patience and stronger long-term orientation compared to others. The tendency for patience is highest in Germanic and Nordic countries and lowest in African nations, with nontrivial variation between countries.[18]

As individual time preference impacts personal economic success, variations between countries in the extent of their future orientation generate economic differences between them. Economists have demonstrated that more future-oriented countries save and invest more, and they have higher per capita incomes. Nations with more patient citizens experience higher economic growth because they accumulate more physical capital, and their citizens acquire more education.[19]

Considerable differences in average patience levels between countries frequently exist even when these countries face similar economic circumstances and are located in the same geographical region. Take Germany and France, neighboring countries that have similar economic conditions overall. However, the measurement of country-level patience reveals that the average German is more future oriented than the average French person. It can be argued that this distinction in time preference does not reflect a purely cultural difference; instead, something unique could have been happening in Germany versus in France when people were surveyed to determine their time preference. But as mentioned earlier, various surveys conducted at different points in time reveal similar patterns, arguing against the idea that these differences between countries emerge by random chance or by specific economic circumstances related to a particular survey year.

Cleverly designed studies reveal additional evidence that these differences in time preference are reflections of stable attributes of societies. One such study analyzed children aged six to eleven in all primary schools in the city of Merano, which is the second-largest city of the South Tyrol province in the northmost part of Italy.[20] This is an autonomous province, sandwiched between Northern Italy and Southern Austria. The province and its German-speaking population was part of the Austro-Hungarian Empire for centuries until it was occupied by Italy at the end of World War I and annexed in 1919. Since then, Italian population has grown in size in the province.

The autonomous status of the province implies that it has a significant degree of independence from Italy and that it enjoys self-governance. Both German and Italian are official languages of the province, and the population of Merano is evenly split between individuals of German and Italian heritage. The city is segregated in terms of schools, media outlets, and other activities, and residents can use either language in official transactions in government offices. This setting provides a great opportunity to measure the time preference of people who live in the same city, under the same governance structure, and face the same economic circumstances, but differ in their heritage.

Experiments were conducted with school children who received tokens from researchers. These tokens could be exchanged for little presents such as candy, stickers, balloons, wristbands, hairbands, and so on, and more tokens would yield more items. In various experiments, kids were asked if they would like to receive two tokens now or a larger number of tokens (three, four, or five tokens) four weeks later.

The results showed that as the age group of the children increased, the percentage of patient choices (preferring a larger number of tokens to be received in four weeks) also increased. But Italian-speaking kids exhibited less patience than their German-speaking counterparts across all age groups. For example, about 20 percent of the Italian-speaking kids displayed patience in the six to seven age group, while over 40 percent of German-speaking kids of the same age group showed patience. Similarly, among nine- to ten-year-olds, the rate of patience was 40 percent among Italian-speaking kids, whereas almost 60 percent of kids with German heritage in the same age group demonstrated preference for delayed gratification. In other words, there were significant differences between children of German versus Italian heritage. Kids with Italian heritage discounted future rewards more heavily and went after immediate rewards in comparison to kids with German heritage.

Another study in the same spirit compared a sample of Romani people from Southern Spain (Gitanos) to their non-Romani neighbors.[21] Researchers chose five semirural towns in Southern Spain, where the Gitano population accounts for one-quarter of the total population. Once again, because everyone in the study lived in the same city, everyone was facing the same institutional conditions and the same overall economic circumstances.[22] The research design required the participants to make decisions about choosing between 150 euros to be received in one month versus a higher amount (up to 225 euros) in seven months. Participants differed in their personal characteristics. After adjusting for these characteristics, researchers found that Gitanos of Southern Spain discounted the future more heavily in comparison to non-Gitano Spaniards from the same towns.

So, individuals in some countries are more long-term oriented, whereas they are less patient and more today oriented in other countries. The same is true for groups of people who live in the same city but differ in ethnicity or national heritage. Time preference, characterized by the emphasis placed on the present or the future, is a cultural attribute. Importantly, this cultural attribute is an important ingredient for economic development.

Monkeys, Humans, Ecology, and Patience

Scientists have long noticed that the ability to exercise self-control and patience varies not only among humans, but also among other animals. Bonobos and chimpanzees, in particular, exhibit a degree of patience not seen in other animals. As an example, chimpanzees on average wait for more than two minutes to obtain six grape halves instead of immediately eating two grape halves.[23] More generally, some species discount the value of delayed rewards more heavily and prefer smaller but immediate rewards in comparison to other species.

The source of this variation in patience has been subject to inquiry in various fields, ranging from psychology to biology, and researchers identified the ecological environment as an important determinant of patience among animals. An interesting study compared two closely related primates: common marmosets and cotton-top tamarins. These two types of monkeys have similar body and brain sizes, social behavior, and mating systems. Their life history trajectories are also similar. However, experiments conducted using these monkeys have shown that marmosets exhibit significantly more patience. When presented with small but immediate food options versus larger but delayed food offerings, they revealed significantly more self-control and waited for the delayed reward. Cotton-top tamarin monkeys, in contrast, were much less patient and chose smaller but immediate rewards.

This difference in patience is attributed to the ecological environment. In their natural habitat, the primary food source for marmosets is gum. Marmosets scratch tree bark and then wait for the sap and gum to flow from the tree to eat. Thus, patience has become a trait of marmosets because to be able to eat and survive, they had to be patient. In contrast, cotton-top tamarins feed on insects, which move quickly. Using insects as a food source requires swift action to catch them, followed by immediate consumption. So, the particular habitat and the necessary feeding pattern of cotton-top tamarins promoted immediate gratification. These observations imply that differences in the ecological environment and the associated feeding mechanisms have shaped the evolution of patience and self-control in animals.[24]

Another study, analyzing three dozen different species, showed that brain volume and associated cognition are major predictors of both problem solving and self-control. Also, within primates, *dietary breadth* (the number of different food categories consumed) is an important predictor of patience. These two findings indicate that brain size can lead to a wider range of foods to consume because animals with larger brains have higher levels of cognition and, therefore, they can find a more extensive variety of food sources. At the same time, if the animal's habitat contains a variety of food sources, the consumption of such a variety of food would result in better nutrition, producing larger brains.[25]

But regardless of whether larger brain size and higher cognitive ability result in a broader range of foods being consumed, or consuming a more diverse array of foods causes brain growth and cognitive development, we know that those with more extensive dietary variety have larger brains, higher levels of cognition, and increased self-control. Importantly, it has been shown that, holding brain size constant, dietary breadth increases primate cognition. In other words, animals that have the same size brain differ in their cognitive ability, with those consuming a wider food variety having higher cognition.

The bottom line is that the ecological environment can have both a direct effect on self-control (such as the need to be patient and wait for food vs. the necessity to consume what is captured quickly) and an indirect effect through the better nourishment of the brain.

Returning to humans and their time preference as it relates to the ecological environment, think about a farmer one thousand years ago. Life expectancy at birth was about twenty-five years in those days, and the infant mortality rate was extremely high due to infection and disease. So, if a baby did not die during the first few months of his life, he could live perhaps until the age of fifty. If this person planted an olive tree, it would take up to ten years for it to produce fruit. This means that one-third of this person's adult life would be spent waiting for the olive tree to grow and produce fruit. But olive trees are high-yield crops; they produce a lot of fruit at a consistent rate, decade after decade. Olive trees are also resilient; they do not need irrigation, and they live many hundreds of years. There are olive trees around the world that are more than one thousand years old.

This suggests that growing olive trees centuries ago may have taught farmers patience and the appreciation of future rewards. This mindset of an olive tree farmer would likely have differed from that of another farmer who grew an annual crop with low yield, cultivation of which was associated with uncertainty.

Similarly, a farmer practicing slash-and-burn farming, where crops are cultivated on poor soil for a couple of years before the soil is allowed to rest and recover for a year to make it suitable for agriculture again, would likely have developed a different time preference.

More generally, descendants of different agricultural legacies may have different time preferences today. People whose ancestors were engaged in farming with high crop yields, which in turn provided the opportunity for long-term planning and investment, could be more patient in comparison to the descendants whose ancestors struggled with low-yield farming. This trait could then be transmitted across generations.

This hypothesis has been formalized and tested by economists Oded Galor and Omer Ozak, who have shown that people whose ancestors lived in locations with fertile land and high crop yield have enjoyed more dependable economic growth and that they developed patience and long-term orientation.[26] Crops with longer growth cycles (i.e., crops that take longer to mature) provide more yield; that is, they have higher returns. By analyzing data from nearly ninety nations worldwide, these researchers have demonstrated that countries tend to exhibit greater long-term orientation when their ancestral crops yield higher returns.[27] This finding supports the conjecture that historically, societies developed tendencies for patience and long-term orientation when they were situated in geographical regions conducive to cultivating crops with longer growth cycles but with more output. Individuals in these locations learned that exercising patience was rewarding when they experienced abundant harvests, which translated into substantial returns for their investment of effort and time.

As mentioned in the preceding chapter, analysis of second-generation immigrants also provides valuable insights. Imagine different groups of second-generation immigrants who were born and grew up in the same country but whose parents migrated to this country from various nations around the world. Although these groups of immigrants all live in the same country, it turns out that they differ systematically in their long-term orientation based on their parents' country of origin. Supporting the idea that the type of agriculture is related to time preference, research has shown that if the parents of second-generation immigrants migrated from a country of origin that has high crop yield, the second-generation immigrants are more patient and more long-term oriented compared to other second-generation individuals whose parents came from a country with low crop yield.

These research findings suggest that historical agricultural practices—specifically, the distinction between high versus low crop yields—have shaped the degree of patience and future outlook among the population in those countries, and this trait has been transmitted across generations.

Work Versus Leisure, Individualism Versus Collectivism

A similar study analyzed whether the historical cultivation of different crops in different societies is associated with different preferences between work and leisure across these societies. The question is: If a group of farmers and their ancestors have traditionally grown a particular crop, such as wheat or beans, do they exhibit a stronger or weaker preference for leisure compared to farmers with a history of cultivating a different crop, such as rice or oats?

This inquiry is based on a hypothesis grounded in economic theory, which suggests that higher labor productivity leads to greater demand for labor. As employment increases and working hours lengthen due to this labor demand, preferences may gradually shift from leisure to work. Observing this trend, parents are likely to instill a strong work ethic in their children if they expect their children to work long hours, further reinforcing the shift in preference away from leisure and toward work.

This means that if the historical cultivation method of a particular crop required more labor—because added laborers and extending work hours did not diminish productivity—societies that have traditionally grown that crop are expected to have developed a stronger preference for work.

The researchers calculated the labor share in the production of different crop types using data from the 1886 Prussian Agricultural Census, along with the 1922 US Department of Agriculture reports detailing man-hours per acre for various field crops. Analyses of surveys from over one hundred thousand individuals across various European regions showed that, after adjusting for personal attributes and regional characteristics, those living in areas better suited for labor-intensive crops tend to work longer hours per week. They also express a greater willingness to extend their working hours. Moreover, when responding to the question, "Please rate the importance of work in your life, from 1='Very important' to 4='Not at all important,'" they place greater importance on work compared to individuals from regions where typical crops require less labor.[28]

This indicates that individuals in regions with a history of labor-intensive agriculture have developed a stronger preference for work and tend to work longer hours today, regardless of their occupation.

Historical plough farming technology created a less labor-intensive method of farming, and it was particularly effective in the cultivation of wheat. Some other crops are much more labor-intensive to produce. The contrast between wheat and rice farming is particularly stark. The hours of work required for rice farming are up to three times more than the hours of work needed to grow wheat. For example, behavioral scientist Thomas Talhelm and his colleagues write, "Medieval Chinese people grew both wheat and rice, and they were aware of the huge labor difference between the two. A Chinese farming guide in the 1600s advised people, 'If one is short of labor power, it is best to grow wheat' (quoted in Elvin 1982). A Chinese anthropologist in the 1930s concluded that a husband and a wife would not be able to farm a large enough plot of rice to support the family if they relied on only their own labor (Xiaotong, 1945). Strict self-reliance might have meant starvation."[29]

Because rice farming requires a substantial amount of labor, it requires groups of farmers working together in coordinated ways and taking turns to farm on each other's fields. (A good depiction of this can be seen in the last seven minutes of Japanese director Akira Kurosawa's epic movie *Seven Samurai*.) In addition, cultivating rice in rice paddies necessitates the creation and maintenance of irrigation networks, requiring farmers to collaborate on determining the amount of labor each one will contribute and the effort invested in the communal project of digging and constructing irrigation canals. Another set of coordination challenges includes determining the amount of water each farmer will receive from the irrigation network, specifying when each rice paddy plot will receive water, and addressing the necessary repairs to the irrigation system.

All of this suggests that societies that were historically involved in rice agriculture (because of the reasons dictated by their location on earth and the associated soil and weather conditions) are expected to have developed collectivist tendencies, where group collaboration, adherence to group decisions, and group norms are important for survival, and defectors who behave selfishly are not tolerated.

Wheat farming, on the other hand, does not need irrigation, as regular rainfall is sufficient for a good harvest. Also, planting and harvesting wheat is less labor-intensive compared to rice.[30] For these reasons, wheat farmers do not need to collaborate with fellow farmers to plant and grow their crop. As a result, societies with a historical wheat-growing tradition are expected to have relatively stronger individualistic cultures, placing importance on personal freedom and autonomy and valuing individual independence.

In an interesting research project, psychologists specializing in cross-cultural behavior investigated whether historically rice-growing populations in China have more collectivist cultures in comparison to otherwise similar Chinese populations with historical wheat-farming traditions.[31] People's tendencies toward being individualistic or collectivist can be measured using various methods. A clever one involves asking each person to draw circles representing themselves and their social network (friends) and to connect these circles with lines to indicate the relationships among them. After the drawing is done, researchers measure the horizontal diameters of all circles (in case the circle is not drawn in a symmetric way). They calculate the average diameter of those circles representing friends and compare it to the diameter of the self circle. If a person represents herself with a bigger circle in comparison to how she draws the other circles representing friends, it is taken as an indication of self-importance and symbolic self-inflation. If, on the other hand, the person draws her self circle the same size as she draws the circles of others, this is considered as an indication that others are given equal weight as the self and as a representation of interdependence.

Previous social psychology research, using this method, has found that Japanese people draw themselves not differently from others, and even a bit smaller. British people drew themselves on average three millimeters bigger in diameter. Germans drew themselves 4.5 millimeters bigger, and Americans' self-circles had diameters that were more than six millimeters bigger.

Using this approach, researchers analyzed the drawings of more than 1,100 Chinese individuals. To account for potential differences in local governance structure, climate, and other factors that may be related to both culture and geographic location, they focused on people who live in neighboring counties in five central provinces of China where growing either rice or wheat has been the primary farming activity historically. Evaluating the drawings revealed systematic differences between those who live in counties that are similar to each other in many respects but differ in whether they historically grew rice or wheat. Individuals from wheat counties inflated themselves: Their self circles were 1.5 millimeters larger in diameter in comparison to how they drew the circles of others. People from rice-growing counties draw themselves the same size as or a bit smaller than they drew their friend circles. This result supports the hypothesis that people in historically rice-farming societies have collectivist cultures, whereas those whose ancestral farming roots are in wheat are individualistic.

The relative sizes of the circles representing the self and others might reflect something other than attitudes toward individualism. For example, smaller circles could be associated with humility, implying that more humble individuals might draw their self circles smaller. If this is the case, then the interpretation of the results would change, suggesting that people in rice-growing societies are more humble, while those in wheat-growing societies are more arrogant. However, to the extent that individualism and arrogance can be paired, and collectivism and humility can be paired, both interpretations would convey a similar underlying meaning.

In a different project, the well-known Hofstede individualism index, mentioned in chapter 1, is used to investigate the link between the degree of collectivism in a society today and the type of agriculture practiced by that society hundreds of years ago.[32] The author of the study evaluated various crops historically grown in countries worldwide and determined the amount of labor required to cultivate each crop. Some crops are more labor-intensive to cultivate than others; cultivating such labor-intensive crops, which requires coordination and cooperation among farmers, is expected to have led to the formation of collectivist attitudes in societies that have historically engaged in this type of farming. Conversely, societies with a tradition of less labor-intensive farming, where people worked independently (due to factors such as soil conditions and climate), are expected to have developed individualistic attitudes.

Analyses revealed that people are more collectivist if they reside in countries that have engaged in more labor-intensive crop cultivation.[33] A supplementary analysis involving data from over one hundred thousand individuals surveyed around the world, after accounting for people's age and various attributes of the regions they inhabit, showed that individuals living in different regions of the same country display different levels of collectivist tendencies. This variation is influenced by the labor-intensive nature of the farming environment in their respective regions, with regions characterized by more labor-intensive practices tending to foster higher collectivist tendencies.

What's in a Name?

Sociologists and psychologists view parents giving common first names to their children as prioritizing collective identity over individualism. A common first name signifies belonging to the community and an intention to blend in, while a unique name given to a child reflects a desire to stand out and signals self-reliance and independence. Therefore, the proportion of infrequent names is expected to be larger in more collectivist societies.[34]

The prevalence of unique names is calculated by considering an age group and locality (e.g., zero- to five-year-olds in Louisiana) and the proportion of children whose names are outside of the ten or fifteen most common names. This rate is computed by sex—and because Black Americans have a tradition of using distinct names, it is also calculated by race in the US.

Surveys of children reveal that those with common first names are more likely to value conformist behavior. Using US census records going back to the end of the eighteenth century, it has been demonstrated that settlers of the American frontier gave their children uncommon names. This is true even when analyzing only native-born parents and ignoring foreign names. Unique first names were also disproportionately prevalent in the frontier regions of Canada and Australia.[35] This is consistent with historians' belief that the frontiers attracted settlers with attitudes of rugged individualism.

Such nonconformism and individualism, embedded in settlers, are reflected in the uncommon names they gave to their children.

So, the proportion of common first names in a society is another indicator of its collectivist, as opposed to individualistic, tendencies. The frequency of common first names is particularly noticeable, even to a casual observer, in some nations that rank high on the Hofstede index of collectivism. This is especially true in societies with strong religious traditions, where many individuals are named after historical religious figures.[36]

An intriguing study explored the agricultural roots of collectivism by using the prevalence of unusual first names as a proxy of individualism. A team of researchers analyzed historical agricultural records from US counties dating back to the late nineteenth century to assess the labor-intensity required to grow each crop during that period.[37] For example, cotton needed about 115 hours of work per acre, and sugarcane required about ninety hours of work per acre. In contrast, some other crops like wheat, oats, and barley were much less labor-intensive to grow, requiring only ten to fifteen hours of labor per acre. Using this information and utilizing data on each county's actual crop production, researchers were able to compute the agricultural labor intensity of US counties during the late nineteenth and early twentieth centuries.

Because higher labor intensity in agriculture requires more frequent interactions with, as well as cooperation and coordination between, individuals, locations with more labor-intensive farming (due to the types and quantities of crops produced) are expected to exhibit more collectivist attitudes. Researchers measured the extent of collectivism in each county by calculating the proportion of common names given to babies, determined via census records.

The authors then identified two key events that significantly influenced agricultural production in the late nineteenth century. The first was the mechanization of agriculture, which introduced new machinery that transformed production methods for some crops but not for others. Mechanization drastically reduced the labor required to cultivate certain crops, such as broom corn, sweet potatoes, and cotton. But other crops, which did not need much labor to cultivate in the first place, did not significantly benefit from mechanization.

As a result, US counties experienced varying degrees of decline in agricultural labor intensity, depending on the crops they produced. A comparison of counties between the mid-1800s and 1900 revealed that this decline in labor intensity gave rise to an increase in the share of uncommon first names, signaling an increase in individualism.

A second event was the invasion of the boll weevil, a pest known for its appetite for cotton plants. This insect wreaked havoc on cotton cultivation across America from the 1890s to the 1930s, particularly impacting the South. Many cotton growers, facing the devastation caused by the boll weevil, opted to transition to alternative crops suitable for their land. Given the labor-intensive nature of cotton farming, this transition led to a substantial reduction in agricultural labor intensity in some locations. The timing and the magnitude of this labor shift varied among counties, depending on the onset and severity of the boll weevil infestation and the prior intensity of cotton production in each county.

Researchers discovered that the arrival of this insect and the subsequent decrease in agricultural labor intensity led to an increase in the prevalence of distinctive names given to children in Southern counties. This effect was particularly pronounced in regions that underwent significant declines in labor intensity due to transitioning from cotton to much less labor-intensive crops like wheat and rye.

These findings provide further evidence that individualism versus collectivism as a cultural attribute of a society has roots in the historical agricultural practices of that society.

5 Is Geography Destiny?

The preceding two chapters have demonstrated that geographical attributes of nations, such as soil conditions and type of terrain, have exerted long-lasting impacts on cultural behaviors and beliefs. However, the examples in these chapters may have created the impression that the only determinant of a society's cultural attributes is where that society is located on earth. Is geography destiny?

Some scholars have suggested that the long-term prosperity of a country depends primarily on its geographical location. Economist Jeffrey Sachs has long argued that geography has a direct impact on economic growth, operating through various channels like climate, agricultural productivity, susceptibility to diseases, and availability of natural resources.[1] He suggested that a country's location determines the extent to which it has easy access to the rest of the world. Societies situated near rivers, seas, and oceans have historically enjoyed lower transportation costs, enabling them to have easier access to international trade and to new ideas and innovations originating elsewhere. In contrast, societies located in hot climates near the equator or in regions where climate-driven diseases like malaria and dengue fever are common, faced inherent disadvantages.

Jared Diamond, a renowned geographer, suggested in his Pulitzer Prize–winning book *Guns, Germs, and Steel* that geography is the key to prosperity of nations, albeit for a different reason.[2] He proposed the *axis of orientation* hypothesis, arguing that the east-west orientation of Eurasia permitted easy spread of ideas and innovations across its regions due to the similarity in climate and habitat. Domestication of animals and plants, cultivation techniques, and other innovations were diffused easily on the east-west axis of Eurasia in comparison to the north-south axis of Africa and the Americas.

Early human settlements and pivotal innovations such as the wheel and writing, originating in Mesopotamia around twelve thousand years ago, propagated predominantly along the east-west axis of Eurasia. Consequently, geographical differences between Eurasia and the rest of the world ultimately resulted in variations in technological, military, and economic advancement between continents.

The arguments posited by Sachs and Diamond suggest that certain regions of the world are inherently predisposed to development advantages compared to others. The Middle East stands out as one such area, meeting the criteria outlined by both of these scholars. This region benefits from access to waterways, rivers, and seas, fostering long-distance trade and providing a platform for exposure to ideas and inventions originating from neighboring societies over many millennia. The historical Silk Road, a crucial trade route connecting Europe and India for centuries, passed through this territory.

The Tigris and Euphrates rivers, springing from Eastern Turkey, flow southward through present-day Syria and Iraq, before reaching the Persian Gulf. Mesopotamia, which is the area between these rivers, is referred to as the *cradle of civilization*. The broader region, known as the Fertile Crescent, encompassing Mesopotamia and extending westward toward the Mediterranean Sea, includes present-day Iraq, Jordan, Lebanon, Palestine, Israel, and the southeastern region of Turkey. It was in this region that the Neolithic Revolution took place starting in 10,000 BCE, during which humans transitioned from a hunter-gatherer lifestyle to settled agricultural communities. As its name indicates, the land in this area is fertile and conducive to agriculture.[3]

The Mesopotamia sector of the Fertile Crescent holds the distinction of being the birthplace of pivotal inventions such as the wheel, the plough, and writing. The first important ancient civilizations emerged there, including the Sumerians, who invented writing in cuneiform script, as well as the Akkadians and the Babylonians. These civilizations achieved significant technical and social advancements, ranging from the construction of intricate irrigation networks to creation of the iconic hanging towers of Babylon, celebrated as one of the seven wonders of the ancient world. The Code of Hammurabi is the first known written legal code, developed and implemented by Hammurabi, one of the kings of Babylon, around 1,750 BCE.

Mesopotamia witnessed other milestones in human history, including the signing of the first-ever peace treaty—the Treaty of Kadesh—following a war between King Hattusili III of the Hittite Empire (located in present-day central Turkey) and the Egyptian Pharaoh Ramses II in 1,259 BCE. The first human temple, built in 9,000 BCE, is located in Göbeklitepe, Turkey, in the northeast part of the Fertile Crescent.

However, despite the advantageous initial conditions thanks to its geographic location, most countries in this region struggle today with economic underdevelopment and face a host of social and political challenges, ranging from fragile democracies to human rights violations and the prevalence of violence. In fact, recognizing these persistent problems in that particular geography, many people in the Middle East label the region as *cursed geography*, suggesting that the particular location of the Middle East is perceived not as a blessing but as a curse. Any adverse event in the area is attributed to the "unfortunate destiny of this geography."

The contrast in economic development and various indicators of human well-being between the Middle East and Western Europe and North America, despite the Middle East's more advantageous geographic location, does not invalidate the hypothesis that geography directly influences or facilitates development. However, although important, geography is not the only determinant of economic development and human well-being. Other factors (culture being the most significant one) also contribute to shaping these outcomes.

As discussed in the previous two chapters, geography certainly does influences culture—but it's crucial to reiterate that just as geography isn't the sole factor shaping economic development, geography isn't the sole influencer of culture either.[4] This chapter will discuss how one such factor, violence, impacts the shaping of cultural norms.

Exposure to Violence and Political Participation

In many countries around the world, ranging from Sweden to Turkey, from Australia to Chile, from Estonia to South Korea, citizens are automatically registered to vote in elections once they reach the age of eighteen or nineteen. This is not the case in the United States. Each US citizen makes an individual decision whether or not to register as a voter. Although not every eligible person chooses to register, the propensity to refrain from voting is bigger among Black Americans. For example, 75 percent of white Americans are registered to vote, whereas the voter registration rate is 64 percent among Black Americans.[5]

There are various reasons for this discrepancy, including economic ones. More educated individuals are more likely to be registered voters. Likewise, as household income increases, people become more likely to register to vote. Black Americans have less education and lower incomes on average compared to white Americans. About 5 percent of white Americans have no high school education, but the rate is 10 percent for Black Americans. The rate of those who have at least a bachelor's degree is 24 percent among Black Americans, while more than 30 percent of white Americans have a bachelor's degree or higher.[6] The median income of white households is $77,000, while it is $53,000 among Black households.[7] These income and education disparities partly account for differential voter registration rates between Black and white Americans.

Several other factors contribute to the gap in voter registration rates between Black and white individuals. For instance, one commonly mentioned obstacle to registration and voting is that elections are typically held on Tuesdays, which poses a challenge for Black individuals who are more likely to be employed in jobs with rigid schedules, making it difficult to take time off during the week. However, there are options for early voting, including weekends, prior to Election Day.

Despite the hurdles that prevent or discourage access to voting, it's clear that greater participation from Black voters could significantly impact election outcomes in many communities, potentially affecting the welfare of Black residents. The persistent reluctance of Black Americans to participate in the political process and to exercise their voting rights, as demonstrated by low rates of voter registration, is a cultural pattern recognized by politicians, community activists, and scholars.[8]

Whether present-day Black voter registration is linked to political violence experienced by the Black community more than one hundred years ago has been analyzed by one of my former doctoral students, Jhacova Williams, in her dissertation. The historical background goes back to the Reconstruction Act of 1867, which aimed to address the status of the Southern states and rebuild the political and social landscape of the American South after the Civil War. The act required Southern states to draft new constitutions that guaranteed the right to vote for Black men. Consequently, Black men were able to cast their votes in the 1868 presidential election in Alabama, Florida, Georgia, Louisiana, Mississippi, North Carolina, South Carolina, and Tennessee. The voter turnout among Black men ranged from 70 to 90 percent, and Black Americans started being elected to political office. For example, Black individuals constituted 61 percent of the state delegates of South Carolina, 50 percent of state delegates in Louisiana, and 40 percent in Florida.[9]

These developments prompted violent reactions from the Ku Klux Klan (KKK). To intimidate Black Americans and to discourage them from voting, the KKK used extreme violence, including the burning and lynching of Black individuals. In 1868, the KKK killed more than two thousand Black people in Louisiana, killed two legislators in South Carolina, and assassinated James F. Casey, the president of the Union League, for his and his organization's efforts to register Black voters and to encourage their participation in the political process. As a result of this violence, Black voter turnout quickly declined, but KKK terror exerted on Black Americans continued, which caused the further decline in participation of Black individuals in politics.[10]

That lynchings are aimed at intimidating Black people in order to suppress their desire to be involved in elections is supported by the fact that lynchings were more prevalent in counties with higher percentages of Black voters. This political violence in the South continued for decades, and some Southern counties experienced up to twenty-five lynchings between 1882 and 1930. The lynching rate during this period, calculated as the total number of lynchings between 1882 and 1930 per ten thousand Black residents in 1900, was as high as 169 in some counties. This means that over this fifty-year period, about two of each one hundred Black persons were lynched in some areas. As a consequence of this extreme violence, Black individuals refrained from voting. In 1940, only 151,000 Black Americans in eleven Southern states were registered to vote, which was about 3 percent of the five million Black residents who were eligible as voters.[11]

Using the voter registration data from six southern states that were part of the former Confederacy and for which lynching data are available at the county level, Williams investigated the relationship between the average percentage of Black registered voters in the presidential elections between 2000 and 2012 in each county and the lynching rate of Black people in those counties about one hundred years ago.[12] The statistical analyses were adjusted for historical institutional, social, economic, and political attributes of these counties that may also be related to lynching. The results showed that Black Americans who live in counties that experienced a relatively higher rate of historical lynchings are less likely to register to vote today. On the other hand, a county's exposure to lynching has no influence on the voter registration behavior of its white residents.

Put differently, variation across Southern counties in the rate at which their Black residents were lynched by the KKK between 1882 and 1930 explains the differences in Black voter registration rates across counties today. In locations where Black Americans were exposed to more intense political violence about one hundred years ago, Black residents withdrew from political participation—and the children and grandchildren of the generation that was originally exposed to that violence are reluctant and unwilling to be registered voters today. In other words, the KKK campaign of terror one hundred years ago achieved its objective of intimidating Black voters. The resultant avoidance behavior of Black citizens has been transmitted to future generations, and the corresponding lack of political participation has become a cultural attribute.

Occupational Persistence as Culture

Certain groups of individuals are known for particular skills that lead them to be heavily represented in certain occupations. Although personal economic conditions as well as income and wealth constraints play a substantial role in shaping occupational choices, the intergenerational transmission of occupation-specific skills and knowledge contribute to the creation of a culture of occupational persistence. Perhaps one of the best examples of this phenomenon can be found in the fishing industry.

Although it is possible to acquire a fishing boat, the necessary equipment, and training specific to fishing, true success as a fisherman hinges on access to elusive idiosyncrasies and a specialized body of knowledge cultivated over generations. This knowledge encompasses the intricate relationships between temperature, wind, light, and currents in specific locations, the conditions of the sea bottom, and the behavioral patterns of fish, which can only be gained from people with prior experience. Consequently, the offspring of seasoned fishermen enjoy a distinctive advantage in achieving success compared to newcomers in the field because they inherit the hard-to-observe aspects of the business and the invaluable tricks of the trade passed down through generations of fishermen.

Illustrating this phenomenon, there is a prevalence of individuals with Vietnamese heritage engaged in shrimping in Louisiana and Texas. Following the Vietnam War, immigrants from coastal towns in southern Vietnam, equipped with net-making and fishing skills, arrived in the US. Many of them secured jobs in the shrimping industry and passed down the profession through multiple generations. Research has shown that many occupations and professions are passed down from one generation to the next. For example, if a politician is elected to the US Congress for more than one term, this doubles the probability that he or she will have a relative elected to the Congress in the future. The same is true for the politicians in the Philippines. A parent's enlistment in the US Army increases the likelihood of their children serving in the military by at least 60 percent.[13] Evidence from various countries, including the US and Sweden, shows that a child is much more likely to be an entrepreneur if a parent is an entrepreneur.[14]

The prevalence of a particular occupation among a specific group of individuals, coupled with the enduring nature of this occupation within the group across successive generations, establishes a culture characterized by a preference for that occupation. Of course, intergenerational avoidance of occupations is also possible. It is highly unlikely to encounter individuals of Muslim or Jewish faith working in a pig slaughterhouse, and it is equally unlikely for their children to opt for that profession. This is due to the fact that both of these religions regard pigs as unclean animals, any contact with which is to be avoided.

This brings us to the Kentucky Derby, a very salient aspect of which is its lack of Black jockeys. Over the last century, there have been only four Black jockeys who competed in the Kentucky Derby. In 2000, Marlon St. Julien became the first Black jockey to race in the Kentucky Derby since 1911.[15] And between 2001 and 2025, there have only been three Black jockeys who competed in the derby.

The lack of Black jockeys is not a phenomenon specific to the Kentucky Derby. There are very few Black jockeys in all horse racing in America, and consequently there are virtually no Black jockeys competing in important races, including the Triple Crown (Kentucky Derby, Belmont Stakes, and Preakness Stakes). I will, however, focus on the Kentucky Derby, given its status as arguably the most prestigious horse race in the world. The Kentucky Derby is often hailed as the most thrilling two minutes in sports, offering a prize of approximately $3 million. This sum is distributed among the owners of the horses that secure the top five positions in the race and their respective jockeys, with the winner's share being around $2 million.

One might hypothesize that the underrepresentation of Black jockeys can be attributed to income disparities between Black and white communities.

Becoming proficient in horseback riding as a sport often requires significant financial investment, which could account for the limited involvement of Black individuals in professional horseracing. Given the lower family incomes among Black families compared to white families, it is plausible that financial constraints hinder Black children from learning horseback riding, thereby limiting their prospects of pursuing a career as a professional jockey later in life.

Although this argument has merit, it overlooks the historical legacy of Black jockeys in the Unites States. At the very first Kentucky Derby in 1875, thirteen of the fifteen jockeys were Black individuals, and the winner of that inaugural derby was a nineteen-year-old Black jockey by the name of Oliver Lewis. It has been noted that the earliest Black jockeys were individuals born into slavery or raised as children of slaves who were responsible for tending to horses on plantations and farms where they both trained and rode them.[16] In the following years, more white jockeys entered the race, and on average, about 60 percent of jockeys were white in the first eighteen derbies. Nevertheless, fifteen of these eighteen derbies were won by Black jockeys. So, Black jockeys were very skilled, and they were dominating the sport.

The success of Black jockeys in the late nineteenth century, amid the backdrop of segregation and racism—exemplified by the enactment of Jim Crow laws during this period—prompted a deliberate campaign by white jockeys to oust their Black counterparts from the sport. White jockeys started targeting Black jockeys during races—using their riding crops to hit them or forcing Black jockeys' horses to the railings. For instance, in one of these incidents, Jimmy Winkfield, a prominent Black jockey who won the Kentucky Derby in back-to-back years, was badly hurt and had his ribs cracked at a racetrack near Chicago. These harassment and intimidation strategies of white jockeys, coupled with the reluctance of horse owners to hire Black jockeys in such a hostile environment, resulted in the expulsion of Black jockeys from the US horse racing scene. Some Black jockeys relocated to Europe in search of employment, while others pursued alternative careers in the horse racing industry, such as working in stables. Some others chose to leave the profession altogether.

This dramatic exodus of Black jockeys due to harassment, coercion, and violence has been portrayed as being due to Black jockeys' inability to compete with white jockeys. This narrative is exemplified in a 1905 article in

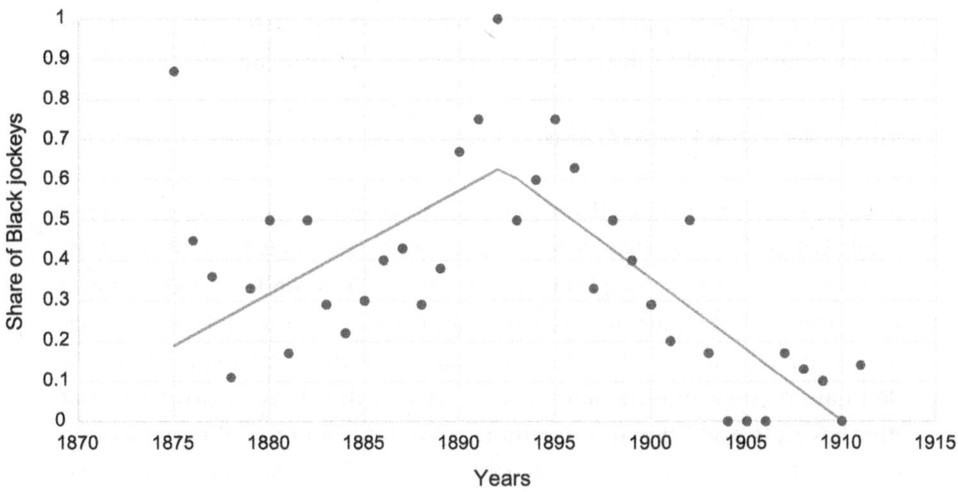

Figure 5.1
Share of Black jockeys in the Kentucky Derby over time

the *Washington Post* titled "Negro Riders on the Wane: White Jockeys' Superior Intelligence Supersedes."[17]

Figure 5.1 displays the share of Black jockeys in each Kentucky Derby between 1985 and 1911. Although there was an increasing trend until 1892, a dramatic reversal took place after that year. The trend line on the graph highlights a steady decline in the percentage of Black jockeys after 1892, dropping to below 10 percent by 1900. This forced exodus of Black jockeys from horseracing had a long-lasting effect: There were zero Black jockeys at the Kentucky Derby for most of the next 120 years.[18]

When one generation experiences harassment and violence due to their aspirations to pursue a particular profession, it is natural for subsequent generations to be deterred from entering that field. As I discussed earlier, compounding this issue is the fact that certain professions, such as horse racing, require specific human capital. The knowledge accumulated over generations cannot be swiftly acquired through formal education or training. Intricate and crucial knowledge about the profession is traditionally passed down to new generations, and if one generation is skipped, it becomes challenging to recover the lost know-how.

This outcome of missing Black jockeys from horseracing is similar to the reluctance of Black individuals to register as voters because of their forbearers' exposure to politically motivated violence a century ago.

African Slave Trade and Mistrust

Suppose you decided to go fishing at a nearby river with your friend from the neighborhood. As you two are walking through the woods towards the river, you see a few of your neighbors approaching. They walk toward you and then stop to chat. After the exchange of pleasantries and a bit of conversation, you say your goodbyes, and each party continues walking toward their destination. A few minutes later, you notice that they have turned back, that they have a few additional companions with them, and that they are following you. The group starts walking faster, comes closer, and before you and your friend can figure out what exactly is happening, they jump you. They start beating you and your friend and try to tie your hands and feet. You and your friend somehow find a way to escape, run away, and enter the nearby forest. In the process, you get separated from each other.

You spend the night and the next day hiding in the forest, carefully making your way back home two days later. Your friend, on the other hand, is nowhere to be found. The word on the street is that the neighbors who attacked both of you captured your friend in the forest, and they sold him to human traffickers who ship such kidnapped individuals to far away destinations for the purposes of organ harvesting or slave labor. You knew that armed bandits, hired by foreign merchants, raided villages to capture people who were then transported by ships to foreign lands, but you had never heard of people kidnapping and selling others from the same community.

Suppose that such incidents become increasingly common in your community, eventually evolving into a regular pattern in which friends and even family members deceive and abduct one another and sell one another into slavery—and this practice continues for several decades.

This scenario is not far from what has been experienced by some communities in Africa during the Atlantic slave trade. It has been documented extensively by historians and ethnographers that as the slave trade progressed, it became commonplace, especially among certain ethnic communities, for individuals to kidnap and sell others, even their own family members, to slavery. As described by Nunn and Wantchekon, German missionary and linguist

Sigismund Koelle wrote in 1854 that almost one in every five slaves was sold by relatives and friends in Sierra Leone. Cultural anthropologist Charles Piot explained the various modes of slave appropriation, including the predatory raids conducted by kingdoms of West Africa against noncentralized societies to capture and enslave their members, and families selling their relatives to slave traders. In particular, he analyzed the Kabre of northern Togo, where it was common for an uncle to sell his nephews and nieces as slaves.[19]

In such an environment, people would naturally develop a culture of mistrust as they would come to view those around them as untrustworthy. The interesting question is whether such a norm of mistrust, if developed, is transmitted through generations so that the descendants of those who were exposed to this environment are still less trusting of others, say, one hundred years after the end of such kidnap-and-sell practices.

Nunn and Wantchekon investigated this question by analyzing the differences in trust levels between individuals in Africa. They found that people who belong to those ethnic groups that were the most exposed to the slave trade in the past display lower levels of trust today to their relatives, neighbors, and members of their ethic group. This finding signifies the enduring, intergenerational effect of distrust due to previous generations' exposure to violence and betrayal. The study also found that trust in local government is diminished among the descendants of those who were significantly impacted by the slave trade. This might be attributable to the fact that, as explained by the same authors, many chiefs were frequently engaged in slave trading or were coerced into selling their own people to slavery. Consequently, the slave trade appears to have undermined trust in local leaders too, which is still detectable long after the end of slavery.

Violence Begets Violence

The examples provided thus far of diminished trust, disengagement from political involvement, and avoidance of a profession illustrate the enduring consequences of violent events that took place at least a century ago. Thus they highlight the persistent, long-term impact of violence. If exposure to violence has a lasting, profound effect on behavior, it is expected that violence also exerts an immediate effect, and it has been shown that this is in fact the case. For example, exposure to civil war makes people more prone to violence and increases their proclivity for unlawful behavior.

Among many examples of research documenting this effect, there is one based on professional soccer in Europe. Soccer is played by eleven players on each team. It involves physical contact, and some moves that require contact are permissible. For example, slide-tackling an opponent who is in possession of the ball is not a foul, so long as the tackler touches the ball first before he makes contact with the opposing player. But if a player commits a foul during his interactions with other players, then the referee intervenes, stops the game, and awards a free kick in favor of the disadvantaged player's team.

Actions constituting unnecessary roughness such as kicking an opponent, stepping on their foot or any body part, making moves that may injure or pose risk of injury to the opposing player, and excessive pushing or pulling of an opposing player during one-on-one challenges are prohibited. In such situations, the referee not only stops the game by calling the foul but also, because the incident surpasses the acceptable standards of a foul, books the offending player by showing him a yellow card. This serves as a warning to the player for the excessive roughness he committed, and it has consequences. A player who receives two yellow cards in two consecutive games is not allowed to play in the following game. If a player receives a second yellow card in the same game, that second yellow automatically becomes a red card, and the player is ejected from the game. In the event of a red card, the team of the red-carded player is not allowed to bring in a new player as a substitute, and the team plays the rest of the game one player down. Red cards also may be issued directly, without the player having previously received a yellow card in the game. When a foul is deemed extremely rough, seems intentional, or poses serious risk of injury to the targeted player, the referee is obligated to show the red card, resulting in the immediate ejection of the player from the game. Red-carded players face further sanctions. All of this means that receiving a card has consequences for the players.

In an interesting study, researchers analyzed data involving more than 2,500 players participating in the world's most prestigious professional soccer leagues: the Premiere League of England, Ligue 1 in France, Bundesliga of Germany, Serie A in Italy, and La Liga of Spain. They also analyzed the games played by these players and their teams in the top European soccer tournament, the UEFA Champions League, in which professional teams from different countries compete against each other to determine Europe's best team each year.[20]

The players analyzed in the study were from seventy different countries, and about 30 percent of them were nationals of African, Latin American, Caribbean, Eastern European, and Middle Eastern nations. Because the country of origin is known for each player, researchers can identify whether there was a civil war in each player's country when the player was young. Civil war, in this context, extends beyond its traditional definition. It relates to wars such as the civil war in Sierra Leone and the Balkan civil war after the collapse of Yugoslavia (involving Serbia, Croatia, Bosnia), but it also includes other violent conflicts such as the Israeli-Palestinian struggle, the Chechen war in Russia, the violence in Northern Ireland, and so on.

The question here is whether childhood exposure to civil war in the home country makes soccer players more prone to violence on the soccer field. Of course, the likelihood of a player receiving a card from the referee depends on many factors. The player's position plays an important role. For goalkeepers, the probability of receiving a card is extremely low, although they can be yellow carded for deliberately delaying the game or similar offenses. In contrast, defensive players and midfielders face higher chances of committing fouls that may result in cards. The player's team and the league in which the team competes are also important, as are the player's age and skill level (it is difficult to measure player skill, but the player's market value for the position in which he is playing is a good indicator).

Analyses have shown that the number of years of civil war in the player's home country when the player was young has a significant impact on that player's tendency to commit rough fouls leading to receiving cards from referees. Two players who are on the same team, are playing in the same position, are of the same age, have the same market value, and originate from countries within the same continent and with similar per capita GDP differ in their proclivity for roughness based on their country's civil war experience. Exposure to civil war violence increases the likelihood that players will act aggressively on the soccer field.

If you remain skeptical about the connection between exposure to civil war violence and subsequent aggressive behavior on the soccer field, consider a different example. This one is from Switzerland. A group of economists have analyzed all crimes committed in Switzerland over an eighteen-year period between 2009 and 2016.[21] Switzerland spans sixteen thousand square miles, placing it between Maryland and West Virginia in terms of land area. There are fewer than nine million people in the entire country. Between 2009 and 2016, Switzerland took in more than thirty-four thousand asylum seekers each year.

For each asylum seeker, Swiss authorities gather comprehensive personal information including age, sex, and country of origin. Authorities also collect detailed information on each crime committed in the country, including the location, date, time, and type of the crime, as well as the identities of the victims and perpetrators. Researchers compared individuals from the same country who migrated to Switzerland in the same year, but who were either (1) born before the civil war in their country and therefore exposed to it or (2) born after the war. These two groups naturally differed in age when they entered Switzerland as they were born in different years. To account for this age effect, the difference in their criminal proclivity in Switzerland is compared to the same difference among asylum seekers from other countries with no exposure to civil war. To give an example, this method involves calculating the difference in criminal activity between two Rwandan cohorts: those born after the 1994 genocide and those who were children during the genocide. The difference in their criminal records is then compared to the crime difference between the same cohorts from countries where neither cohort was exposed to civil war.

Careful statistical analyses showed that asylum seekers who were exposed to violent civil war in their home country before the age of twelve are significantly more likely to commit violent crimes in Switzerland than other asylum seekers who were not exposed to violence.

Importantly, this effect is not observed for property crimes, the main motivation of which is financial. So exposure to violence does not increase the propensity to commit any crime, but it raises the proclivity for violence.

Crimean Tatars

The final example of the impact of violence demonstrates how exposure to a violent event alters trust in three consecutive generations. This example is from the Crimea, which is a peninsula on the northern part of the Black Sea, with an area of about 10,500 square miles, which is about the size of Massachusetts or Hawaii. The Crimea used to be part of the Ukrainian territory after the collapse of the Soviet Union, until Vladimir Putin invaded it and annexed it to Russia in 2014. Over the course of its history, the Crimea has been ruled by the Byzantine Empire, Ottoman Empire, and Russian Empire. Its population consists of people of various ethnicities. Crimean Tatars are one of these ethic groups. They are of Turkic origin and speak a Turkic language. The majority of Crimean Tatars are Muslim.

During World War II, in the summer of 1941, Germans launched an attack on the Soviet Union. As part of their advance, they occupied Crimea in 1942. German occupation lasted until May 1944, when the Soviet Red Army drove out Germans from the peninsula. Immediately afterward, on May 18, 1944, Joseph Stalin gave the order for forced deportation of the entire Tatar population from the Crimea to various eastern territories of the Soviet Union on the allegations of collaboration with Nazi Germany during the war and "mass treason." Historical records indicate that there was no Tatar collaboration with the Nazis and that this mass deportation was part of Stalin's broader policy of population relocation and suppression of minorities.

Between May 18 and 22, 1944, the entire Tatar population of about two hundred thousand individuals were forcibly removed from their homes. Historians write that families were given ten to fifteen minutes to collect their belongings that could be carried by hand, often in the middle of the night.[22] Most Tatars were transported by cattle trains under terrible conditions to Soviet Central Asia, primarily to Uzbekistan, Kazakhstan, and the Ural region. The estimate of casualties during and soon after the deportation due to starvation and disease ranges from 20 to 50 percent.[23]

Almost half a century later, after the dissolution of the Soviet Union in 1991, Ukraine declared its independence as a nation, and the Crimea became part of the newly independent Ukraine. This allowed the Tatars to come back to Crimea from various locations in Central Asia and elsewhere to which they were exiled.[24]

In a creative research study, political scientists surveyed randomly selected Crimean Tatars who were in their seventies in 2014.[25] These individuals were toddlers or young children in 1944, so they are the members of the first generation exposed to Russian forced deportation. Researchers also interviewed two randomly selected children of these individuals, who are members of the second generation. Finally, two children of each second-generation member were randomly selected to be interviewed. This research design allowed for tracing down the family tree for each family by linking three hundred first-generation Crimean Tatars to six hundred individuals of the second generation and more than one thousand members of the third generation, from twenty-three towns and almost 190 villages throughout the Crimea.

The intensity of the first generation's exposure to violence is measured by the number of their family members who died during the train journey to the deportation destination or shortly afterward. Researchers asked all participants questions to gauge their trust in fellow Crimean Tatars (with the possible answers *trust none, trust only some, trust the majority, trust all*). The same questions were posed to determine their trust in Russians. The difference between these two responses measures the extent of *in-group trust*—that is, the extent to which Crimean Tatars trust their fellow Tatars more than they trust Russians.

Survey participants were also asked whether they consider themselves or their relatives to be victims of the Russian political system today. Similarly, they were asked whether they felt fearful about their future after Putin's troops annexed the Crimea to Russia. Finally, they were also asked whether they thought that Chechens and Dagestanis, who were fighting against Russia at the time of the survey, were radicals or whether they were freedom fighters trying to gain independence from Russia.

The results showed that among the first-generation Crimean Tatars who lost a larger number of family members during the deportation when they were kids, in-group attachment to fellow Tatars was higher, feelings of victimhood were stronger, and the perception of the Russian threat was bigger.

Researchers have found that among the second-generation Crimean Tatars, the attachment and trust to their fellow Tatars, the intensity of their belief that Tatars are the victims of the Soviet State, and the fear and distrust of Russia was stronger for those whose parents experienced more intense victimization (bigger casualties during the Russian forced deportation in 1944).

These effects were also observed among the third generation. The grandchildren of those who faced worse violence during the deportation seventy years ago have stronger in-group attachment and more negative attitudes toward Russia today. They are also more likely to support the Chechen and Dagestani separatists and are less likely to support Russia's annexation of the Crimea.

These findings reveal that severe violence affects the beliefs and attitudes of those who were the targets of this violence, and that these beliefs and attitudes are transmitted to future generations. This, of course, sheds light on the cycles of violence experienced around the world, the long-lasting war between Israelis and Palestinians being a prominent example.

In summary, exposure to violence transforms preferences, beliefs, and behaviors, and these changed preferences, beliefs, and behaviors are passed down to future generations. Therefore, violence leads to cultural change and creates ripple effects that are evident in subsequent generations.

6 Institutions and Culture

In this chapter, I will demonstrate how institutions can change culture. Examples will include political institutions, legal institutions, and economic systems. I will show how institutions influence cultural attributes such as trust, dishonesty, and family living arrangements. I will also discuss how the effectiveness of institutions depends on culture and how institutional differences emerge from cultural variations.

Empires

Think about a city one hundred miles away from the city in which you live. Perhaps some of your relatives or friends live in that city; perhaps you do business with people in that city. Now imagine that a war breaks out, at the end of which a border is created between your city and the other one. Your city remains on one side of the border, governed by one kingdom, and the other city lies on the other side of the border, governed by a different kingdom. These two kingdoms have different kings and queens, different governance styles, and different political and judicial structures. People enjoy varying degrees of personal freedom, and they are exposed to different levels of government bureaucracy and corruption, depending on which side of the border they find themselves.

Presume that people in these cities live under these two different regimes for two hundred years or more. Then, one day, these kingdoms collapse, the border disappears, and both cities come under the control of one single state. From that point on, the residents of both cities live under the same governance style for one hundred years.

If we were to survey people living in these two cities today, a full century after the collapse of the kingdoms under which their ancestors have lived, would we detect systematic disparities in their attitudes that cannot be ascribed to personal characteristics such age, sex, income, education, and so on, but could potentially mirror the institutional frameworks to which their predecessors were once subjected?

The question posed here can be decomposed into two parts:

(1) Did differences in institutions of these separate kingdoms, such as the quality of their government, the efficiency of the legal system, and the extent of bureaucratic corruption, exert an influence on the behaviors and beliefs of their inhabitants?

(2) Were these behaviors and beliefs pervasive enough to constitute a cultural attribute to be transmitted across generations so that significant differences are observed between descendants of these two cities even one hundred years after the collapse of these kingdoms?

If the response to the first question is in the negative, then the answer to the second question must also be in the negative. If institutions in these kingdoms failed to shape behaviors and beliefs, then there is no belief to be transmitted to future generations that can be attributed to the impact of institutions.

Should the response to the second question be "no," it remains unclear whether (1) the institutions in these kingdoms had no influence on the attitudes and behaviors of those who lived within them, or (2) the institutions indeed altered behaviors and attitudes, but these influences were insufficiently potent to persist across multiple generations.

But if the response to the second question is affirmative, then we can reasonably conclude that the institutions of these kingdoms exerted substantial and enduring influence over the behaviors and beliefs of their populace. Furthermore, this influence was potent enough to shape cultural characteristics that have persisted through generations and are discernible in the present-day descendants of these kingdoms' inhabitants.

To find an answer to this inquiry, economists analyzed people who belonged to the same nationality and ethnic group, but whose descendants happened to live under the rules of different empires, just as the thought experiment described earlier. These empires are the Habsburg Empire (also called the Austro-Hungarian Empire), the Ottoman Empire, and the Russian Empire.[1]

Although its territory expended and shrank over its reign, as is the case with any empire, the Habsburg Empire in various centuries ruled lands that comprise modern-day Austria, Hungary, Northern Italy, Slovenia, Slovakia, the Czech Republic, parts of Poland and Ukraine, Belgium, the Netherlands, Serbia, Croatia, Bosnia and Herzegovina, and parts of Romania. At its height, the Ottoman empire ruled the area that is modern-day Turkey and most of the Middle East and Arab peninsula. The Ottoman Empire's European territories included modern-day Greece, Romania, Serbia, Bosnia and Herzegovina, Montenegro, Kosovo, Albania, Bulgaria, North Macedonia, and parts of modern-day Ukraine. The Russian empire, at its height, occupied European territories covering modern-day Ukraine, Poland, Romania, Belarus, Estonia, Latvia, and Lithuania.

As the list of territories ruled by these three empires makes clear, the Ottoman and Russian Empires bordered the Habsburg Empire for centuries, and various parts of Eastern Europe were ruled by these empires over centuries. To investigate the existence of the long-term effects of institutions, researchers analyzed the differences in individuals' beliefs, examining if these beliefs were influenced by whether their ancestors were governed by the Habsburg Empire as opposed to Ottoman and Russian Empires.

The study surveyed people who live in today's Montenegro, Poland, Romania, Ukraine, and Serbia. The border of the Habsburg Empire cut through these countries before its collapse in 1918 following World War I. This meant, for example, that the grandparents and great-grandparents of some Romanians who reside in present-day Romania lived under the rules of the Habsburg Empire, governed by its bureaucrats and facing the rules of its courts. Some other Romanians, on the other hand, live today in locations that were under the rule of the Ottoman Empire for centuries, and they were exposed to its bureaucracy and courts. Similarly, there are hundreds of towns in Poland, Macedonia, Montenegro, Ukraine, and Serbia that are located on both sides of the old Habsburg Empire border.

Historians documented differences in the institutional structures and quality of government between the Habsburg Empire and the empires of the Ottomans and the Russians. The Habsburg Empire provided significant local autonomy and freedom of governance to the cities and territories under its crown. The Habsburg Empire is considered the prototype of a federation, a *Vielvölkerstaat* (state composed of many people) that respected the identity and local differences of various parts of the empire.[2] The bureaucracy of the Habsburg Empire was respected by the population as it was considered reliable, fair, honest, and hardworking.[3] Because the Habsburg bureaucracy was decentralized and was perceived as honest and effective, it is plausible that Habsburg rule promoted people's trust in local governance.

The Ottoman Empire, on the other hand, was characterized as a system in which the subjects had no political influence. Secular education was absent, and bribery was widespread and deeply ingrained within the institutional system. As documented by historians, corruption was systemic at all levels of government.[4] The Russian Empire shared similar traits, featuring centralized political authority and rampant bureaucratic inefficiency and corruption. The system of serfdom existed in Russia until the mid-nineteenth century.

Researchers analyzed people who currently live in 180 towns that are located around the old Habsburg border in Poland, Ukraine, Romania, Serbia, and Montenegro.[5] Because these towns are on average only 200 km apart from each other, they have similar geographic conditions and the same ethnic makeups. But some of these towns were governed by the Habsburg Empire in the past, while others were under the rule of the Ottoman or Russian Empire.

Surveys were administered to gauge individuals' trust in courts and police. People were also asked about their experience with corruption in the provision of local public services in their towns—for example, "In your opinion, how often is it necessary for people like you to have to make unofficial payments/gifts to courts?" The same question is also asked about bribing the traffic police.

Responses to these questions could, of course, depend on people's personal attributes as well as the local characteristics of their towns. Careful statistical analyses, adjusting for the influence of peoples' personal characteristics and other potential factors, revealed that individuals who are residents of the same country but who live in different towns only a short distance away from each other exhibit lower trust in courts and the police if their town has the heritage of the Ottoman Empire or the Russian Empire as opposed to the heritage of the Habsburg Empire. Similarly, people who live in towns with Ottoman or Russian Empire heritage are more likely to pay a bribe to the courts or to traffic police officers.

Interestingly, there was no difference between these two groups regarding their answers to this question: "Generally speaking, would you say that most people can be trusted, or that you can't be too careful in dealing with people?" This means that the difference between the Habsburg Empire and the Ottoman or the Russian Empire regarding the corruption of the courts and the bureaucracy of these empires did not influence people's general trust of others, but the differences in the institutional quality of these empires had a targeted impact on the extent to which people distrust contemporary institutions such as the courts and the police.

These results indicate that individuals' perceptions and beliefs, such as trust in the system of government, are formed by their experiences living under different empires and being exposed to these empires' governance styles and institutional systems. These beliefs, reinforced by repeated interactions with local bureaucracy over multiple generations, are passed down from parents to children and remain ingrained in the descendants of these empires even generations later.

Communism Versus Capitalism

What would have happened if people were exposed to different institutions and governance styles for a shorter period of time, such as fifty years? This type of experiment took place in Europe during the twentieth century. After World War II, Germany was divided into four sectors by the US, France, Great Britain, and the Soviet Union. These sectors eventually evolved into two separate countries: West Germany and East Germany. West Germany became a sovereign nation, the Federal Republic of Germany, with Bonn as its capital. East Germany, under the name of the German Democratic Republic, had East Berlin as its capital and was controlled by the Soviet Union. West Germany had a democratic government and a Parliament, while East Germany was a communist state under Soviet influence. The presence of communist ideology in state institutions in all facets of life in East Germany and the practice of indoctrination using schools and the media led to dramatically different preferences of East Germans compared to West Germans.

The reunification of West and East Germany occurred in October 1990 as the Soviet Union was collapsing. East Germany was absorbed into the Federal Republic of Germany, and the political and economic systems of West Germany were adopted in the newly unified country. This means that a German child who was fifteen years old and who happened to live in the Eastern part of the country at the end of World War II would have spent the majority of her life, until the age of sixty, living under the communist regime of East Germany. Her child, born under this regime, would have also grown up and spent most of his childhood and adult life until around age thirty-five to forty under the same communist government.

In 1992, two years after the unification of Germany, a survey was conducted, asking Germans who used to live in either East Germany or West Germany to provide their views on the following statement: "It is the responsibility of the government to reduce the differences in income between people with high incomes and those with low incomes." Stark difference in opinions was surfaced. Whereas 66 percent of residents of former West Germany stated that they agreed or strongly agreed with the statement, the rate of agreement surged to 89 percent among those who lived in East Germany until its collapse. In other words, those who were exposed to the communist regime of East Germany were much more inclined to hold the belief that the government should wield a potent influence in mitigating income disparities between individuals.[6]

Of course, style of government and quality of institutions depend on the culture of a society. A society that has a cultural tendency to enjoy hierarchy and tolerate corruption will choose a different political structure compared to another society with opposite cultural tendencies. But this is not true in the case of East and West Germany. Initial cultural preferences played no role in the establishment of institutions in these two nations after World War II. Germany was divided into two segments after the war by the Allies, and the communist system of East Germany was not chosen by its residents; rather, it was imposed by Soviet occupying forces. Those who ended up on the Eastern side of the border were culturally no different from those who became residents of West Germany.[7]

A similar analysis utilized a survey administered seven years after the unification, and again five years later. Adjusting for the differences in the respondents' income levels as well as other personal characteristics, ranging from age to gender, from marital status to education, researchers found significant differences between East and West Germans.[8] In the study, people were posed the question: "At present, a multitude of social services are provided not only by the state but also by private free market enterprises, organizations, associations and private citizens. Who should be responsible for the following areas?" The respondents were then provided with various scenarios, such as "Financial services in case of unemployment," "Financial services in case of illness," or "Financial security for old age." Options available for the respondents to choose regarding who should provide these services included "state only," "state mostly," "state and private sector," "mostly private sector," and "only private sector." Thus, survey respondents could reveal their preference for the extent of government involvement versus the provision of these services by the private sector.

In all responses to these various questions, individuals who lived in the former East Germany prior to unification revealed stronger preferences for state provision for financial services. On average, they were 60–100 percent more likely to declare that "only the state" or "mostly the state" should provide financial services, compared to those who lived in West Germany. These findings reveal that the East German communist regime altered the social preferences of people who lived under that regime, even though the regime lasted for only fifty years and impacted no more than two generations of East Germans.

Not surprisingly, the length of exposure to the regime and therefore the duration of indoctrination determines the strength of preferences, as evidenced by the analysis of different age groups. East Germans of all ages exhibited stronger progovernment attitudes compared to their West German counterparts of the same age. However, the gap in progovernment attitudes between East and West Germans was more pronounced among the older cohorts.[9] This means that a political regime and the associated ideology as an institution modify how people view the world, and the longer people live under that regime, the stronger is the impact on people's beliefs and preferences.

Legal Institutions and Culture

Imagine somebody borrowed a substantial sum of money from you but failed to repay it. You took the matter to court to seek resolution, but the legal process dragged on for ten years before the judgment was finally reached. This means that when you factor in the legal expenses you had to bear and the gradual erosion of the money's value due to inflation over those years, even if you win the case, you will only be able to recoup a fraction of your loan in real terms.

Consider a different scenario, in which you purchase a used car with the understanding that all components are in reasonable working order—but it turns out that the car's brakes are faulty, which leads to a serious accident just days after the purchase. You initiate a lawsuit against the seller to seek compensation for the damages incurred. Although the seller is undoubtedly liable for concealing the car's defect, he bribes the judge overseeing the case, and you lose the case as a result.

If situations like these typify the legal system, what implications would they hold for society? The answer is straightforward. If court cases are not resolved quickly, and if the legal system is plagued with corruption, which results in uncertain case outcomes despite the evident legal merits, then individuals subjected to such a legal system will inevitably seek alternative means to navigate around it. These alternative means would involve acts that bypass or violate laws, ultimately resulting in a society in which dishonesty and disregard for the law become pervasive and tolerated. That is, low-quality judicial institutions would cultivate a culture of dishonesty.

In a research project, my colleagues and I analyzed the extent to which the quality of judicial institutions impacts individuals' dishonest and criminal acts and people's acceptance of such conduct.[10] Our study, which was also mentioned in chapter 1, leveraged comprehensive data from individuals who live in twenty-five European countries. The survey included up to fifty-four thousand participants, depending on the specific question at hand, and aimed to gauge the extent of their dishonest and criminal acts over the preceding five years. The questions included scenarios such as the following:

"In the last five years have you over-claimed or falsely claimed government benefits such as social security or other benefits?"

". . . . have you sold something second-hand and concealed some or all of its faults?"

". . . . have you bought something you thought might be stolen?"

". . . . have you made an exaggerated or false insurance claim?"

". . . . have you offered a favor or a bribe to a public official in return for their services?"

". . . . have you misused or altered a card or a document to pretend to be eligible for something you were not?"

In addition, the respondents were asked about their attitudes toward the acceptability of dishonest and illicit acts. This was accomplished by measuring their level of agreement on a scale from 1 to 5, ranging from strongly agree to strongly disagree, with statements such as "Citizens should not cheat on their taxes" and "If you want to make money, you can't always act honestly." Likewise, participants were prompted to express their perception of the level of wrongdoing on a scale of 1 to 5, from "not wrong at all" to "definitely wrong," for actions such as these:

"Selling someone something second-hand and concealing some or all of its faults"

"Buying something you thought might be stolen"

"Making an exaggerated or false insurance claim"

"A public official asking someone for a favor or a bribe in return for their services"

Each of the twenty-five countries in the study has had the quality of its judicial system evaluated by assessments of the independence of its judiciary as well as the impartiality of its courts. Organizations such as the World Bank and Transparency International evaluated and rated each country on a scale from 0 to 10, measuring the extent to which the judiciary of the country is independent from the political influence of members of its government, citizens, and firms. Similarly, the impartiality of the courts is evaluated by determining whether the legal framework of the country is not subject to manipulation and whether it is based on a clear and neutral process.

Countries are also appraised based on the effectiveness of their legal framework in facilitating private businesses to resolve disputes and on the ability to contest the legality of government actions and regulations. This evaluation considers whether the judicial system is susceptible to inefficiency and manipulation or if it operates efficiently, following a transparent and neutral procedure.

Detailed analyses of the data reveal that an increase in the quality of a country's judicial institutions reduces the dishonest and criminal acts of the residents of that country. Elevated judicial quality also diminishes the likelihood of individuals considering dishonest and unlawful actions as acceptable behavior. People differ in their proclivity for dishonest and illicit behavior and in their propensity to consider such behavior as acceptable even if they live in similar countries (in terms of per capita income, average country education, population size, democratic maturity, the size of the government, the extent of individualism vs. collectivism, etc.) and even if they have the same personal characteristics (including age, gender, education marital status, religiosity, household income, urban vs. rural residence, etc.). Those who live in countries with low judicial quality are more prone to illicit behavior and are more tolerant of illicit and dishonest acts. This means that some of the permanent differences observed between countries in terms of their citizens' inclination toward dishonesty and illegality are in part driven by the low quality of judicial institutions in those nations.

Institutional quality, measured by judicial independence and the impartiality of the courts, helps shape people's beliefs and behaviors regarding their tendency toward dishonesty and inclinations for illegal behavior. Inefficient and corrupt judicial systems foster a culture of dishonesty. However, it can be argued that inefficiency and corruption of the judicial system of a country emerges in the first place because of undesirable cultural characteristics in that country. If the cultural tendency of the society is to tolerate corruption and dishonesty to begin with, then it is conceivable that the members of the judicial system would be inclined to be corrupt as well. In this situation, the relationship between institutions and culture is more complicated because institutional quality would impact individuals' behavior, which can ultimately translate into cultural change—but at the same time, the prevailing culture can influence the manner in which institutions function and operate.

To shed light on this potential complication, we can make use of the fact that the structures of judicial systems exhibit variations across nations. For example, in some systems, judges and prosecutors can be appointed by the government without undergoing the scrutiny of any other party, while in other systems they can only be selected through a competitive and transparent examination process. Legal systems exhibit variation in other aspects as well, such as whether appointments to the highest court of the nation involve a judicial council, whether judges are appointed for life, and the types of procedures applied for the removal of a judge from the bench. These procedural rules are designed by laws and are sometimes embedded in the constitutions of countries. In the same research paper, we have shown that these different types of institutional regulations and guidelines enhance or impede the efficiency, fairness, and integrity of the judiciary—and this alteration in the efficiency and integrity of the judiciary in turn translates into a change in the behavioral patterns of the people, as described previously. More specifically, a variety of statistical analyses, teasing out and adjusting for the mutual dependence of culture and judicial institutions, indicate that institutional quality, measured by judicial independence and the impartiality of the courts, helps shape both the beliefs and the behaviors of people regarding their tendency toward dishonesty and inclination for illegal behavior. More efficient and less corrupt judicial systems foster a culture of honesty.

You Tend to Cheat If the Institutions in Your Country Are No Good

Institutions also shape personal attributes that are often assumed to be inherent and fixed, such as honesty. In the following discussion, I will demonstrate that poor institutional quality in a nation can drive its residents toward dishonesty, cheating, and corruption.

To shed light on the link between institutional attributes of nations and the extent of dishonesty, a group of researchers conducted experiments with more than 2,500 undergraduate students from twenty-three countries.[11] Participants sat in a cubicle and were asked to roll an electronic die twice on a computer but report only the first roll without anyone watching. They were told before the experiment that they would get paid according to the outcome of the roll. If the subjects report rolling a 1, they receive the equivalent of one dollar; if they report that the roll was 2, they receive the equivalent of two dollars; and so on. The higher the roll, the larger the amount of money they receive. But if the roll is a 6, they receive nothing. This means that reporting a roll of 6 would provide no money to the subject. Money received was not in dollars but in the currency of the student's country, and it was adjusted so that the purchasing power of each money unit was the same everywhere.

Although the experiment cannot infer whether a particular subject is dishonest, it can identify the prevalence of cheating in a group of subjects. Because each side of the die is equally likely to end up on the top after a roll, each number has a one-in-six probability of occurrence, but number 6 receives no money. This means that the average earnings of the group are expected to be $2.50. This is because of the following calculations: Suppose we have a group of sixty participants. Under full honesty, about one in six of the participants in this group (ten individuals) would roll a 1 and receive one dollar each. Another ten individuals (another one-sixth of the group) are expected to roll a 2 and receive two dollars each, and so on. Around one-sixth of the group would roll a 6 and receive zero dollars. So, the average earning of the group under full honesty would be around $2.50.

It turns out that the average earnings in this experiment is never $2.50 regardless of the country in which the experiment is conducted. The average claim of earnings everywhere is greater than $2.50, and the mean across the twenty-three countries is $3.30. This means that people everywhere tend to cheat and try and take advantage of the system when their actions are anonymous.

However, the extent of cheating varies across countries. Average earnings, based on subjects' self-declarations, is about three dollars in Germany, Sweden, the UK, and Lithuania. It jumps up to about four dollars in Morocco and Tanzania. Other countries are scattered within this range. For example, the average claim is about $3.50 in Poland, Turkey, and Vietnam.

Another way to identify dishonesty in this experiment is to calculate the proportion of subjects in each country who reported having rolled a 6. Recall that a roll of 6 earns no money. Because a roll of 6 can happen for one out of each six rolls (a probability of 1/6, or 16.6 percent), subjects from a country can be considered honest if the proportion of rolls of 6 they reported is closer to 16.6 percent. As the proportion of reported rolls of 6 becomes smaller, the dishonesty of the subjects becomes worse.

Again, there is significant variation in this measure of honesty across different countries. In Austria, Malaysia, Germany, and Slovakia, 13–15 percent of subjects reported rolling a 6, even though such a declaration meant they received no money. In contrast, the rate of such truthful declarations is lower—around 7–8 percent—in the Netherlands, the Czech Republic, Turkey, Indonesia, and Guatemala. This rate drops further to 5 percent in China, Italy, and Colombia, and it falls to less than 2 percent in Morocco and Tanzania. This is yet another example highlighting that intrinsic honesty varies greatly across countries.

In addition to documenting cross-country differences in the tendency to lie for financial gain, the same study also analyzed the relationship between the average level of dishonesty exhibited by participants and the institutional characteristics of their respective countries. Institutional quality was measured by the prevalence of political fraud, tax evasion, and corruption in each country. Each of these items represents a different aspect of rule-breaking, with higher prevalence indicating more widespread rule violations, fostered by low institutional quality. Analyses revealed that participants in these experiments claimed having won more money if they lived in countries with higher incidence of rule violations (more political fraud, more corruption, more tax evasion). Similarly, the fraction of people reporting no earnings in the experiment was lower in countries with elevated rule violations.

In other words, variations across nations in their citizens' dishonesty are related to disparities in the quality of institutions between these nations, reflected by the extent of political fraud, tax evasion, and corruption.

Retirement Income and Family Living Arrangements

In some societies, it is customary for adult children to live with their parents after marriage, serving as a form of insurance for parents in their old age as children are expected to take care of parents. In matrilocal societies, a married couple resides with or near the wife's parents. Indonesia is a good example. Some of its forty-five ethnic groups practice matrilocality, while others do not. A recent study examined how the introduction of a government pension program in Indonesia influenced family living arrangements.

In 1977, Indonesia introduced a retirement program for employees, initially implemented in specific regions of the country before expanding nationwide. This program provided a lump-sum payment to individuals upon their retirement after age fifty-five. The researcher of the study used data from the Indonesian census that contain information about members of each household. The research design involved comparing individuals who missed the eligibility for the coverage of the pension plan to those who were covered by it. The analysis showed that the introduction of the plan did not affect older people's likelihood of living with their daughter during retirement if they are members of ethnic groups that do not practice matrilocality. In these ethnic groups, the probability of parents living with the adult daughter was the same before and after the implementation of the retirement program. This means that when parents do not have a cultural tradition about residing with their adult daughter, their propensity to live with her family is not influenced by whether or not they have additional financial power, provided by the retirement program. However, for individuals from those ethnic groups that *do* practice matrilocality, the plan reduced their likelihood of living with their adult daughter in old age. In other words, having financial means in retirement, provided by the pension plan, impacted the cultural practice of matrilocality by decreasing the tendency for parents to live with their adult daughters.[12]

The study conducted a parallel analysis for Ghana, which established a comparable retirement program in 1972, allowing employees to receive benefits after the age of fifty for women and fifty-five for men. In contrast to Indonesia, patrilocal customs are prevalent among some ethnic groups in Ghana, in which parents traditionally live with their adult sons in their old age. This custom's prevalence varies across the fifty-three ethnic groups of the country.

Analyses revealed that the introduction of the retirement plan in Ghana had no impact on the likelihood of parents cohabiting with their adult sons among ethnic groups that do not practice patrilocality. However, among ethnic groups that traditionally practice matrilocality, the propensity of parents to live with their adult sons has decreased. This demonstrates that the same type of institutional reform—that is, providing financial support to older adults—has altered this cultural practice in Ghana as it did in Indonesia. So, the prevalence of a cultural practice related to multigenerational living arrangements has responded to financial incentives created by institutions in two different countries.

Property Rights and Beliefs in Individualism

In the early 1980s, approximately 1,800 families settled on what they believed to be state-owned wasteland in the metropolitan area of Buenos Aires, Argentina. Each one of these squatter families occupied a parcel of land of roughly three hundred square meters (about 2,700 square feet). It was later discovered that this area did not belong to the state but was comprised of thirteen separate, privately owned tracts. However, despite several attempts to evict the occupiers and demolish their dwellings, these efforts were unsuccessful.[13]

In the mid-1980s, the government of Argentina decided to expropriate the land from its legal owners, providing them with financial compensation, and then give the parcels to the squatters already residing on them. Eight of the thirteen landowners accepted the government's proposal, enabling the squatters on these tracts to receive their titles by 1989. However, the remaining landowners challenged the proposed compensation amount in court, claiming it was inadequate. These legal battles persisted for twenty years without resolution.

Argentinian economists surveyed squatter households in 2003 while the court cases were still ongoing.[14] Unsurprisingly, squatter households on each parcel of land were very similar in personal attributes, such as the age of the household head, the level of education of residents, and the characteristics of the parcel, regardless of which parcel they occupied. The only difference was that some squatters got lucky because the owners of their parcels agreed to the government's deal. Consequently, squatters on these parcels obtained their legal land titles and became landowners. In contrast, other squatters were unlucky because the owners of their land went to court, leaving these squatters in limbo without receiving the rights to the property they occupied.

Survey results showed that squatters who obtained land titles tended to hold more individualistic beliefs aligned with free markets compared to squatters without land ownership. For instance, when asked whether success could be achieved individually or required group support, those who were granted land titles were 30 percent more likely to believe in individual success. Similarly, this group was 34 percent more inclined to agree that "Having money is important for happiness," compared to squatters who had waited twenty years for land titles but had not received them.

Because who received a land title and who didn't was random, and because there are no other observable differences between the groups, it is reasonable to conclude that these differences in beliefs across the two groups arose because one group obtained property rights to their parcels and the other did not. In essence, having property rights influenced individuals' beliefs about individualism versus collectivism and the importance of wealth.

Christians, Jews, Moneylending, and Anti-Semitism

Religions have established rules for determining the behavior of their adherents. For example, the Catholic Church banned usury for its clergy after the First Ecumenical Council in Nicaea (present day Iznik in Turkey) in 325 CE. The Second and Third Lateran Councils in 1139 and 1179, respectively, reiterated the church's condemnation of usury, and extended sanctions to any Catholic who lent money at interest. But this prohibition did not apply to Jews, who were permitted to lend money at moderate interest rates. The Lateran Council of 1215 forbade Jews from engaging in moneylending at "high and immoderate" interest rates, which implied that Jews were granted by Christian authorities the privilege of conducting lending activities at low and moderate interest rates. Consequently, moneylending became a primary occupation of the Jews in many parts of Europe after the thirteenth century.

The Protestant movement, which began with the actions of Martin Luther, a German monk and theologian, transformed the religious and economic landscape of Europe. The Protestant Reformation spread rapidly after publication of Luther's *Ninety-Five Theses* in 1517. Although Luther initially condemned all forms of usury, he later permitted moderate interest rates under certain conditions. Meanwhile, John Calvin played a pivotal role in relaxing the prohibition on lending at interest, marking a significant departure from traditional Christian teachings on usury. This shift reshaped economic practices in Protestant regions, paving the way for greater acceptance of interest-based lending. The tolerance of the Protestant religion for moneylending, coupled with Protestants' emphasis on education, opened the doors for them to compete with Jews in the moneylending business.

This development meant that in Catholic-majority regions of Germany, market dynamics remained largely unchanged: Jews continued to complement Catholic economic activities by providing financial lending services. However, the situation was different in Protestant-majority areas. Because Protestants were permitted to engage in money lending, Jews became both substitutes and competitors in the financial sector. This growing economic competition heightened tensions, fueling conflicts between Protestants and Jews and leading to a significant rise in anti-Semitism and violence in regions with large Protestant populations.

Analyses of data from 1,300 German cities for the period of 1300 to 1600 CE have demonstrated that pogroms against Jews rose significantly in the sixteenth and the seventeenth centuries (after the Protestant Reformation) in Protestant cities, as opposed to Catholic cities.[15] This indicates that strong anti-Jewish sentiment was driven by the emergence of the Protestant Reformation, which opened the door for Protestants to compete with Jews who were already established in the moneylending business. The number of anti-Jewish books published in German cities in each decade between 1450 and 1600 is another indicator of anti-Jewish attitudes during that period. Analyses have also revealed that the number of such books published jumped following the Protestant Reformation in Protestant cities, compared to Catholic cities.[16]

These findings reveal that anti-Semitic acts and attitudes rose more strongly in Protestant areas of Germany relative to Catholic areas after the Protestant Reformation. Thus, they indicate that the surge of anti-Semitism was related to the Jews being in economic competition with the Protestants following the Protestant religion permitting its adherents to enter the moneylending business.

Two underlying elements of the discussion in this section warrant emphasis. First, I considered religion a form of institution here. This perspective is logical because, as discussed in chapter 1, religion can be considered a social institution. Similar to the function of the other formal institutions of a society, religion determines the rules that aim to regulate its adherents' ethical persuasions and behaviors. Therefore, an alteration in the rules and regulations dictated by religion is a modification of the institutional structure. At the same time, prevalent religious beliefs are part of the culture.

The second element pertains to the attitudes and conduct directed toward other races, ethnic groups, and religions. Insofar as these attitudes and behaviors are pervasive in a society and endure over long periods of time, they become integral components of that society's cultural characteristics. This means, for example, that persistent prejudice and racism constitutes a cultural attribute of a society.

The examples provided in this chapter demonstrate that any variations in institutions, whether they pertain to the style and the quality of government or the particular tenets of religion, exert long-lasting influences on individuals' beliefs and behaviors, reflecting the impact of institutions on culture.

The Complex Relationship Between Institutions, Culture, and Prosperity

When discussing the influence of institutions, originally emphasized by Douglass North, it is important to underscore a hypothesis developed by economists Daron Acemoglu, Simon Johnson, and James Robinson, who broadly classify institutions into two categories: inclusive institutions and extractive ones. If society's institutions are *inclusive*, then the playing field is level for everyone, underpinned by adherence to the rule of law. Economic and political participation has no barriers, and there exists a well-functioning and participatory democracy, accompanied by protection of people's property rights. In contrast, *extractive* institutions concentrate power and wealth in the hands of a few, often at the expense of the broader population. These institutions tend to limit property rights and restrict political and economic participation.[17]

As their name implies, extractive institutions are designed with the intension of siphoning a society's economic resources in order to channel them to particular groups. This institutional design creates an environment of uncertainty and insecurity that discourages innovation and investment: Individuals lack confidence in the security of their property rights and the potential rewards of their efforts. Acemoglu, Johnson, and Robinson argue theoretically and provide empirical evidence showing that countries with inclusive institutions are more likely to experience long-term economic growth because inclusive institutions provide a conducive environment for technological progress, human capital accumulation, and efficient resource allocation.

Although the proposition suggesting a direct causal influence of institutional quality on economic outcomes and economic development is quite compelling, it is also evident that the effectiveness of any institution is contingent upon the cultural environment within which it operates. As I mentioned earlier in the book, two societies might have the same institutional framework of formal rules and regulations, but the execution of these rules can differ based on cultural factors. For instance, in the United States, the alignment of state or federal laws and regulations with the constitution undergoes rigorous examination and public discourse, frequently culminating in resolutions by the Supreme Court. Examples range from state laws regulating women's access to abortion to laws regarding financial contributions to political campaigns.

Conversely, in some countries, there is little to no public concern over whether government actions comply with the constitution. A striking example is former Turkish president Turgut Özal's infamous remark in 1991 that "nothing happens if the constitution is violated once," which drew no significant public backlash, illustrating how adherence to institutional rules is determined by the cultural context in which those institutions operate.

One demonstration of the impact of culture on the effectiveness of institutions is provided by economist Deirdre McCloskey, who references a case presented by Acemoglu and Robinson.[18] The example mentioned by these authors involves government-provided health care in India, where the delivery of services is plagued by health care staff absenteeism. Nurses frequently fail to report for duty, resulting in healthcare facilities being closed most of the time. To solve this problem, a system change was devised in the Udaipur district of Rajasthan. The new structure introduced time clocks that would time stamp the entry and exit dates and times of the staff at health care facilities.

This, of course, constituted a transformation of the institutional framework as it modified the "rules of game" and established incentives aimed at curbing absenteeism. Although the intention behind this specific alteration in incentives was to decrease absenteeism and potentially establish a fresh norm of showing up for work, nothing changed in practice. Nurses collaborated with their superiors; the time stamp machines encountered "issues" and were frequently "broken"; and the absenteeism of nurses remained unaffected.[19]

Acemoglu and Robinson interpret this as an example of an extractive institution—the government's health care delivery system—resisting change. Yet another, more realistic, viewpoint is offered by McCloskey: There was in fact a change in institutional structure. The introduction of the time-stamping system and the associated sanctions represented a change in institutional design. Yet this institutional reform failed because of the cultural context in which it was implemented. McCloskey contends that "[the failure of the new incentive scheme] was rather about a lack of an ethic of self-respecting professionalism among the nurses."[20]

The upshot is that institutions create incentives, but their impact on individuals' behavior depends on a receptive cultural context and the credibility of those incentives. If the ensuing behavioral change becomes long-lasting, it can register as cultural change. For example, driving while intoxicated is illegal everywhere. But the enforcement of rules against drunk driving varies from country to country. Suppose there is general acceptance of drunk driving in a community, and drinking and driving is considered permissible conduct, at least under certain circumstances.[21] If the penalties for drunk driving are made more severe, then the only way this would result in behavioral change is if law enforcement permanently enforces these stricter penalties. If the prevailing culture is characterized by acceptance of corruption and is lenient toward drunk driving, then raising penalties for intoxicated drivers would likely lead to an escalation in bribes offered by drivers to police officers, with no significant alteration in the extent of drunk driving behavior. So, the effectiveness of institutional reform is contingent upon particular attributes of the culture that interacts with that institution.

How Do Institutions Emerge and Evolve?

Acemoglu and Robinson state, "The low education level of poor countries is caused by economic institutions that fail to create incentives for parents to educate their children and by political institutions that fail to induce governments to build, finance, and support schools and the wishes of parents and children." They further write, "All economic institutions are created by society. Those of North Korea, for example, were forced on its citizens by the communists who took over the country in the 1940s, while those of colonial Latin America were imposed by Spanish conquistadors."[22]

Acemoglu and Robinson convincingly argue that the choice of institutions is determined by the political power struggle between different groups in the society that would gain or lose in different ways from the adoption of different institutions. They state that institutional differences impact not only nations' prosperity but also how wealth is distributed and who holds power in those societies. An example given by these authors is the Congo under the leadership of Joseph Mobutu between 1965 and 1997. Mobutu created a highly extractive set of economic institutions, which allowed him and his supporters around him to become extremely wealthy. For example, "Mobutu built himself a palace in his birthplace, Gbadolite, in the north of the country, with an airport large enough to land the supersonic Concorde jet, a plane he frequently rented from Air France for travel to Europe. In Europe he bought castles and owned large tracts of the Belgian capital of Brussels."[23]

Meanwhile, people endured extreme poverty, and the country remained in dire economic shape for decades under Mobutu's rule. This example of the Congo is provided to make the point that the political power struggles in a country can result in an outcome in which the winners of that struggle may establish economic and political institutions that serve their own interest, even if these institutions are detrimental to the overall economic development and prosperity of the country.

The Democratic Republic of the Congo is a very poor country. According to World Bank data, about 75 percent of Congolese people lived on less than three dollars per day in 2023.[24] Given that the per capita income in 1990 was about $400, the cost of chartering a Concorde jet from Air France for a round trip to Europe by Mobutu that year was likely equivalent to the total annual earnings of an entire Congolese city with three thousand residents. So, an important question is: Why did such blatant corruption and such an extraordinary level of theft of public resources, persisting for so long, not trigger strong public outrage and lead to Mobutu's overthrow?

There are likely multiple reasons that people fail to respond to such blatant misconduct and abuse of office. One factor could be the ethnolinguistic fragmentation of Congo, which may make it difficult for different ethnic groups to cooperate and unite against a corrupt regime, especially if some of these groups are aligned with the leader of the regime. But the cultural context in which institutions operate also plays an important role. In some societies, a dysfunctional system that harms the economic and social well-being of most residents might provoke strong reactions, while in others, similar reactions may not materialize. I recall a conversation with a taxi driver in Istanbul, who, when asked about his views on well-known instances of government corruption, responded with a Turkish idiom: *Bal tutan parmağını yalar,* which translates to, "He who holds honey licks his fingers." This phrase implies that those in positions of power are entitled to benefit from their roles. Essentially, the taxi driver viewed corruption as a natural state, almost as an immutable law of nature. If this sentiment is widespread as a cultural trait, we would not only expect people to refrain from complaining about ineffective institutions and politicians who exploit them but also anticipate that individuals will replicate this behavior themselves when given the opportunity.[25]

There may be a large group of individuals who are harmed by corruption and malfeasance in society yet still expect to benefit from corruption in the future. For example, in a parliamentary system with two major parties (or two groups of parties) that have roughly equal support among voters, if members of the government are engaged in corruption and the benefits of corruption trickle down to lower ranks, including voters who support the ruling party, then the opposition party and its supporters may have little reason to push for institutional reform. They might anticipate gaining power in the future and hope to engage in similar corrupt practices themselves. This creates an equilibrium in which corruption and misuse of resources persist, with no incentive for the median voter to seek change.[26]

A comparable situation is observed in the US in a different context. Low- and middle-income individuals often oppose income-redistribution policies that involve taxing high-income earners, despite the fact that such policies could benefit lower-income groups. This attitude is commonly thought to stem from the belief in the "American Dream," which suggests that hard work can lead to upward economic mobility. This belief is a well-known American trait. John Steinbeck described the working poor in America as "temporarily embarrassed millionaires."[27] He suggested that many working-class individuals oppose income redistribution because they view their current financial situation as temporary and believe they will soon achieve greater wealth. This perspective leads them to resist redistribution policies, seeing them as a threat to their future economic well-being.

Economic research has shown that upward intergenerational mobility in the US has stalled for some time now and is no longer stronger than in Europe. Nevertheless, Americans' belief in their potential to achieve a rags-to-riches story persists. This enduring perception continues to drive their resistance to redistributive policy proposals.[28]

In summary, the way institutions function and how they evolve over time are influenced by the cultural attributes of society. To conclude this chapter, I will provide an example from economic history that illustrates how different cultural attributes lead to different institutional designs.

A study by Avner Greif analyzed two societies that specialized in trading goods during the eleventh and twelfth centuries.[29] The Maghribi traders were Jewish merchants who migrated from Iraq to the Maghrib region of North Africa (present-day Tunisia and the surrounding areas). They were involved in long-distance trade in the Mediterranean. The Genoese traders were based in the city-state of Genoa in Italy, and they too navigated through the Mediterranean. Both the Maghribis and the Genoese used the same naval technology (ships and navigation equipment) and traded similar goods. There was, however, one main difference between them. The Maghribis were part of a collectivist culture, whereas Genoese are best described as belonging to an individualistic culture.

According to Greif's research:

> The Maghribis were *musta'ribun*, that is, non-Muslims who adopted the values of the Muslim society. Among these values is the view that they were members of the same *umma*. This term, although translated as "nation," is derived from the word *umm*, meaning "mother," reflecting the basic value of mutual responsibility among the members of that society. . . . In addition, the Maghribis were part of the Jewish community, within which it is a prominent idea that "All Israel is responsible for every member." . . . In contrast, Christianity during that period placed the individual rather than his social group at the center of its theology. It advanced the creation of "a new society based not on the family but on the individual, whose salvation, like his original loss of innocence, was personal and private."[30]

This cultural difference manifested itself in different forms. For instance, as stated by Greif, historical records show that Maghribi merchants shared trade information among themselves by exchanging letters filled with commercial news, gossip, and other relevant details. In contrast, the Genoese did not share information with each other and were secretive about their business dealings. These collectivist versus individualist attributes led to the emergence of different organizational structures. As trade expanded to more distant locations, a merchant had the option to either hire an agent from his own "circle," who would travel or relocate abroad, or to employ a local agent from the foreign trade center to manage various aspects of the business on behalf of the merchant. When they expanded their trade, the Maghribi traders employed other Maghribis as agents and relied on informal collective sanctions and enforcement mechanisms to enforce contracts and arrangements among themselves. The Genoese, on the other hand, started hiring non-Genoese people as agents. Consequently, they developed mechanisms to organize and enforce contracts between traders and agents that increasingly involved non-Genoese individuals. Similarly, the Genoese developed bills of lading, which formalized the transaction of goods being shipped and the parties involved in the trade. Maghribi merchants did not utilize this contractual mechanism even though it was known to them. Instead, they relied on other Maghribis who traveled on the same ship carrying the merchandise to perform that function.

In the end, because the two societies had different cultural makeups, they ended up with very different institutional structures, even though they started off with the same technology and were operating in the same market.

7 Language and Culture

My House Versus Our House

I was the coach of my daughter's soccer team during her elementary and middle school years. The team would practice on Tuesdays and Thursdays after school and play games on Saturdays. The kids would frequently carpool to the practice field or to the game. When I drove them, I would overhear them chatting in the back seat, talking about the events of the day. Sometimes they would try to organize play dates during these rides. A typical invitation would be extended by one of the kids via the question: "Do you guys want to come over to my house after the game?"

This phrase always struck me as odd because none of the kids lived alone. They all lived with their families. They had parents, and some of them had siblings. So, when a kid invited her friends over to "my house," she was actually inviting them to her family's house, which was home to her, her parents, and her siblings.

The source of my surprise is related to the fact that I grew up in Istanbul, Turkey, where nobody invites anybody to "his house" or to "her house" unless the person who extends the invitation is single and lives alone. So in Turkey, the question takes the form, "Do you want to come to *our* house?" This acknowledges the fact that the house is shared by the entire family. That people don't refer to their residence as "my house" in Turkey is because in that context using the words "my house" implies that others who also reside in the same space are excluded. In contrast, in the US, using the phrase "my house" simply means "the place where I live," without any connotations of exclusivity or ownership.

One avenue through which culture and language are linked is through the conception of the individual. The question, posed as, "Would you like to come to *my* house?", reflects an *individualistic culture* in which the individual places herself in the center by using the words *my house* in reference to *the house in which I live*. If the same question is phrased as, "Would you like to come to *our* house?", it implies the house where my family and I live, emphasizing the *collectivist* sentiment. As discussed previously, in individualistic cultures, individuals take a central role in their affairs, and they are responsible for their actions. In contrast, in collectivist cultures, individuals are part of their social network, which is an important part of personal identity.

Another interesting difference between English and Turkish, related to the culture of individualism, is the use of pronouns. In English, the pronoun *I* may not be dropped from the sentence *I am going*, because the remaining words, *am going*, do not constitute a proper sentence. In contrast, the first-person pronoun may be dropped in Turkish. The sentence *Ben gidiyorum* means "I am going," with *Ben* translating to "I." If the pronoun is dropped, the sentence becomes *Gidiyorum*, which means the same thing; it is still grammatically correct, and the verb inflection makes it clear that the act of going is done by the singular first person (me).

In other words, to express the idea of going someplace in Turkish, you would normally say *Gidiyorum*, omitting the first-person pronoun, because the Turkish language downplays the person performing the action. Only if you wanted to emphasize yourself as the person undertaking the action would you include the pronoun, and say ***Ben** gidiyorum*.

There are many other languages, in addition to English, that do not permit pronoun dropping, such as Hungarian, Danish, French, Hausa (Nigeria), Czech, Dutch, German, and so on. But pronoun dropping is allowed in Italian, Greek, Turkish, Spanish, Romanian, Polish, Arabic, Hebrew, Kikuyu (Kenya), Mandarin (China), and Japanese, among others.

The difference between languages in their license to drop first-person pronouns reflects cultural values associated with individualistic and collectivist societies. As you will recall from the discussion in chapters 1 and 3, Hofstede's widely used individualism index assigns a value to each country: A higher value on the index represents a more individualistic culture, and lower values are associated with collectivist societies.[1] Using this index, an analysis of sixty languages worldwide revealed an interesting regularity: Nations tend to exhibit higher levels of individualism (having higher values on Hofstede's individualism index) if their language does *not* allow pronoun drop (as in the case of English, French, and German), while countries where pronoun drop is permitted (such as Turkish, Italian, and Polish) tend to have collectivist cultures.

In other words, languages which mandate the inclusion of the word *I* in the sentence *I am going* are more commonly found in individualistic societies. In contrast, languages spoken in collectivist societies often allow for the omission of the word *I* in the same sentence. This indicates that a fundamental aspect of culture (whether it is individualistic or collectivist) is reflected in the language used by a society.[2]

To establish the link between language and economic outcomes, a study examined the linguistic structures of countries across the globe. It revealed that in countries where the language allows for pronoun drop, corruption is more prevalent, democracy is weaker, civil liberties and political rights are more restricted, and respect for property rights and enforceability of contracts are weaker.[3]

The individualistic versus collectivist tendencies of a society are even reflected in the insults prevalent in each society. In an interesting study, social psychologists analyzed how the types of insults and curse words vary between collectivist and individualistic communities.[4] University students were recruited from three different cities in Italy: Catania in Sicily, Bologna in central Italy, and Trieste in northern Italy. It is well-known that people in southern Italy and Sicily have a strong collectivist culture, whereas the dominant cultural orientation in northern Italy is individualistic. The students in all three locations were asked to write down any insults and swear words they could think of, regardless of whether they would use these words themselves. Researchers then classified these insults and curse words as either individualistic or relational. *Individualistic insults* are those that attempt to assault an individual's physical and mental attributes by using derogatory terms and phrases, as well as sexual insults targeted at a person. *Relational insults* are those that target an individual's relatives and the members of that person's presumed group. Examples of relational insults include such phrases as *Che venga una colpa a te e a tutta la raza tua*, which can be translated to English as "May a curse come upon you and your entire family." Other examples of Italian relational insults are *V***te e 36 dei tuoi parenti*, which means "Go f** yourself and your thirty-six relatives," and *Vacca di tua sorella*, which translates to "Your sister is a cow."

It turns out that the proportion of relational insults among all insults and curse words used was significantly higher in Catania compared to Bologna or Trieste. Even though all participants lived in Italy, those who reside in the collectivist culture of Sicily are more predisposed to verbally attack the associated group of a person (family and relatives) when they want to insult that person. In contrast, people in the more individualist northern Italy are less likely to use such relational insults. In those cases, insults are directed toward individuals.

Respect for Hierarchy

Languages also differ in the attention paid to the status of the individual being addressed. In some languages, there are distinct second-person pronouns reflecting the relationship between the speakers and the person spoken to. As an example, in German, the informal *Du* is used to address people who have a close relationship with the speaker, such as friends or children, while the formal *Sie* is used for people with higher social status, the elderly, or strangers. For instance, to ask a friend "Can you come here?" in German, you would say *Kannst du herkommen?*, while to ask the same question politely to a person of higher status, you would say *Können Sie herkommen?*. The same differentiation exists in French (*Tu* vs. *Vous*), Turkish (*Sen* vs. *Siz*), and many other languages. There is no such differentiation in English, where *you* is the only second-person pronoun. The question would be formulated as *Can you come here?* regardless of whether you were talking to a best friend, to your boss, or to the president of the United States.

Languages with second-person differentiation are those that pay attention to the hierarchy of power in society: These languages have specific ways for lower-status individuals to address higher status ones and vice versa. Linguists determined that more than one-third of the world's languages have politeness distinctions, and in some languages the politeness distinction is quite detailed and complicated. Several South Asian languages, for instance, have multiple second-order pronounces that are used in a sentence based on the status of the addressee. The Hindi language of India contains three distinct levels of second-person pronouns, which differ in their formality. In the Marathi language spoken in the Maharashtra state of India, *tu* is used for family members and friends, *te* and *he* are employed when speaking to people of a higher social status, and the extra formal and polite *apan* is used when speaking to teachers and priests.[5] Similarly, the Moldavian, Lithuanian, and Japanese languages have multiple second-order pronouns.

Why do some languages have a politeness distinction in how the second person is referred to? Part of the answer lies in the structure of a society. Some societies are more egalitarian, whereas others are more hierarchically structured. The caste system in India is a prime example of a hierarchical structure, where an individual's place in the hierarchy is inherited from their parents and cannot be changed. The caste affects the individual's social interactions, treatment by others, occupational opportunities, and even marriage choices.[6] More broadly, different societies have different levels of hierarchical social structures. The extent of the hierarchy is part of the culture of a society, and the factors that shape cultural patterns also affect the degree of the hierarchy.

Rigid social hierarchy creates differences in power, authority, and status between groups of people. In hierarchical societies, individuals who are ranked in the lower echelons of the hierarchy are expected to show deference to those in higher echelons. For instance, in a hierarchical society like Turkey, to insult or to speak disrespectfully about the president of the country is considered a criminal offense, punishable by imprisonment. This is in contrast to a much less hierarchical society like the US, where there are no legal consequences for any type of language, including the use of obscenities directed at the president.[7]

I remember my surprise during my first week in the US while attending graduate school when I heard the department secretary calling a prominent professor, who was also the department chair at the time, by his first name. I was in disbelief when I heard her referring to him as "Mike" instead of "Professor Grossman." In contrast, in Turkish society, it is extremely uncommon to address one's supervisor in an informal manner, let alone by their first name. This is primarily due to the deep-rooted cultural significance of the social hierarchy, which is reflected in the language norms and practices.

Attitudes toward hierarchy across societies can be measured using the World Values Survey. This is a widely used international survey administered in repeated intervals around the globe to assess people's beliefs, values, and attitudes. Among the many questions included in this survey, respondents are asked which qualities parents should emphasize for their children to learn at home. The question is posed as follows: "Here is a list of qualities that children can be encouraged to learn at home. Which, if any, do you consider to be especially important?" Of the options they were given, if respondents chose "Obedience" or "Religious Faith", they are considered to have a stronger hierarchical orientation. Conversely, if they prioritize "Independence" or

"Determination and Perseverance," then they are considered to have a lower hierarchical orientation.

Averaging people's responses within each country produces a measure of the hierarchical orientation of countries. Using this indicator, it has been shown that if the people of a country have a stronger hierarchical orientation, that country's language involves second-person differentiation politeness (e.g., as in German, French, Hindu, and Turkish). Conversely, when the language of a country does not differentiate between formal and informal second-person pronouns, the people of that country are less hierarchically orientated.[8] In other words, how a person of a high socioeconomic status is addressed in a language reflects the extent of the hierarchical structure of the society that speaks that language.

Language and Economics

The discussion so far in this chapter has been about language as an indicator of culture. But economics is involved in the mix as well, because scientific studies have shown the following:

- Corruption has a negative impact on economic development. Similarly, if a country has weak democracy, if civil liberties and property rights are not protected, and if the rule of law is not enforced, then that country's economic development is hindered.
- Individualism versus collectivism, as a cultural attribute, influences a country's level of corruption, the functioning of democracy, the rule of law, the protection of civil liberties, and property rights. Collectivist and hierarchical cultures impede economic development because they prioritize conformity to a group and loyalty to supervisors over independent thinking and dissent, thus stifling freedom of thought and innovation.
- The language structure of the country is a marker of whether the country has an individualistic or collectivist culture. A country's hierarchical structure can also be inferred from its language.

These three bullet points collectively imply that a country's linguistic structure can serve as a predictor of its economic development, as the structure of language reflects cultural characteristics that influence economic development. In other words, the linguistic features of a society provide insights into that society's cultural traits, such as individualism versus collectivism and the degree of respect for hierarchy, which in turn have an impact on the economic landscape of the society.[9]

Language, Patience, and Economic Success

As discussed in chapter 4, patience and the ability to delay gratification is an important ingredient for economic success. And just as different individuals are more or less patient, the same is true for countries. People in some countries are, on average, more future oriented than those in other nations.

Suppose we select a large and diverse group of adults from a particular country, including men and women, young and old, rich and poor, those who work in different occupations, those with different ethnicities, those with varying levels of education, and so on. By measuring each person's time preference and taking their average, we can obtain an indicator of that country's time preference. Residents of German and Nordic countries are more patient compared to those in Anglo/American countries. This latter group, in turn, is more patient than individuals in Asian countries, while people in Southern and Eastern Europe, Latin America, and the Middle East demonstrate even lower levels of patience than those in Asia. Residents of African nations exhibit the least amount of patience.[10]

So we know that people in some countries are more future oriented than those in other countries. But what does language have to do with the propensity for being patient versus being present oriented? An economic study provided evidence that the structure of the future tense of a language has an impact on how speakers of that language view the future and how they make decisions and trade-offs between now and the future.[11]

Languages differ in the way they differentiate the future from the present. Some languages identify the future in their grammar, while others don't. For example, in English, the word *will* in the statement *I will do that* emphasizes that the action is going to take place in the future. The same is true in Turkish, where *Yapacağım* means *I will do that*; here, the verb inflection . . . *acağım* underlines that the action will take place in the future. In contrast, in German, *Ich mache das* means both *I will do that* and *I am doing that*. In other words, English and Turkish clearly separate the future from the present, while German does not.[12]

When the structure of a language differentiates between the future and the present, does this divergence shape the way its speakers think about the future? More specifically, if the grammar of the language distinguishes the future from the present, does that lead the speakers to dissociate themselves from the future and underestimate its significance?

Linguists refer to the way a language marks the future as its *future time reference* (FTR). A *strong FTR* describes the grammar of a language that makes it obligatory to mark future events. Conversely, a language that does not require the speaker to differentiate between the present and the future has a *weak FTR*. Languages in this latter category are "futureless" because they express the present and the future in the same way. For example, Estonian falls into this category. *I will go to school* is translated as *Ma lähen kooli* in Estonian, where *Ma* means *I*, *lähen* stands for *will go*, and *kooli* means *to school*. But *I am going to school* is also *Ma lähen kooli*; that is, the present tense is used to describe both present and future actions in Estonian.

Similarly, Finnish does not have a grammatical structure to indicate the future tense. Instead, future actions are often marked through context or through the use of adverbs such as *tomorrow* or *later*. *Tänään on aurinkoista* and *Huomenna on aurinkoista* mean "it is sunny today" and "it will be sunny tomorrow," respectively. *Tänään* means today, and *Huomenna* means tomorrow. The verb in both sentences is *on*, which means both "is" and "will be."

There are many futureless languages around the world. In addition to German, Finnish, and Estonian, mentioned earlier, other examples of such languages include Japanese, the Cantonese and Mandarin languages of China, Norwegian, Sudanese, Swedish, Icelandic, Indonesian, and many African languages.

To investigate the link between how a language refers to the future and the economic behavior of people who use that language, economist Keith Chen employed data from the World Values Survey for about 140,000 individuals from seventy-six countries.[13] His analyses accounted for several attributes of these individuals along with the characteristics of their county of residence. Chen also was able to compare individuals who live in the same country and share the same personal characteristics but differ in the language they speak. In addition, he analyzed another dataset, focusing on about forty thousand people from thirteen European counties.

The findings showed that people who speak a futureless language, in which there is no obligatory future time reference, were more likely to engage in future-oriented behaviors. In these languages, the present and the future are referred to in the same manner. Speakers of such languages save more and accumulate more wealth by retirement. They are also less likely to smoke, more likely to be physically active, and less likely to be obese. In other words, they invest in their health more. By analyzing the savings rates of OECD countries, the author similarly found that countries with languages that do not distinguish between the present and the future save on average 5 percent more of their gross domestic product.

So language influences how people think about the future and make decisions involving trade-offs between the present and the future. When a language's grammar distinctly separates the future from the present, its speakers tend to view the future as more distant. In contrast, in languages that use the same sentence structure for both present and future events, speakers perceive the future as being not far away and behave accordingly.

Language and Economics: Market Specialization

Language impacts how people perceive concepts and interpret the world, which in turn influence culture and the economic environment. At the same time, the manner in which language is spoken is a cultural attribute, and it interacts with the economic environment. An interesting example is provided by linguistic anthropologist Elinor Ochs Keenan. In her analysis of the Malagasy language spoken in Madagascar, she explains how social norms of conduct are intertwined with speech patterns.[14] As a social norm, people in Madagascar are expected to avoid open and direct confrontation with each other. If an individual puts another in an uncomfortable position by insult, verbal hostility, or other direct confrontation, then the aggressor is shamed and sanctioned by the community. These sanctions take the form of being shunned, being gossiped about, and even being cut off from the community. Along the same lines, direct expression of anger and disagreement is considered unacceptable. If there is disagreement between two individuals, they do not confront each other; instead, each person explains their grievance to their associates, and these associates communicate the issues to the other side. In other words, as a social norm, disputes are resolved through intermediaries to avoid confrontation in Madagascar, and direct criticism or direct accusation is not an acceptable behavior. This communication style as a cultural norm serves the purpose of not putting another person in an uncomfortable position, which in turn aims to preserve communal harmony.

However, this norm does *not* apply to Malagasy women, who communicate their anger toward others openly. In contrast to men, they speak directly to articulate their feelings and express their criticism of others. When speaking in a straightforward manner and even getting involved in face-to-face encounters, Malagasy women do not face disapproval of the community. Importantly, this dichotomy between men and women is used as a tool in social interactions. For example, in an anecdote described in Keenan's article, children playing soccer damaged the wall of a house in a village. The homeowner told the villagers politely that he requested the damage be repaired. When no action was taken, he went to the village square with his wife, who publicly confronted the villagers and angrily demanded that the repairs be made. She was not condemned by the villagers for her outburst. Although this type of behavior would be inappropriate for a man, it is considered acceptable for a woman.

This disparity raises the question of why it is deemed acceptable for women to express their opinions to, criticize, confront, and disrespect others, while the same behavior is viewed as unacceptable for men. One possible explanation for this discrepancy maybe the specialized roles of men and women in economic transactions. In Madagascar, women typically dominate the marketplace as sellers, and buying and selling often involves intense negotiations. As merchants, women are well-versed in bargaining and confrontation, whereas men are more likely to sell fixed-price items like meat. When both husband and wife are merchants, the husband handles the weighing and money transactions, while the wife handles negotiations.[15] This suggests that women's role as bargainers and sellers in village markets may have led to a social norm that allows them to use confrontational speech patterns without facing consequences in other areas of their social lives.

Of course, it is possible that the difference in speech patterns between men and women has emerged for other reasons in distant past and that the society has embraced direct speech from women while discouraging it from men. Society's acceptance of women's direct speech might have then created an advantage for them in the marketplace, as their assertive and confrontational speaking style facilitated effective negotiating and bargaining. This might have led women to assume the roles of sellers and negotiators in village markets. But the main point here is that the difference in speech patterns between men and women, as a cultural attribute, is associated with the difference in their labor market specialization.

Language and Personal Responsibility

You may have come across videos of cats or dogs interacting with objects, breaking them or spilling contents onto the floor. In these videos, the owner approaches the animal and asks: "Did you do this?" The charm of such videos lies in the animal's seemingly taken-aback reaction to this accusation, characterized by a behavior that seems to exclaim: "Who? Me? Of course not!" In essence, the appeal of the video emerges because of the animal's disavowal of any responsibility in the incident, despite the evidence indicating otherwise.

The knee-jerk reaction to avoid responsibility for an undesirable result may be a natural response for many species, including humans, but the inclination to deny any involvement in a negative outcome is deeply ingrained in certain languages. For example, in the event of a car accident resulting in a broken leg, an English speaker would typically describe the situation by saying, "I broke my leg in the accident." In contrast, a Turkish speaker would express the same situation by saying, "My leg broke." Even if he had partaken in a foolish act, such as dancing on a high wall while intoxicated, leading to a subsequent fall and a broken leg, he would still describe the incident as, "My leg got broken." In other words, although the individual bears complete responsibility for his injury, this event would not be articulated in Turkish by the phrase *I broke my leg* due to the implication that the person deliberately caused harm to his own leg.[16]

Similarly, if a person accidently knocks over a glass of water at a dinner table, in English she would describe it by saying, "I spilled the water." In Turkish, the same incident instead would be described by the person saying, "The water got spilled." So the structure of the Turkish language downplays the role of the person involved, thereby reducing their personal responsibility. In contrast, the English language emphasizes the person's involvement, even if he has little or no real responsibility in causing the event.

The linguistic attribute of denying agency and responsibility is not limited to Turkish. It exists in other languages as well, such as Spanish and Japanese. As an article by Fausey and Boroditsky note in the *Psychonomic Bulletin & Review*, "For example, in Spanish nonagentive expressions with the clitic *se* are often used to describe accidents (e.g., '*Se rompió el florero*', translating roughly as '*The vase broke itself*')."[17]

In an interesting study, videos of sixteen different events were viewed by English-speaking and Spanish-speaking participants. Each scenario was presented in two variations: one where an action was performed intentionally, and the other where the same event occurred accidentally. For instance, in one version, an individual sat at a table and deliberately tore a page from a notebook; in the alternate version, someone sat at a table, flipped through a notebook, and accidentally ripped a page. Another instance involved a person intentionally popping a balloon with a tack in version 1, while in the second version a person tried to place tacks into a container and accidentally popped a balloon in the process.[18]

Participants in the study were asked to write descriptions of the scenes after watching each video. In the case of intentional events, both English and Spanish speakers depicted them as equally agentive. This means that all participants ascribed responsibility for the incidents to the involved agent using descriptions like "He popped the balloon" and "He ripped the page." Both English and Spanish speakers remembered equally well the agents involved in these incidents. On the other hand, when it came to accidental events, English speakers were more likely to attribute the event to the agent involved and remembered the agent involved in the event better than Spanish speakers did. Spanish speakers were less prone to attribute responsibility to the agent. Similar results are obtained by comparing English-speaking and Japanese-speaking subjects.[19]

Thus, in certain languages, like English, expressions often revolve around individuals carrying out actions, even when describing unintentional incidents. In contrast, speakers of languages like Turkish, Spanish, and Japanese refrain from specifying the person involved, even when describing events for which the person bears responsibility, resulting in a reduced emphasis on that person's accountability. Turkish broadcasters who comment on soccer games on TV often describe a missed shot at the goal by saying "the ball went out," as if the ball decided to go out on its own, rather than stating that "the player kicked the ball out."

The tendency to admit responsibility for action thus is muted in some languages. This inherent tolerance for avoiding accountability, stemming from language structure, can shape behaviors and can eventually become a cultural trait. To elaborate further, if Mike breaks the vase, but the language convention describes the situation as "the vase broke," then it becomes easier for Mike to avoid acknowledging his role in the incident. Similarly, if a CEO leads his company into bankruptcy, the implications and the degree of accountability varies depending on whether society describes the event as "He bankrupted the company" or "The company went bankrupt."

Language and Cognition

An important question is whether language has a direct influence on culture. The conjecture that language has a causal impact on culture stems from a hypothesis in linguistics and psychology that language affects the way people think and process information. Although this hypothesis has been challenged, a large and growing body of recent work has been producing compelling evidence that language may influence cognition because language shapes the way people think.[20]

An interesting line of research makes use of cross-linguistic differences in color perception and analyzes the connection between color terms and cognition. Various languages contain up to eleven different words for describing colors. But many languages have no names for pink, orange, grey, or purple. Some languages have one term describing the group of green, blue, and yellow, and at least twenty languages have only three or four words for colors.[21]

Of course, the emergence of color terms in a society is related to the socioeconomic and ecological environment. My university's colors are gold and purple—not yellow and purple. But an isolated society that has no access to gold as a precious metal would have no word for gold as a color in its vocabulary. The Turkish language contains *blood red* as a specific shade of red. This could be because of the legacy of many wars over four hundred years, during which the Ottoman Empire conquered the Middle East, North Africa, and Eastern Europe. In contrast, *blood red* is not the name of any standard shade of red in the US, although various shades of red have their specific names.

Having distinct words for different colors seems to influence how the human brain processes information about colors. Research has shown that if various shades of a particular color are all called by the same name, speakers of that language think of these shades to be similar when they see them, and that they are more likely to confuse these colors in comparison to people who speak a language in which these color shades have different names.

The Russian language, for instance, has two distinct and obligatory words for blue and dark blue. The Russian word *goluboy* describes light blue, while *siniy* is the specific name for dark blue. The same distinction exists in

Turkish, where *mavi* means blue, and *lacivert* denotes dark blue. In English, on the other hand, there is no universally accepted word for dark blue. Although *navy blue* refers to a particular shade of dark blue, it is not a standard definition, and it is unlikely that two English-speaking individuals would call the same color "navy blue" when presented with a particular shade of blue. In contrast, in Turkey and Russia, when young children learn their numbers, letters, and colors, they learn that the color blue has a name, and that dark blue is represented by a different name.

When Russian and English speakers were tested for color differentiation between twenty shades of blue, ranging from the lightest to the darkest, Russians were found to be faster to tell the difference between two shades of blue when these shades were in different linguistic categories in Russian (one siniy and the other goluboy), compared to when the two shades of blue were in the same linguistic category (both siniy or both gouboy). English speakers' ability to differentiate between color shades was not impacted by whether the color was in the light blue or dark blue range. This indicates that how colors are named in a language can impact how the differences in colors are perceived by the human brain.[22]

Consider another example of how language alters perception. In some languages, such as Turkish, there is no grammatical gender system. Both people and objects are referred to as *it*. Many languages, on the other hand, assign masculine, feminine, and neuter genders to mark objects. In English, a boy is referred to as *he* and a girl is *she*. Inanimate objects are referred to as *it*. In some languages, certain inanimate objects have genders too. For example, in German, a car is neuter (*das Auto*), but a tree is male (*der Baum*), and a bridge is female (*die Brűcke*). Spanish is another language in which inanimate objects can have masculine or feminine gender.

Researchers made use of the fact that some of the same words have different genders in Spanish and German to design a clever experiment that investigated whether the gender assignment of words has an impact on people's perceptions.[23] German and Spanish speakers were given the same words, which have different gender classifications in these languages. When asked to describe these words using adjectives, there were significant differences between how they were perceived by Spanish versus German speakers. For example, the word *key* is masculine in German (*der Schlűssel*) and feminine in Spanish (*la Ilave*). German speakers described keys as hard, heavy, jagged, metal, serrated, and useful. Spanish speakers, on the other hand, described keys as golden, intricate, little, lovely, shiny, and tiny. The word *bridge* is feminine in German but masculine in Spanish. German speakers described bridges as beautiful, elegant, fragile, peaceful, pretty, and slender, while Spanish speakers thought bridges were big, dangerous, long, strong, sturdy, and towering. This example demonstrates that the particular structure of a language has an influence on how the speakers of that language perceive the world around them.

It is also not difficult to see that a system of symbols, as part of a language, can have an effect on cognition. For instance, as pointed out by linguists, a society that insisted on using Roman numerals, instead of Arabic numbers, would have a very difficult time making progress in algebra and calculus and reaching the associated cognitive gains. Cognition improves even in chimpanzees when they are taught abstract symbolic systems.[24]

Language seems to affect how we perceive concepts, including time. Speakers of different languages differ in whether they think about time as a distance or as a quantity.[25] There are even differences between speakers of different languages regarding the perception of the direction in which time moves. If the language is written from left to right, then speakers of that language think of time as moving from left to right. If the language is written from right to left (as in Arabic and Hebrew), then people who speak that language think time as moving from right to left.[26]

Language Alters the Anatomy of the Brain

Over the past two decades, research in neuroscience has revealed the brain's remarkable ability to change its structure both functionally and physically. This capability, known as *neuroplasticity*, enables the brain to reorganize itself in response to environmental stimuli, cognitive challenges, and behavioral experiences.[27] In this section, I will discuss the influence of language on neuroplasticity; I will explore the findings of this neuroscience research further in chapter 11 when examining the impact of education on culture.

Recent studies have uncovered a new dimension of neuroplasticity, demonstrating that learning a second language brings about both functional and anatomical changes in the brain. Specifically, it has been shown that individuals who speak two languages (bilingual people) demonstrate greater creativity than those who speak only one language (monolingual people). This creativity advantage has been observed in both children and adults.[28] Bilingual children and adults also exhibit higher levels of cognitive flexibility compared to their monolingual peers, and bilingualism has been linked to a significant delay in the onset of dementia and the development of neuropathological conditions.[29]

Bilingualism impacts *executive functions*—the mental processes required for concentration and focused attention—particularly in situations where relying on automatic responses, instincts, or intuition may not be effective.[30] As stated by cognitive neuroscientist Adele Diamond, using executive functions requires effort. "It is easier to continue doing what you have been doing than to change, it is easier to give into temptation than to resist it, and it is easier to go on 'automatic pilot' than to consider what to do next."[31] Higher-level executive functions encompass cognitive skills such as planning, reasoning, ignoring irrelevant information, and problem-solving. Numerous studies have shown that bilingual individuals exhibit stronger executive functions compared to monolingual ones.[32]

An important question is whether the brain structure of bilingual people is genetically different from that of monolingual people, enabling them to have an executive function advantage and to acquire a second language more easily. A related concern is whether differences in the socioeconomic environments of monolingual and bilingual people may account for the cognitive differences observed between the two groups. Researchers addressed these issues in various ways, such as comparing infants raised with two languages from birth to those raised with only one language and examining individuals with similar socioeconomic backgrounds who differ in whether they speak one or two languages.[33] These analyses, once again, revealed that speaking more than one language changes the brain and that this effect is unlikely to be related to genetic differences.

Additional fascinating insights have emerged from research utilizing neuroimaging technology to study the brain. This research uses structural magnetic resonance imaging (MRI) technology to examine the brain's anatomy, precisely capturing the physical characteristics of brain tissue and any anatomical changes resulting from language learning. A typical approach involves selecting a group of individuals to undergo language acquisition and analyzing how their brain structure is altered after the training, in comparison to before. These changes are then contrasted with those occurring in the brain of a comparable control group that did not undergo language training during the same time period. Studies have revealed structural changes in various parts of the brain as a result of language acquisition. For instance, learning a second language has been shown to increase the gray matter volume in the left inferior parietal cortex (IPC).[34] This region of the brain works as a multifunctional hub, integrating higher-order cognitive functions such as language processing, mathematical reasoning, working memory, and attention. It plays a crucial role in understanding grammar, semantics, and syntax, and it also supports numerical cognition, arithmetic, and the integration of sensory and cognitive information. Thus, acquiring a second language boosts the IPC's gray matter volume, improving overall cognitive abilities.

Technical reasoning skills, including understanding the physical world and visuospatial imagery, are influenced by a subregion of the IPC known as *area PF*. These skills can be evaluated through tasks such as building a paper airplane or constructing a tower with wires.[35] Research indicates that the cortical thickness of area PF is related to higher technical reasoning abilities.

The cortex, the brain's outer layer, consists of gray matter and plays a crucial role in information processing and cognitive functions. The thickness of the cortex provides insights into the density and organization of neurons and their connections within specific brain regions. Numerous studies have shown that cortical thickness is strongly associated with overall cognitive performance and intelligence.[36] This relationship between cortical thickness and intelligence has been observed even in chimpanzees.[37] Importantly, it has been shown that cortical thickness increases with language learning.[38]

These findings, taken together, imply that engagement with a second language alters the brain's structure by increasing gray matter volume in specific regions, including the cerebral cortex. This structural change enhances cognitive abilities, particularly in areas such as memory, attention, and executive functions. As a result, bilingual individuals often demonstrate improved skills in abstract thinking, problem-solving, working memory, planning, and decision-making.

The straightforward implication is that members of two societies with identical genetic makeups could develop different brain structures if one society encourages learning a second language while the other discourages it. Structural modifications in the brain, induced by bilingualism, would likely make individuals in the former society cognitively more advanced than those in the latter.

It is crucial to emphasize that this cognitive difference between societies is not due to genetic factors but is instead driven by changes in the brain structure associated with learning. Therefore, societies with cultural norms that hinder language learning are likely to experience cognitive disadvantages compared to those that actively promote learning a second language.

Another important point is that changes in brain biology are not limited to learning a second language. Increases in brain's gray matter volume, and the associated improvements in cognition and intelligence, can result from learning in general. We will revisit this topic in chapter 11 when discussing the role of education in cultural change. For now, it is worth noting that it has even been suggested that a significant portion of the differences between Western, educated, industrialized, rich, and democratic (WEIRD) societies and the rest of the world can be attributed to variations in brain structure, influenced by the higher prevalence of advanced literacy in WEIRD societies.[39]

Does Language Change? Can It Be Changed?

The discussion in this chapter highlights the connection between language, cognition, and economic behavior. Differences in linguistic structures impact how the brain processes and interprets information, which in turn impacts decisions and behaviors. The structure of a language also embodies information about cultural patterns of behavior. Put differently, a language reflects the cultural attributes of a society that speaks that language, and these cultural attributes have an impact on people's economic and social well-being in that society.

At the same time, language is influenced by the economic and social history of a society, and it evolves over time. For instance, in English, the second-person pronoun distinction used to be made by using informal *thou* and formal *ye*. Between the seventeenth and eighteenth centuries, this distinction evolved into a single *you*, the both formal and informal second-person pronoun used today.

Language can also change rather quickly due to external influences. An example is a shift that has been observed recently in some countries, which has been attributed to the use of social media.[40] The impersonal nature of communicating on social media platforms such as X (formerly known as Twitter) resulted in a sense of equality among the users, which has minimized the perceived socioeconomic status gap between them. This trend, coupled with the need to write shorter phrases quickly on these platforms, appears to have negatively impacted the attention paid to both grammar and vocabulary use, as well as the use of the second-person pronoun's politeness distinction. To the extent that these shifts lead to a permanent decrease in the range of vocabulary and a weakening of grammatical accuracy, it will have a harmful effect on cultural complexity.[41]

Scholars have recently started investigating the impact of social media on language use. Out-of-vocabulary words (made up by the users of social media), how they spread, and their sociolinguistic properties have become a research domain. Studies in computer science and operations research have demonstrated that Twitter/X users influence one another not only in the content they share but also in their language and syntax. This research explores how ideas and communication patterns spread among users, suggesting a mechanism for the horizontal transmission of culture within the same generation.

The impact of social media on language is important because aspects of language, such as the range of vocabulary, are influenced by social media, which in turn has the potential to affect the depth and nuance of communication across all aspects of society, including politics, sports, and arts. If a language loses its complexity due to the loss of vocabulary, this will have a direct impact on culture through the way individuals communicate. It will also have an effect, albeit in the long run, via the diminished cognition of those who use the simplified language.

To make the point about the importance of vocabulary clearer, note, for example, that most languages contain words for cardinal directions such as north, south, east, and west, as well as words to describe locations and directions based on a body's position in space (such as left, right, behind, and so on). Certain languages, however, contain only absolute spatial terms, such as north and south, and no relative terms, such as left and right, as in some of the Aboriginal Australian languages.[42] This makes it necessary for the speakers of such languages to keep track of their absolute orientation in describing situations (e.g., "I am writing with my south hand"). It is not difficult to see how this would make it difficult to communicate with others.

More generally, if a language lacks a word for a concept, then it is difficult to develop a discourse about that concept. For example, if the language has no word for *ethics*, it would be difficult to discuss or express concerns about unethical conduct. It follows that societies without a word for ethics may be at a disadvantage when it comes to identifying, addressing, and preventing unethical behavior—say, that of their political leaders.

In his classic novel *Nineteen Eighty-Four*, George Orwell describes a society where a new form of language, called *Newspeak*, is created by the rulers of the society. This new language is a derivate of the original one; it is designed with the goal of having a limited vocabulary to restrict freedom of thought. For example: "[In Newspeak] there was no vocabulary expressing the function of Science as a habit of mind, or a method of thought, irrespective of its particular branches. There was, indeed, no word for 'Science.'"[43] Similarly, Newspeak has no words for *more*, *greater*, or *better*. Instead, the suffix *plus* is used for anything better than *good*. Thus, the word *plusgood* is used in this language instead of greater or better.

What George Orwell described in this dystopian novel seventy-five years ago appears to be actually happening, at least in some societies. A notable example is the transformation in the use of the Turkish language over the last two decades. The depth of Turkish vocabulary has been enriched over centuries by adopting words from other languages, such Persian, Arabic, and those with Latin origins, as a natural result of centuries-long interactions with other societies through trade, diplomacy, and conflict.

The Turkish language contains words of different intensity to describe a given feeling, different verbs identifying subtle differences in action, and different adjectives capturing nuances. But there has been a transition to limited vocabulary in this rich and complex language, which should otherwise lend itself easily to the expression of subtlety and finesse. For instance, Turkish language contains many adjectives describing the gradation from *good* to *excellent*. Some of them, in some arguable order of strength, are *iyi*, *çok iyi*, *fevkalâde*, *hârika*, *hârikulade*, *mükemmel*, *müthiş*, *muhteşem*, *muazzam*, and *şahane*.

Yet for the most part, Turks are now using only *iyi* (good) and *çok iyi* (very good), both in written and spoken language. The remaining adjectives in this spectrum are seldom used. Instead, they are replaced by *süper*, which has the same meaning as *super* in English.

Any change in the sophistication of a language, including the depth of its vocabulary, is likely influenced not just by what is being taught in schools but also by role models, including political leaders, peers, and media content exposure. So, language, as an element of culture, is subject to horizontal transmission within the same generation.

In summary, the language of a society carries the signs of cultural attributes of that society. Also, the complexity and sophistication of a language influence culture by shaping abstract thinking, development of concepts, and cognition. In chapter 10, we will explore the contagion of undesirable behaviors that may ultimately evolve into negative cultural attributes. Decline in linguistic complexity and sophistication is an example of this phenomenon. Media personalities and political leaders play a crucial role in this process as their use of limited vocabulary and slang often encourages others to adopt similar speech patterns. This reflects a natural dynamic of cultural evolution, in which individuals tend to mimic those they perceive as successful or influential.

8 Morality

How Do You Get on a Subway Car?

One of my international doctoral students invited her parents to America for her graduation. They subsequently traveled together for a couple of weeks for vacation. Afterward, she shared with me how her father was restless each time when they had to join a queue, whether it was at a Starbucks coffee shop or at an airport boarding gate. He always wanted to cut the line, despite her daughter's warnings against it, and kept asking her why other people were not doing the same.

Attempting to cut in line, when people have formed a well-defined queue by lining up one behind the other, is a brazen action. But when there is not a clear line, sneaking in and skipping the line becomes easier. One example of such an environment is subway platforms. I have taken the subway during rush hours in many densely populated cities, including New York, London, Paris, Tokyo, Lisbon, Hong Kong, and Istanbul. The beginning of each scene is the same. You purchase a token or a subway card, pass through the turnstile, and wait on the platform for the next subway car. Because the place that each subway car will come to halt at the platform is usually marked, people tend to gather around these spots.

What takes place when the subway arrives and pulls into the station varies by city. Usually, people on the platform scurry toward the doors of the subway car, but what unfolds thereafter depends on the city. In some cities, individuals waiting on the platform rush to the doors and try to enter the subway car as soon as the doors open, disregarding the passengers who are inside and need to exit. This of course creates quite a bit of chaos, involving unintended physical contact, followed in some cases by verbal exchanges between passengers. In some other cities, the process of exiting and entering the subway is more or less orderly, but there is still variation from city to city. For instance, in some places, when the subway doors open, people on the platform create a narrow pathway for those inside the train to get off, allowing for the simultaneous entry and exit of passengers. In other cities, individuals on the platform wait around the doors until after all the passengers who wish to disembark have completely exited the subway car.

But what I saw in Tokyo was different. While waiting for the subway to arrive, people on the platform lined up in two rows, to the right and to the left of where each car was expected to stop. When the subway arrived and the doors opened, those waiting in line on the platform did not move but waited until the passengers in the car got off. They then entered the subway car, preserving their order in the line. So in Tokyo, the convention dictates that the person who is the first in line enters the subway before others, while those who arrive later follow in sequence. In other cities, there exists a social acceptance, albeit to varying degrees, of joining the back of the crowd awaiting the subway car and then pushing and shoving one's way into the car.

This, of course, is a resource-allocation problem at its core. Everyone pays the same ticket price, but some passengers inevitably end up receiving a smaller benefit in return. Some individuals enter the subway car before others, and they get to sit down during the ride to their destination. Others have to stand up in a crowded subway car. Still others cannot manage to squeeze in before the doors close and have to wait for the next subway train to arrive in order to try and get on again. This problem emerges in the first place because the demand for seats is greater than the supply, but it is generally not cost-effective for the subway authority to increase the supply of the service (such as adding more cars or operating the trains more frequently) in order for every passenger to have a seat or stand comfortably without feeling cramped like sardines in a can.

So in this circumstance, a societal ethical norm of acceptable behavior determines how to allocate seats. If we accept the premise that individuals who arrive earlier should have the right to board the subway before those who arrive later, then the varying patterns in different cities' subway platforms indicate that in certain societies, people freely violate their fellow passengers' rights and steal their place in line, while this behavior is not as prevalent in other societies.

In the same vein, writer Tim Parks, who has lived and worked in Italy, mentions in one of his books the Italian *il furbo* personality, which refers to a person whose crafty and shrewd actions have often the intension of gaining advantage over others.[1] As colorfully described by Deirdre Nansen McCloskey, il furbo's habit to sneak into ticket lines at train stations would get him likely harassed and attacked by grandmothers in Germany and by concealed-gun-carrying men in America.[2] Italians are resentful of il furbo, who steals their place in the ticket line, but they do not react, arguably because the act of the il furbo gives them the justification to act as an il furbo themselves sometimes.

This Italian il furbo character exists in some other countries also. In Turkey, he is called *uyanik*. The word *uyanik* would translate to English as a "vigilant person" or "alert person," but the real meaning of the persona is not someone who is alert, vigilant, or smart. An *uyanik* is someone who tries and finds ways to get around the rules to create an advantage for himself. Needless to say, he would feel no remorse for his actions.

As an example of Turkish uyanik behavior, imagine a narrow, two-way, inner-city street like the ones you would find in many old European cities. The vehicle traffic is not too heavy on this street, but there are always cars in motion, and sometimes bigger vehicles such as buses or delivery trucks pass through as well. This means that if there is some obstruction in one lane, like street repair, congestion arises because vehicles in both opposing lanes have to take turns and coordinate their moves around the blockage.

There are various shops along this street, such as bakeries, butcher shops, and grocery stores. If you are driving along this street, notice a store, and decide to purchase something, finding a parking space becomes a challenge. Because the street is narrow and there is no place to park your car, you need to drive away, find a parking space somewhere, perhaps a couple blocks away, walk to the store, and then walk back to your car. But if you are a uyanik person, you can stop your car in front of the store, put the hazard lights on, and stroll into the store to do your shopping. This of course creates a traffic bottleneck, but you are not phased. You are content that your car's flashing emergency lights reveal to the world that the inconvenience you created is temporary. And what is the big deal about the two minutes of congestion created by your car anyway?

So as a uyanik, you decided to appropriate a public good (a street meant for the free use of everyone) as your own personal space to avoid a short walk between your car and the store. The traffic jam and the discomfort and wasted time your behavior has created for others are not concerns for you. Interestingly, other drivers who are affected by this behavior do not confront the uyanik, and the store owner doesn't tell the uyanik that he won't be served so long as his car is blocking the traffic. All of this occurs because this behavior is deemed acceptable, and people anticipate that they themselves may engage in similar actions at some point in the future.

Why are these kinds of behaviors more prevalent in some societies and not in others? The answer lies in the variations in ethics and morals between them. But why are ethics and morals different in different societies, and how does economics play a role in shaping these differences? We will explore the answers in this chapter.

What Does a Referee's Wrong Decision Mean to You?

Imagine that you are watching an important soccer game between your favorite team and its rival. With the score tied, the referee awards a penalty kick to your team in the final minute of the regulation time. The player taking the penalty kick scores, and your team wins the game. However, the penalty awarded by the referee was the wrong call. Had the referee made the correct decision and not blown the whistle, the game would have ended in a tie. For those who are not familiar with soccer, we can translate this scenario to other sports. For instance, assume that the referee did not see a hold or some other rule violation committed by your football team in the last fifteen seconds of the game, and as a result your team ended up scoring a touchdown, winning the game.

How would you react to this situation? Would you overlook the incorrect decision and be happy that your team won the game, or would you acknowledge that your team's win was unjust and feel uneasy and unhappy about it? Maybe you might assess this scenario as a random event that is part of the game and something not worth fretting over—so let's explore another hypothetical situation. Suppose that your child has applied to be enrolled in a school or to be a member of a sports club or some other organization. Although there are many applicants, there is only one open spot. Your child has fine qualifications, but some other applicants are better qualified. However, the person making the admission decision is a friend of yours, and she chooses to admit your child instead of one of the better-qualified applicants. How would you feel about this outcome? How would you feel if the reverse happened? That is, how would you feel if your child was the most qualified applicant but the decision-maker chose a less qualified child due to a sense of camaraderie with that child because they were associated with the same group?

Or consider a situation in which you are a teacher, grading the exams of your students. Would you favor the students who are of the same race or ethnicity as you and give them higher grades than they deserve? If you were a judge in a criminal court, would you be more lenient toward the defendants who share the same background as you?

In other words, do you tend to categorize the world into us versus them and make decisions based on varying criteria depending on who stands to gain, or do you apply a uniform set of rules to all groups and circumstances? In the heart of these questions lies the concept of *universal morality*. That is, are you a person who has a single universal moral standard for fairness and for right versus wrong, which is applied to any situation regardless of who gains and who loses, or do you apply different moral standards to different situations depending on whether the outcome is advantageous to yourself or to the group to which you feel connected?

Before we get too agitated about immoral or unethical behavior, we should recognize the long history, in several fields ranging from evolutionary biology to evolutionary psychology and philosophy, trying to explain the moral foundations of human behavior. The question of "Where does morality come from?" is inherently difficult to answer, and it has been agonized over for centuries, going back to Confucius and Greek philosophers. But a hypothesis developed by social psychologists Jonathan Haidt and Craig Joseph stands out. Haidt and Joseph point out the similarity of moral judgments across societies on the one hand, and the variation in morality between them on the other hand. This opens the pathway to an understanding of the determinants of moral virtue. In a series of convincing articles, Haidt, Joseph, and their colleagues argue that morality has two components.[3] First, it is innate and hardwired into human psyche; second, it is influenced by the human environment. The innate component is the result of the forces of evolutionary biology. Over the course of hundreds of thousands of years of evolution, humans have developed instincts and intuitions that promoted their survival. These inborn tendencies include such elements as caring for vulnerable offspring; sensitivity to suffering; perceptiveness of reciprocity, fairness, and cheating; recognition of strength and appreciation of the power hierarchy; and emphasis on purity and avoidance of disease and waste products.

Another innate human attribute is the preferential treatment of those who are part of the group, such as blood relatives and other humans who share similar attributes. These innate components exist in all human beings as they are built into the human mind during the process of evolution. They make humans predisposed to certain behaviors and influence people's approval or disapproval of others' actions.

Haidt and his colleagues argue that these natural tendencies interact with the environment, and this interaction leads to the emergence of different types of moralities in different societies. In other words, although all humans start off with the same "factory settings" and therefore with the same tendencies for loyalty, reciprocity, caring, and preferential treatment of those who belong to the same group, these foundations are shaped by environment. This leads to the formation of different moral norms in different societies. Following the analogy used by these authors, this is similar to the emergence of different cuisines in different countries. Even though all humans have the same biological tongue structure, which has five taste receptors (for sweet, salty, sour, bitter, and umami), different societies have created different types of cuisines that please these taste receptors differently. The properties of different cuisines around the world depend on both environmental factors, such as the climate, geographical location, and access to different food and spice sources, and on the creativity of the people of those societies, despite the fact that the underlying factory settings are the same in all humans for the taste receptors on their tongues. Along the same lines, the argument goes, although all humans have the same inborn moral tendencies, different moralities have emerged in different societies due to the impact of various economic and environmental factors.

The evidence for innate moral tendencies can be found not only in humans but also in other primates. Ethologists have long identified that apes have some of the same inherent building blocks of morality as humans, such as empathy and compassion for those in pain, the understanding of power hierarchies, and a tendency for reciprocity.[4] Coming back to humans and human behavior, as described in the beginning of this chapter, it has been well-documented that people have an inclination for being biased in favor of those who are "similar" and who belong to the same group. Humans tend to show preference toward those with whom they identify, such as friends, relatives, and those who share similar attributes, like people of the same race or ethnicity. This phenomenon, known as *in-group bias*, has been substantiated by scientific research in several academic fields, including economics—in both my own research and that of other economists.[5]

Studies in experimental psychology shed light on the potential foundations of this in-group favoritism, reinforcing the argument that there are likely evolutionary reasons for it. This fascinating work reveals that humans have inborn compassion and empathy for those who look like themselves. Insights are obtained from experiments done with young children, infants, and babies around the world. In-group preference is observed in five-year-old children. Even babies as young as three months old demonstrate a significant visual preference for faces from their own ethic groups and own race. It has been found that infants treat others well if these others look similar to the infants and that others are treated poorly by infants if they look dissimilar. Experimental psychologists Neha Mahajan and Karen Wynn reach the conclusion that a central feature of human psychology is humans' pervasive tendency to divide their social world into *us* and *them* and to hold more positive beliefs about those who are similar.[6]

Based on these findings, psychologist Paul Bloom states, "Kin has always mattered; it makes perfect Darwinian sense to favor someone who looks like you, because that individual is likely to share more of your genes."[7] But, importantly, it has also been recognized that what matters is not so much people's inborn preference for their own race or ethnicity. Instead, people have a natural tendency to associate themselves with a group and then treat the members of that group favorably in comparison to those who are nonmembers.

A striking line of experimental research in social psychology has shown that when people are *randomly* assigned to groups, they start favoring the members of their group even though they have no reason whatsoever to do so. For example, imagine we randomly divide people into two groups. We give the members of the first group yellow t-shirts and call them the *the Yellows* and give the second group green t-shirts and call them *the Greens.* The only difference between people is the color of the t-shirt they are wearing, yet such arbitrary and meaningless social groupings produce in-group preference. People allocate more resources to those who are in their group and treat them more favorably compared to those who are members of the out-group.[8] Likewise, individuals belonging to the out-group are subjected to negative treatment. In-group bias in punishment was detected even among children. When six-year-olds are randomly divided into two groups, they inflicted more punishment on members of the out-group for perceived unfair behavior in comparison to punishment applied to in-group members for the same behavior.[9]

Dozens of research articles have documented that once the notion of a *group* was introduced, the subjects discriminated against those assigned to another random category. For example, imagine an experiment in which adults are presented with a series of abstract paintings and are instructed to rank them based on personal preference. Subsequently, these individuals are randomly divided into two groups. Those in the first group were told that their ranking of paintings revealed that they liked the paintings of Paul Kell, while the second group was told that their ranking indicated a liking for Wassily Kandinsky paintings, although of course none of this was true because the groups were determined randomly. Subsequently, participants were asked to distribute a sum of money among members of both groups. It turns out that people allocate more money to fellow members of their own group (those who they believed liked the same painter), even if doing so does not benefit them personally.[10]

The upshot is that evolutionary forces have produced instincts in humans to favor those who belong to the same in-group. This inborn tendency and the resultant coalition among the members of the group enhanced trust and improved cooperation. Thus in-group favoritism was beneficial to individual survival as well as to the economic well-being of the community in primitive societies.

Nature Versus Nurture

Even though humans seem to be hardwired for evolutionary reasons to favor and prefer others who are like themselves and who belong to the same group, and although arbitrary assignment to a group triggers preference for the members of that in-group, these intrinsic preferences are weaker in some societies and stronger in others.

An extreme form of in-group preference and distrust of the out-group was documented by political scientist Edward Banfield.[11] After spending a year in a remote village in Southern Italy after World War II and observing and documenting the behavior of the villagers, he identified an extreme version of in-group favoritism: People trusted only their nuclear families as their in-group. Others, including neighbors and other villagers, were considered as out-group members and were treated with distrust and suspicion. Banfield explained that the goal of people in that community was to maximize the material, short-term advantage of their nuclear family and assume that all others will do likewise. He created the term *amoral familist* for those who behaved this way. Banfield documented that in this setting, no one would do anything to improve the interest of the community; nobody became involved in public affairs, and nobody checked on public officials to see if they performed their jobs.

An amoral familist who is an office holder will take bribes when he can get away with it. But whether he takes bribes or not, it is assumed by the society of amoral familists that he does. Because there is no trust in others, effective organization and deliberately concerted action is very difficult. As a result, this extreme in-group bias, in which nobody trusts anyone or cooperates with anyone, produced undesirable outcomes, including poor governance and terrible economic conditions for the village.

This type of extreme in-group bias, where only members of the immediate family are trusted, is probably not very common—but where do people draw the circle of trust? To investigate this question, we can turn to the World Values Survey, mentioned in previous chapters. In this survey, people around the world are asked the following question: "Could you tell me whether you trust people from your family completely, somewhat, not very much, or not at all?"[12]

If the survey respondent selects either "completely" or "somewhat," it indicates trust of family members. The same question is then posed two more times replacing "People from your family" with "People from your neighborhood" and then "People you know personally." By considering survey respondents' answers to these three questions, the extent of trust people place in their in-group can be assessed. Using these data, I assigned a value of 1/3 to respondents who trust only one of the three (family, neighbors, or someone you know personally). Those who trust two of the three groups received a value of 2/3, and individuals who expressed trust in all three groups were assigned 3/3. By calculating this ratio for each survey respondent in a particular country, an average value can be obtained, which can be converted to an index, ranging from 0 to 100. Higher index values indicate stronger trust of the in-group in that country.[13]

The same survey participants were also asked about their level of trust toward (1) "people they meet for the first time," (2) "people of another religion," and (3) "people of another nationality." By calculating the average of the affirmative answers to these three questions, we can similarly ascertain the degree of trust individuals place in outsiders (the out-group).

The larger the difference between in-group and out-group averages, the greater the discrepancy in the extent to which people trust in-group members over the out-group. For example, people in both Sweden and Northern Ireland exhibit a high degree of trust to their in-group members, with an index value of 97 in Sweden and 96 in Northern Ireland. However, the value of the out-group trust index is only 73 for the Northern Irish, compared to 88 for Swedes. So the gap between in-group trust and out-group trust is nine points in Sweden, but it is twenty-three points in Northen Ireland. This indicates that, compared to the Swedes, the Northern Irish exhibit stronger preference for their in-group relative to their out-group.

If residents of a particular country trust the out-group as much as they trust their in-group, the difference between the index values of in-group and out-group will be zero—but it turns out that the value of this difference is positive in every country. This means that people in every country trust their in-group—such as family, neighbors, and people they know personally—more than their out-group, which includes strangers, individuals of different religions, or those from other nations. In other words, morality is not universal; instead, people everywhere exhibit in-group preference.

However, although people in every nation tend to favor those who are similar to them, this tendency presents itself to varying degrees in different societies, as displayed in figure 8.1. In countries located at the bottom of the graph, people trust insiders only slightly more than they trust outsiders. Trust of the in-group over the out-group becomes bigger as we move up the graph. For instance, the gap between in-group and out-group trust levels is twenty points in Canada and thirty-one points in Portugal.

The figure reveals that many countries diverge quite substantially from universal trust and morality. In Armenia, Pakistan, Malaysia, Mongolia, Georgia, and Albania, the gap is fifty to fifty-five points, revealing that people in these countries trust in-group members substantially more relative to outsiders. The relative lack of trust of outsiders is higher in Tajikistan, Greece, and South Korea, with the difference between in-group and out-group trust being around sixty-four points. China is the extreme case, with a seventy-four-point gap between in-group and out-group trust.

Turks too trust to their in-group members significantly more compared to outsiders, with a notable fifty-three-point trust disparity between the

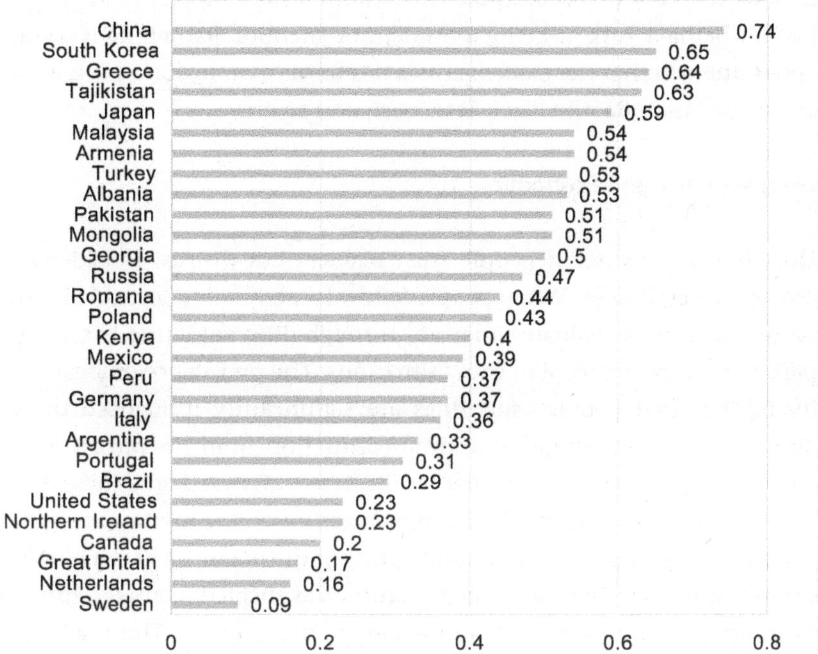

Figure 8.1
Difference between in-group and out-group trust in various countries

two groups. When I take a taxi in Istanbul, Turkey, and engage in a conversation with the driver, it is typical for him to ask the question, "*Sizin memleket neresi?*", which translates to English as "What is your country?" Because there is no conceivable way for the driver to think that I am not a Turk (because I don't speak Turkish with an accent, nor do I look non-Turkish), this question seems odd. But what is really meant by that question is, "What is your city of origin?" The underlying intention of the driver is to determine my hometown, or the city of origin, to understand if I belong to the same in-group as him.

The population of Istanbul has grown tremendously over the last twenty-five years, reaching fifteen million. A substantial portion of this population consists of people whose parents or themselves were born in some other region of the country and migrated to Istanbul. Thus, the question "What is your city of origin?" reflects the taxi driver's curiosity about whether the passenger belongs to his in-group. The critical point here, of course, is that the taxi driver does not consider the customer as belonging to his in-group just for being a Turk or being a resident of Istanbul. Rather, he is trying to determine whether the passenger has ties to his own region of origin, such as Eastern Anatolia, the Black Sea Coast, and so on.

Local Morality and Economics

Does it really matter if people trust insiders but distrust outsiders? The answer is, yes, it does. When people follow local morality instead of universal morality, they evaluate situations through different lenses based on the parties who are involved in those situations. The prevalence of local morality implies that people's identities are significantly influenced by their affiliation with the in-group and differentiation from the out-group. Circumstances that involve outsiders are assessed, analyzed, and judged using different criteria compared to circumstances involving in-group members.

Strong in-group preference and distrust of the members of the out-group can result in parochialism, which manifests as suspicion, antagonism, and hostility toward those who do not belong to the in-group. This is an impediment to a well-functioning modern society and a detriment for economic development as well as prosperity for a variety of reasons. Divergence from moral universalism would lead to inefficient and incorrect allocation of resources, such as hiring or doing business with an unqualified person simply because he is a member of the in-group. Distrust of outsiders would reduce the tendency to cooperate with them, and people would be less eager to engage in economic transactions with those who are considered outsiders. If morality is not universal, then justice and fairness would apply differently to kin, friends, and community members (or some other version of the "clan" or "tribe," such as people in the same geographic area) compared to outsiders, such as strangers, foreigners, or people who belong to another religious or ethnic group. Distrust of outsiders is likely to lead to discrimination against individuals in the out-group.

When people operate with local morality driven by in-group preference, they not only have less trust toward outsiders compared to their in-group but also exhibit a reduced inclination for equal altruism toward everyone. Instead, individuals tend to prioritize allocating resources to those who are in their in-group. For example, a study analyzed the views of approximately twenty thousand adult Americans on the appropriate level of government welfare spending. Individuals' support for welfare spending was assessed based on their responses to questions about whether they believed government welfare spending (assistance to those in need) was too high, about right, or too low.[14] After controlling for respondents' various personal attributes—including race, age, education, marital status, number of children, household income, and location—it was shown that individuals were more likely to support welfare spending as the proportion of welfare recipients from their own racial group increased in their community. In other words, all else being equal, and regardless of their own income status, individuals are more likely to support government welfare spending when a larger share of welfare recipients belongs to their racial in-group.

Similarly, recent research provided evidence on this point by surveying about sixty-four thousand individuals from sixty countries to determine how they would distribute the local currency equivalent of $1,000 between two hypothetical individuals who have the same standards of living.[15] The question posed to the respondents was: "How much of the $1,000 would you give you to [Person 1], if the rest goes to [Person 2]?" The first hypothetical person in the question was listed as a person in the family, a friend, someone of the same religion, or someone with the same ethnicity (an in-group member), while the second individual was listed as a random stranger from the same country or a stranger from another country (an outsider).

Analyses revealed nontrivial differences between countries in the extent of their residents' generosity toward someone from their in-group versus toward someone in the out-group. People everywhere allocate a larger fraction of the money to the person who is the member of their in-group compared to a socially distant stranger. But in some countries, people came close to a fifty-fifty split between the in-group and out-group allocation, whereas in some other countries people allocated a substantially larger share to the in-group. For example, Chinese people on average allocate 75 percent of the money to their in-group and 25 percent to the out-group. In Uganda and Algeria, the split is about seventy-thirty in favor of the in-group. And people in such countries as Mexico, Cameroon, Venezuela, and Jordan allocate 60 percent of the money to their in-group, leaving 40 percent to outsiders.

To gain a view of the potential costs of local morality, an insightful study analyzed the decisions of over 2,800 loan officers in India, who evaluated more than 113,000 loan applications.[16] In addition to factors that determine a loan's creditworthiness and risk, such as loan amount, duration, and annual interest rate, the data also included personal attributes like the social group (Hindu vs. Muslim) and caste of both the lender and borrower. The analysis found that, all else being equal, lenders were more likely to approve applications from borrowers in their own social group. This in-group favoritism had significant consequences. Because lenders were more inclined to approve risky borrowers simply because they belonged to the same group, this behavior resulted in higher default risks of loans, and lower returns for the lending institutions.[17]

In summary, in-group preference and favoritism based on ethnicity, race, religion, or political affiliation—along with the resulting nepotism and inefficient resource allocation—lead to an increase in polarization and decrease in intergroup cooperation. This, in turn, results in governance challenges and imposes economic costs on society as a whole. The issue becomes more severe as the number of in-groups increases. When people prefer that government-provided economic and social benefits go to their own racial, ethnic, or religious group—regardless of merit—coordination and governance become more challenging as demographic diversity grows. In other words, if subgroups exhibit a tribal mindset, localized morality, and strong in-group preferences, then the quality of government and economic performance may deteriorate as group fragmentation rises in society.

What Predicts Local Versus Universal Morality?

The fact that there is substantial variation across nations in the extent of universal morality raises the question of what the proximate mechanisms of this variation are. In what types of societies are people more likely to exhibit universal morality, and in which societies are they more inclined toward favoritism and preferential treatment of their in-group?

Individualism and Morality

Figure 8.2 displays the correlation between local morality and individualism based on data gathered from a cross section of fifty-three countries. The horizontal axis represents the degree of individualism in each country, measured by Hofstede's index, where a higher value indicates stronger individualism and lower values represent a more collectivist orientation. On the vertical axis, local morality is depicted as the difference between trust

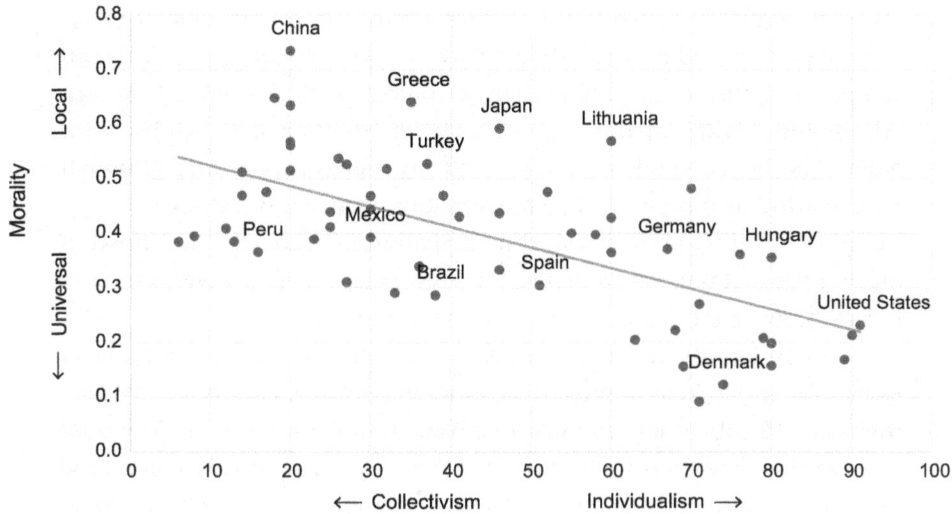

Figure 8.2
Relationship between morality and individualism-collectivism in various countries

in the in-group and out-group. Larger values signify a higher degree of local morality, and smaller values represent stronger universal morality.

Each data point on the graph represents the combination of the extent of local morality and individualism for a specific country. The straight line is the best statistical fit to these data points, illustrating the average relationship between individualism and local morality across countries. The graph reveals that countries with higher levels of individualism (bigger values on the horizontal axis) tend to exhibit lower levels of local morality (smaller values on the vertical axis). Conversely, countries with stronger collectivist attitudes have stronger local morality. This is not surprising as in collectivist societies opinions are commonly held by the community instead of being distinctive to an individual, and individuals have a strong emotional connection to the group and a willingness to collaborate with others. As a result, loyalty to the group and the strength of local morality is stronger in collectivist societies.

Note that individualism is not the same as selfishness. In fact, collaboration among individuals for the benefit of the common good is more prevalent in individualistic societies. This is important because cooperation among genetically unrelated individuals is critical in dealing with a wide range of problems related to the group's well-being. For example, if everyone cooperated and changed their behavior to reduce their fossil fuel consumption slightly, then climate change would be easier to tackle. However, self-interest might motivate individuals to let others change their behavior while they themselves do nothing, benefiting from others' efforts. Although participating in protests and demonstrations against a dictator carries the risk of physical harm, widespread participation increases the likelihood of ousting the dictator. Yet from a self-interest perspective, it may seem safer to stay home, relying on others to take action instead.

Now consider the following game, played with four players. Each player receives twenty tokens, representing a monetary value. Players are told that they can contribute any number of tokens to a common pool. The total contributions are then multiplied by 1.6 and divided equally among the players. This multiplication process simulates the return to an investment. Here, the collected tokens provide a 60 percent return. A player's income at the end of the game is the tokens she kept and didn't contribute, plus her share of the multiplied pool.

Suppose everyone contributed their twenty tokens to the public good. The total contribution would have been eighty tokens. Multiplied by 1.6, this would have yielded 128 tokens. Dividing this amount among the four players would have given each player thirty-two tokens. Therefore, if each player contributed all twenty of their tokens to this public good project, they would each end up with thirty-two tokens.

Let's assume you as Player 1 contributed four tokens to the common pool and kept sixteen, while each of the other three players contributed twelve of their tokens to the common pool and retained eight. The total contribution to the pool is forty (4+12+12+12), which becomes sixty-four tokens when multiplied by 1.6. These sixty-four tokens are then divided equally among the four players, so each player receives sixteen tokens from the investment pool. At the end of the game, Players 2, 3, and 4 each end up with twenty-four tokens (sixteen from the pool plus eight tokens they each kept), while you end up with thirty-two tokens (sixteen from the pool plus sixteen tokens that you kept).

So if all players contribute a certain amount while you contribute less, you end up better off compared to them because you still benefit equally from the returns of their contributions. This is a classic free-riding problem, similar to the ones described earlier in which one avoids contributing to the group while reaping the benefits of others' efforts. If everyone cooperates, total gains for the group will be higher, and this gain would be equally shared among all players. However, there is an obvious incentive for any one individual to contribute less to increase their own benefit.

Suppose the game described here is played not just once but ten times in a row, with the same group of four players. This would allow players to observe the outcomes of each round and adjust their behavior in subsequent rounds based on the actions of others.

When this public goods game was played with 1,100 participants from sixteen countries, it was observed that individuals in more collectivist societies were more inclined to take advantage of others by contributing less to the common pool. This behavior and the adjustment made by other players produced outcomes that were less beneficial for everyone. Over ten rounds, average contributions were notably lower in cities like Muscat (Oman), Athens (Greece), Istanbul (Turkey), Riyadh (Saudi Arabia), Samara (Russia), and Minsk (Belarus) compared to cities associated with more individualistic cultures according to the Hofstede index, such as Boston (US), Copenhagen (Denmark), Bonn (Germany), Zurich (Switzerland), Nottingham (UK), and Melbourne (Australia).[18]

Consider a real-life example of the same idea of cooperation between genetically unrelated individuals. If you're in a taxi and notice the driver changing lanes without signaling, and you ask why he isn't using his blinker, he might explain that signaling would prompt drivers in the next lane to speed up and block him from moving in front of them. Therefore, signaling creates an obstacle, so he chooses not to signal and instead changes lanes abruptly. Because others prevent him from changing lanes, the taxi driver reciprocates by not letting other drivers in. This creates a dangerous situation in which all drivers must stay alert and constantly monitor the cars around them. The result of these strategic interactions is that no one signals, everyone tries to cut each other off, and cooperation breaks down. This leads to a chaotic situation: Drivers remain vigilant but face a higher risk of accidents compared to a scenario in which everyone uses their turn signals. Although the optimal outcome for society would be for all drivers to signal, the lack of cooperation leads to disorder. If you travel around the world, you'll notice that this type of behavior is more common in collectivist societies, where "others" are seen as outsiders who cannot be trusted.

Rule of Law and Morality

Figure 8.3 illustrates the correlation between the level of local morality and the strength of the rule of law across different countries. *Rule of law* measures the extent to which people have confidence in and abide by the rules of society, including the quality of contract enforcement, property rights, the police, and the courts, as determined by the World Bank.[19] The horizontal axis measures the percentile rank, depicting each country's ranking, with 0 corresponding to the lowest rank and 100 indicating the highest-ranked country in the rule of law dimension. Countries that are located to the right on the horizontal axis have a stronger rule of law. As revealed by the graph, nations that uphold the rule of law tend to have stronger universal morality. Conversely, in countries where morality is local (higher values on the vertical axis), adherence to the rule of law tends to be weaker.

It is of course not straightforward to make the claim that the prevalence of the rule of law has a direct causal impact on universal morality in a country. Nevertheless, it is reasonable to suggest that a corrupt legal system and poor rule of law compel individuals to seek alternative means for resolving disputes and ensuring contract enforcement. In such situations, individuals might enhance their economic well-being by prioritizing loyalty to their in-group, placing trust in and providing support to fellow in-group members.

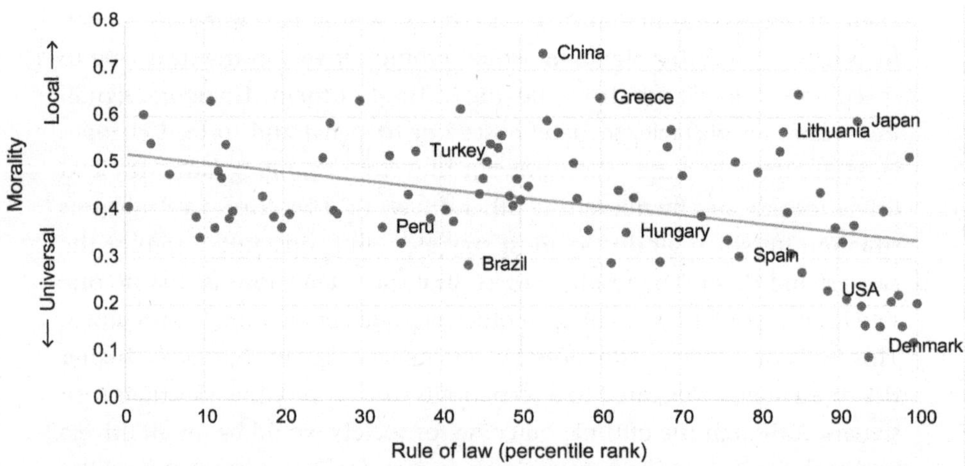

Figure 8.3
Relationship between morality and rule of law in various countries

Therefore, a weak rule of law in a country may enhance the intensity of in-group connections and bolster the strength of local morality.

Income and Morality

Figure 8.4 displays the plot of country-level per capita income (measured horizontally) and the extent of local morality (measured on the vertical axis). It shows that countries are richer when the extent of universal morality is stronger. As mentioned earlier, in societies where local morality is prevalent, people trust in-group members more than those who are outsiders, and insiders are treated more favorably than outsiders.[20] This in-group favoritism generates a host of inefficiencies in economic resource allocation and production, leading to lower incomes. At the same time, it is also plausible that economic development and rising per capita incomes prompt societal changes that compel or encourage a shift away from in-group preferences and toward universal morality. In this scenario, economic progress may catalyze a transition from local to universal moral principles. Thus the negative association observed in figure 8.4 between per capita country income and the prevalence of local morality may arise from (1) the hinderance that local morality poses to economic development, (2) the diminishing inclination toward local morality as countries progress economically, or (3) a combination of both factors occurring concurrently.

Ancient Production Technology and Kinship Structure

Another factor that explains whether local versus universal morality is more prevalent in a society is the ancient production type of that society. Research has identified transhumant pastoralism as a contributing factor to the extent of local morality. *Transhumant pastoralism* involves the community-driven movement of livestock, such as cattle, camels, or sheep, across various grazing lands in search of better pasture and water sources. This practice exposes people to challenging and perilous environmental conditions, underscoring the essential nature of cooperation and mutual support within the community for survival. Anthropologists suggest that this type of environment and the associated economic production system give rise to closely bonded kin groups as well as a sense of skepticism and hostility toward outsiders.

Indeed, analyzing data from ninety-seven countries around the globe, it has been shown that historical reliance on transhumant pastoralism is a

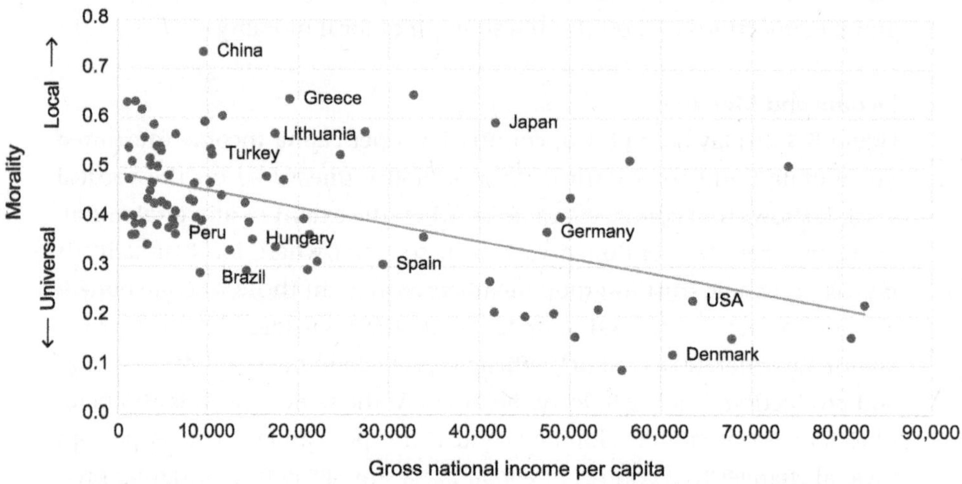

Figure 8.4
Relationship between morality and per capita national income in various countries

strong predictor of greater in-group relative to out-group trust.[21] People in countries with a historical tradition of transhumant pastoralism are more likely to trust their in-group (relatives, neighbors, and people they know) compared to the out-group (people met for the first time, people of other religions, foreigners). Conducting a parallel analysis with data from forty thousand individuals who reside in thirty-three different countries provided the same result and showed that individuals with ethnicities historically linked to transhumant pastoralism exhibited lower levels of universal morality compared those who live in the same country but have ethnicities that are not linked to pastoralism.

A similar result was obtained by another group of researchers who focused on sub-Saharan countries, making use of the fact that many African societies have been organized around kinship structures.[22] Individuals are deeply connected to their ancestry in these *segmentary lineage societies*, and the lineage is traced and recorded through the patrilineal (male) or matrilineal (female) blood line. Economic, social, and political interactions and affairs of individuals take place within the context and under the influence of their lineage. This structure fosters strong relationships and dependency between the members of a given lineage, which constitutes the in-group.

This implies that trust of family members would be enhanced, but trust of non–family members would be diminished for individuals who are members of ethnic groups with a strong tradition of such segmentary lineage structures. By analyzing twenty-five thousand individuals who belong to 145 ethnic groups from twelve countries, it was found that people in ethnic groups that traditionally had a segmentary lineage structure exhibit higher levels of trust for their relatives compared to nonrelatives. Put differently, a segmentary lineage structure and the resultant strong connections between individuals who belong to the same blood line reduce the propensity for universal morality.

In summary, there are differences in innate moral tendencies between societies. The extent to which people take advantage of others and how they perceive the application of societal rules varies from one nation to another. Specifically, the way people treat those outside their in-group differs significantly across societies. In some communities, concepts like fairness, honesty, and adherence to the rule of law are applied differently to those within the in-group versus those outside it. The in-group can include family, kin, or any group that shares common traits, such as race, political affiliation, religion, or region.

Considerable distrust of outsiders leads to various social issues, such as a lack of cooperation between different groups, hostility, and a reduced willingness to engage in interactions, including economic ones.

There are evolutionary biological reasons underlying humans' innate tendency to trust insiders and distrust outsiders, and in every nation people's trust in their in-group is stronger than their trust in the out-group. Thus, morality is not universal anywhere. However, the extent of these natural tendencies has evolved differently across societies, and the difference in the level of trust between the in-group and out-group varies tremendously across countries That is, the extent of local versus universal morality varies significantly across societies, and factors such as income levels, the quality of institutions, and economic conditions are related to the type of morality that a society embodies.

9 Persistence and Change

This chapter presents cases illustrating the persistence of cultural beliefs, providing evidence for their transmission across generations. It will also provide some examples pinpointing the underlying reasons for such persistence. It is important, however, to note that persistence does not imply perpetual existence, as culture is subject to change. In fact, the second part of this chapter and the next two chapters will discuss the mechanisms through which cultural transformations can occur.

Cultural Transmission from Parent to Child

Although it may be self-evident that cultural beliefs and preferences are passed down through generations, it is nevertheless important to provide evidence of parent-to-child transmission. One approach is to use survey data obtained from both parents and their children to identify patterns of transmission of beliefs, preferences, and attitudes. Various studies along these lines examined young adults and their parents in different countries and revealed that risk-averse parents are more likely to have risk-averse children. Similarly, children's level of patience is influenced by their parents' patience, and parents' trust in others has a strong impact on their child's inclination to trust others.[1] Parents, of course, pass on their genes to their children, and genetics can influence children's behaviors, including their willingness to take risks and trust in others. The importance of genes versus the family environment is at the heart of the broader debate about nature versus nurture. Behavioral geneticists, sociologists, psychologists, and economists have been trying to determine the relative importance of genes and the environment on individuals' personal attributes and behavioral patterns using a variety of creative methods.

Perhaps the most compelling evidence in this group of nature-nurture studies comes from analyses of adoptees. Extensive datasets linking biological parents, adoptive parents, and adopted children provide important insights into the relative importance of the inherited prebirth factors (nature) and the family environment in childhood (nurture). Research has shown that both factors play a significant role in intergenerational transmissions. For example, a comprehensive analysis of about 7.5 million randomly selected persons from the Swedish population, including all adopted individuals in the country, has shown that male adoptees are more likely to commit crime if their biological parents have criminal records. However, their criminal activity is also influenced by their adopting parents' criminal record.[2] Another study, again based on adopted Swedish children and their biological and adoptive parents, has revealed that the attributes of both prebirth factors (genes inherited from biological parents) and postbirth factors (attributes of the adopted parents) contribute to intergenerational transmission of earnings and education.[3] These and many other studies indicate that both nature and nurture play important roles in explaining the intergenerational correlation of personal traits and behaviors. However, the relative influence of each depends on the specific behavior being analyzed.

A related approach is to study second-generation immigrants. Born and raised in a different country from their parents' country of origin, these individuals live and work within the political, legal, economic, and cultural framework of their destination country. They face the same economic incentives, constraints, and institutional structures as native-born residents. However, if cultural traits are passed from parent to child, then the cultural attributes of their parents' country of origin would continue to influence their behavior, even in their new environment.

As an example, suppose that certain cultural beliefs systematically differ among Italians, Turks, Russians, and Moroccans. If immigrants from these nations bring their cultural attributes to a destination country and pass them on to their children, then these second-generation immigrants would exhibit the same systematic differences in beliefs and behaviors as those observed between Italians, Turks, Russians, and Moroccans in their respective home countries.

Numerous studies, based on this idea, have consistently found evidence of cultural values and behavioral patterns being transmitted across generations. For instance, an analysis of data from thirty different nations showed that immigrants tend to support income redistribution policies more strongly if their countries of origin also have a strong preference for such measures. When first-generation immigrants were asked whether they agreed with the statement, "The government should take measures to reduce income disparities," their responses were positively correlated with the prevalence of such views in their home countries. Likewise, first-generation immigrants were more likely to vote for center-left political parties advocating income redistribution if they came from nations where support for such policies is stronger.[4] Importantly, this pattern also holds among second-generation immigrants. The preferences for income distribution prevalent in their parents' home country continue to shape the view of second-generation immigrants and to influence their tendency to support political parties that advocate income redistribution.

People in different countries hold different perspectives on the value of leisure. Questions such as "Indicate how important leisure time is in your life," "Do you agree or disagree that people who don't work turn lazy?", "Do you agree or disagree that work should always come first even it means less spare time?", and "Are generous holidays are important in a job?" elicit systematically different responses across countries, revealing stark differences in how people perceive the importance of leisure across different societies.

By analyzing second-generation immigrants in twenty-six European countries whose parents originated from forty-seven different nations, one of my studies found that the preference for leisure in the parents' country of origin influences both labor market participation and weekly working hours among their adult children. More specifically, comparing migrants from different origins within the same destination country reveals that second-generation immigrants from nations with a stronger preference for leisure work fewer hours than those from countries where leisure is valued less—an effect that is particularly pronounced among women. In other words, the cultural attitudes toward leisure in parents' countries of origin are reflected in the labor market behavior of their children.[5]

Although cultural preferences remain generally stable across two generations, analyses of four consecutive generations of immigrants in the US reveal a nuanced pattern of cultural persistence. While certain preferences and beliefs remain largely unchanged across all four generations of immigrants (parent, child, grandchild, and great-grandchild), others gradually converge to cultural norms and beliefs prevailing in the US.

Consider statements such as "A working mother cannot maintain a strong bond with her children" or "Women are not fit for politics." Immigrants are more likely to agree with these statements if the sentiment in their country of origin aligns with that same statement. However, across successive generations, their responses gradually shift toward the American norms. The gap between immigrants and the typical American narrows with each generation, though it remains detectable even among fourth-generation immigrants.

This country-of-origin effect persists across multiple generations in other cultural aspects as well, such as views on family relationships (e.g., accepting multiple generations living together) and religiosity (e.g., prayer frequency and beliefs about the afterlife). On the other hand, certain crucial cultural traits, such as the belief about whether people can be trusted, tend to converge more quickly with the average American viewpoint.[6]

An interesting study provides evidence on the intergenerational transmission of beliefs spanning hundreds of years, focusing on the belief in witchcraft.[7] Toward the end of this chapter, I will discuss the subject of witchcraft and witch killings as a cultural phenomenon prevailing today, notably in sub-Saharan Africa. Beliefs in witchcraft were even more widespread in Africa during the era of the slave trade from the fifteenth to the nineteenth centuries.

Between ten and twelve million African captives were transported across the Atlantic, and, as highlighted by the author of the study, over 96 percent of them were brought to Latin America and the Caribbean as slaves. Brazil alone received five million enslaved Africans.[8] It's well-documented that these enslaved individuals brought their beliefs in witchcraft with them, and these beliefs evolved to cope with the harsh realities of slavery. Specifically, the slave trade appeared to have reinforced beliefs in witchcraft as the hardships of enslavement were frequently attributed to the actions of witches, sorcery, and malicious religious forces.

The descendants of millions of African slaves who were brought to Latin American countries during the slave trade have integrated into these societies. This raises the question of whether their ancestors' belief in witchcraft is still evident among these individuals today. To investigate this question, the study utilized a survey given across seventeen Latin American nations, the purpose of which was to gauge the prevalence of various beliefs, including witchcraft.[9] Survey participants indicated their racial and ancestral backgrounds as Afro-descendant or Black, white, indigenous, or mestizo. *White* referred to European ancestry, while *mestizo* indicated a blend of African,

European, and indigenous heritage. Around 20 percent identified themselves as white, 13 percent as indigenous, 57 percent as mestizo, and 10 percent as Afro-descendant.

In this comprehensive analysis of Latin American and Caribbean nations, about 70 percent of Afro-descendant individuals expressed belief in witchcraft. The statistical analysis considered various factors that could influence individuals' superstitious beliefs, such as education, being in poverty, age, gender, urban or rural residence, country of residence, and geographical characteristics (like elevation and proximity to coasts, which could be related to the intensity of slave labor used in that location in the past). After accounting for all these factors, the results revealed that descendants of Africans were nearly 10 percent more likely than whites to hold beliefs in witchcraft today. In other words, the individuals who were captured in Africa, enslaved, and brought to Latin America have passed down their beliefs in witchcraft through successive generations, so their descendants today differ from other residents of the same countries in the intensity of their belief in witchcraft.[10]

Long-Term Persistence: Dragon Children of China

Some cultural beliefs persist for very long periods of time–in some cases, for centuries. One example is the belief in China about the superiority of children born in the Year of the Dragon. In China as well as some other East Asian countries, people believe in the existence of twelve zodiac signs—in order of appearance, Rat, Ox, Tiger, Rabbit, Dragon, Snake, Horse, Sheep, Monkey, Rooster, Dog, and Pig. Each zodiac sign covers one year based on the Chinese lunar calendar, which is ten to twelve days shorter than the Western Gregorian calendar. Thus each zodiac sign appears approximately every twelve years.

It is believed that people who are born in a given zodiac year will possess the innate attributes of that particular sign. Those born in the Year of Tiger, for instance, are believed to be brave, independent, adventurous, and competitive. Those with the Sheep sign are believed to be mellow, gentle, follower types.

The Dragon is considered to be special among all zodiac signs. The Dragon is the symbol of good luck and power in China, and individuals born in the Year of the Dragon are believed to be destined for greatness and good fortune. Chinese parents want their babies born in a Dragon year. Consequently, marriages go up in China during the two years before a Dragon year, and the number of births spike during a Dragon year.

The year 2024 marked another Dragon year, running from February 10, 2024, to January 28, 2025. It was anticipated that there would be approximately one million more births during this Dragon year compared than would typically occur in another zodiac year.[11] China has a population of 1.4 billion people, and there are about ten million births per year, so an extra million births represents a significant bump even in this populous nation.

For an economist, it is obvious what will ensue when the birth rate jumps up so dramatically in a Dragon year: These "Dragon kids" are destined for a rough ride in life. When they reach school age, their classrooms will be more crowded because their cohort size is larger. There will be more pupils per teacher, which will result in lower educational quality for them. When they graduate from high school and take the university entrance exam, which determines whether they are allowed to attend a university and which ones, Dragon children will face stiffer competition. This is because there will be one million extra kids taking the exam for the same limited number of university freshman slots. Finally, these Dragon children will have a more difficult time in the job market simply because the supply of workers will be larger in their cohort due to the sheer fact that there are an extra million same-age peers competing for the same jobs.

So things should be worse, not better, for those born during any Year of the Dragon. When people observe these difficulties faced by Dragon kids, they should revise their beliefs about the good fortune and greatness supposedly destined for those born in a Dragon year. Even if those born in a Dragon year have no worse life outcomes compared to those born in other zodiac years, there is absolutely no reason to expect them to be more successful.

Although being born in a particular zodiac year should have no bearing on one's success in life, the fact that this belief has persisted for hundreds of years raises an important question: How can such a belief continue to survive across generations when it is clearly unfounded? How can a superstitious cultural belief as scientifically baseless as this endure for centuries?

The answer lies in the following statement: Beliefs, even those that are scientifically incorrect, can turn into reality by people's actions, which can then sustain those incorrect beliefs for generations, creating a self-fulfilling prophecy that can be very long-lasting. The belief in Dragon children is a prime example.

In a research project, my coauthor Han Yu (who happens to have been born in a Dragon year) and I analyzed a sample of Chinese individuals and found that those born in the year of the Dragon were nearly 20 percent more likely to have a college diploma compared to those born just a few months earlier or later and thus under a different zodiac sign.[12] In China, students take a centralized university entrance exam that determines the university in which they are allowed to enroll. This is an exam taken by more than ten million high school seniors each year. The exam takes nine to ten hours, spread over multiple days, and measures students' knowledge in a variety of subjects. Analyses of the university exam scores of about three thousand randomly selected students from fifteen universities in Beijing have revealed that students born in a Dragon year score almost 2 percent more than other students on this test. This is a substantial effect, which makes a significant difference in whether a student will be admitted to a university and in the quality of the university.

Another set of analyses in the same project focused on about fifteen thousand Chinese middle school students from nearly 440 classrooms across 112 schools in twenty-eight districts of China. Because the school starting age cutoff (September 1) does not perfectly align with the zodiac year cutoffs, students in the same classroom can belong to different zodiac signs. For example, a particular entry cohort includes children born between September 1, 1999, and August 31, 2000. This twelve-month period spans the zodiac years of the Rabbit and the Dragon, with February 5, 2000, marking the cutoff day between the two. A child born in January 2000 is considered to be born in the Year of the Rabbit, whereas a child born in March 2000 is born in the Year of the Dragon. However, both children start school in the same year and are in the same class.

Analyses of midterm exam scores in mathematics, Chinese, and English revealed that middle school students born in the Year of the Dragon had higher test scores compared to their peers in the same classroom who were born under a different zodiac sign. This result held even when controlling for factors such as the student's sex, the presence of siblings, their parents' education and occupation, and family income. So middle school students perform better if they are born in the Dragon year. But how could this be? Could it really be that the Dragon sign has a mystical impact on people, making them successful? Perhaps the centuries-old belief about the superiority of those born in the Year of the Dragon is correct!

It turns out that parents hold the key to solving this puzzle. Parents of Dragon children are not different from those of other children. They are not more educated, nor do they have more income compared to other parents. But they have significantly higher expectations of their kids in comparison to other parents. For instance, when asked, "What educational degree do you expect your child to achieve?" and "What occupation do you expect your child to have in the future?", parents of Dragon children display consistently higher expectations about their child's future educational achievement, and they were more likely to express a belief that their child will be a scientist, an engineer, a company executive, or a leader at national or governmental institution. They are also significantly more confident than other parents that their kids will have an overall bright future.

Parents of Dragon children not only have high expectations for their kids, but they also invest more time and money in their upbringing compared to other parents. They are more likely to enroll their children in kindergarten and show greater involvement in their education. They also tend to communicate regularly with teachers to discuss their child's progress. In addition, they refrain from assigning household chores to their children during the week or even on holidays, as Dragon children are expected to focus on their schoolwork.

These high expectations placed on Dragon children and the ensuing investment in their education produce demonstrably high academic achievement, which becomes evident to society. Ultimately, these achievement differences between Dragon children and other children reinforce the belief in the superiority of Dragon children. Even though Dragon children are no different from other children, the belief in their superiority makes them in fact successful, creating a self-fulfilling prophecy.

It is not difficult to imagine situations in which the opposite of the Dragon superstition holds true as well. If a cultural belief accepts the inferiority of a particular group of people, such a belief can turn into a self-perpetuating reality through society's low expectations of this group and the resultant attitudes toward the group. Imagine if society perceived children with blue eyes as less intelligent than other children and believed that these children did not need to be educated because they were unlikely to succeed in school anyway. In this environment, parents of blue-eyed children would not have incentives to invest in the quantity and quality of their children's education, which would then make these kids fall behind their peers in cognitive development. This would in turn reinforce the false belief about blue-eyed individuals being inherently less able than other people.

Persistence of Anti-Semitism

A second example of persistence spans six hundred years, beginning in fourteenth-century Europe, when the Black Death wiped out half of the continent's population. With no knowledge of how the disease spread and no cure available, fear and uncertainty ran rampant. In search of an explanation, scapegoating emerged. In some parts of Europe, minorities—particularly Jews and Romani people—were blamed for causing and spreading the epidemic. This fueled widespread fear and hatred, leading to violent attacks against Jewish communities, with some individuals killed or even burned alive at the stake.

Six hundred years later, in the 1920s, Adolf Hitler and the Nazi Party were rising to power in Germany. In the 1928 election, the party's platform was heavily centered on anti-Semitism, with Hitler blaming Jews for the country's problems. Researchers analyzed regional voting records from that election and found a striking pattern: The areas where Jews had been murdered at higher rates during the Black Death epidemic six hundred years earlier were the same regions that showed the strongest support for the Nazi Party in 1928. This suggests that anti-Semitic sentiment from the medieval era endured in these localities for more than six centuries.[13]

Another example begins with the 1928 German election and extends to the twenty-first century. In a study, my coauthor and I analyzed a large sample of Germans who were surveyed in 1996 and 2006.[14] The survey contained very detailed information about individuals' personal attributes, such as their age, education, income, occupation, religion, and more. In addition, the survey included questions aimed at assessing anti-Semitic sentiments. Specifically, Germans were asked how much they agree or disagree with various statements about Jews.

Twenty-two percent of Germans supported the idea that "Jewish people living in Germany should not have the same rights as other Germans in every respect." Twelve percent concurred, "It will be unpleasant to have a Jewish person as a neighbor." Twenty-five percent of Germans declared, "It would be unpleasant if a Jewish person married into my family," and 46 percent agreed, "Many Jews try to profit today from the history of the Third Reich, and they try to make Germans pay for it." When asked about their agreement with the statement, "Due to their behavior Jews are not completely innocent of their persecution," 17 percent of Germans expressed agreement.

Analyzing people's responses to these anti-Semitic statements, we found that, taking into account their personal attributes, economic circumstances, and the economic conditions of the regions in which they live, individuals residing in those areas of Germany that provided stronger support for the Nazi Party in the 1928 election are more likely to express stronger anti-Semitic sentiments today in comparison to similar individuals residing elsewhere in Germany.

In other words, the level of voter support for the Nazi Party in a given location in 1928 predicts the extent of anti-Semitic sentiments in the same area eighty years later, suggesting that these attitudes are passed down through generations and remain persistent.

Does Exposure to "Others" Reduce Prejudice?

As demonstrated by the preceding examples, and as the history of humankind reveals, prejudice against those who are perceived as different can prevail and endure in a society, often becoming a cultural trait. Beginning with this section and continuing in the following two chapters, we will explore the mechanisms by which cultural attributes, including prejudice, can be transformed.

It has been suggested that prejudice against "others" could potentially be reduced through contact and interaction with those others. However, research results are mixed regarding whether such exposure and engagement can actually diminish prejudiced sentiments and negative attitudes. Although some scholars report that exposure leads to a decrease in prejudice, others observe no effect or even an increase in prejudicial feelings following exposure. Moreover, a substantial body of research spanning fields like sociology, economics, and political science consistently indicates that as the ethnic and racial diversity of a community grows, the level of trust among individuals in that community decreases rather than increases.

The reason for the mixed evidence lies in part in the concept of how exposure to others can influence prejudice, developed seventy years ago by psychologist Gordon W. Allport. The conjecture is that interpersonal contact can lead to a positive change in attitudes and a decrease in prejudice only under specific conditions. First, both individuals involved should have equal status (unlike a student and a teacher, an employee and a boss, etc.). Second, they should be working toward a common goal. Furthermore, it has been shown that the interaction should be cooperative and noncompetitive, and it should be sanctioned or supported by a law, authority, or established custom. It has been argued that if these criteria are not met, interpersonal contact may not lead to a reduction in prejudice.

Naturally, it is difficult to come across or establish situations in which all these conditions are satisfied. Moreover, research has shown that interpersonal contact can backfire, potentially exacerbating intergroup prejudice instead of alleviating it. This happens when the contact is *negative*, meaning it is perceived as harmful, causing physical harm, or eliciting feelings of being demeaned or threatened. In fact, it has been argued that negative interactions contribute more significantly to increasing prejudice than positive interactions do to reducing it.[15]

But, when interpersonal contact is *positive*, it not only reduces prejudicial sentiments but can also disrupt the transmission of prejudice from parent to child. Research in psychology has shown a strong correlation between parents' racist attitudes and those of their children, indicating the intergenerational transmission of racism, especially between parents and adolescents. However, studies also reveal that this transmission weakens when adolescents have positive interactions with members of out-groups, highlighting the transformative effect of positive interpersonal contact on prejudice.[16]

An analysis of the effect of interacting with others who share the same status and collaborate toward the same goal was conducted using cadets from the US Air Force Academy.[17] In their first year, students are randomly placed into groups known as *squadrons*, each comprising thirty students who study, dine, play sports, and undergo military training together. These cadets also share living quarters in the same dormitory. At the end of their first year, cadets are reassigned to a new squadron with a different group of peers and must select a new roommate for their second year at the academy.

Researchers examined the impact of exposure to Black peers during the first year on white cadets' attitudes toward Black students in the following year. Specifically, they investigated white students' willingness to choose a Black peer as a roommate in their second year. The analysis revealed that white males who interacted with high-ability Black peers during their first year at the Air Force Academy were more inclined to select a Black roommate in their second year. (*Ability* here refers to high school success and SAT scores.) On the other hand, exposure to Black peers with average or lower abilities had no effect on white cadets' willingness to choose a Black cadet as a roommate, highlighting the nuanced impact of contact with others.

A similar study conducted with members of the Norwegian military examined the impact of integrating women into this traditionally male-dominated environment. In an eight-week boot camp, researchers randomly assigned female recruits to some squads while excluding them from others. After the boot camp, male soldiers who trained with female recruits exhibited more egalitarian attitudes, showing improved beliefs about the performance of mixed-gender teams. They also expressed a greater inclination to believe that household chores should be equally shared between men and women. However, these effects were short-lived, dissipating after six months, suggesting that when exposure to another group is brief, the effects may not be permanent.[18] So exposure to others appears to be effective in reducing prejudice and discrimination, but only under certain conditions. This arguably explains the persistence of prejudice and mistrust among racial and ethnic groups in the United States and elsewhere despite the fact that communities have become more diverse and integrated over time.

Of course, others can be defined not just by race or gender, but also by income. A study focusing on Indian students in seventeen elite private schools in Delhi, India, analyzed whether exposure to others of different income levels mattered.[19] The vast majority of private schools in Delhi are situated on land that was leased by these schools from the state at a lower rate in perpetuity. In 2007, these schools came under a court order to enforce an agreement made with them by the government, which required the schools to also cater to economically disadvantaged students in exchange for the land grant. Consequently, private schools started admitting poor students beginning in 2007, and by the order of the court they reserved 20 percent of their seats for students from poor households.

These low-income students did not pay tuition or fees; instead, the government partially compensated the schools. Because there was excess demand for these schools by poor households, these students were admitted by lottery, and they were randomly allocated to classrooms. On average, economically disadvantaged students had household incomes at the twenty-fifth percentile of the Indian consumption distribution, while affluent students' households were situated at the ninety-fifth percentile. In terms of US standards, this translates to roughly $23,000 per year for the former group and $200,000 for the latter.

The researcher who conducted the study analyzed a wealth of data collected from approximately 2,400 students from these schools five to seven years after the first cohort of students began attending them. Analyses revealed that having a poor classmate made rich students more eager to volunteer for a charity for disadvantaged children. The results of an economic game played by the students showed that rich students who were exposed to poor students were more generous: They shared a larger proportion of the money given to them in the game with an anonymous player.[20] Furthermore, being part of economically diverse classrooms led rich students to discriminate less against poor students. Also, a cleverly designed experiment, as part of the same study, revealed that rich students who were exposed to poor classmates were less willing to be teammates with another rich and less-athletic student over a poor but athletic student.

Positive Exposure

The results of the study on Indian students imply that children's perceptions of the other may be more malleable compared to adults. However, positive exposure can influence prejudice even for adults and even in the short run. An interesting study analyzed racial prejudice among soccer fans in England. The authors of the study investigated the impact of the prominent soccer player Mohamed Salah, who transferred from the Italian soccer club Roma to the Liverpool soccer club in 2017 for 39 million euros.[21] Salah is an elite Egyptian soccer player and known to be a practicing Muslim. His success on the soccer field continued after joining Liverpool, garnering tremendous fan support.

As an illustration of Liverpool fans' dedication to Salah, the authors of the study offer some of the songs chanted during the games and in pubs.[22] For example:

> If he scores another few
> I will be a Muslim too
> If he's good enough for you
> He's good enough for me
> Sitting in a mosque
> That's where I wanna be

Mohamed Salah
A gift from Allah
He's always scoring
It's almost boring
So please don't take
Mohamed away

Researchers of the study found that after Salah joined Liverpool, hate crimes dropped by 16 percent in Liverpool compared to other comparable cities in England. Also, Liverpool fans cut their anti-Muslim tweets by half compared to the fans of other soccer clubs after Salah's arrival at Liverpool. The strong impact of Mohamed Salah is no doubt the result of his high visibility as a celebrity coupled with his uncommon success as a professional athlete. Nevertheless, this finding underscores the influence of positive exposure on prejudiced feelings.

Another example of positive exposure is the case of Black American GIs in the UK during World War II. Leading up to the invasion of Normandy on June 6, 1944, there was a large buildup of American troops in the UK, reaching 1.5 million troops before D-Day. About 150,000 of these troops were Black Americans. American troops were located in various places in the UK, and because there were not enough military bases to accommodate them, troops were stationed throughout the country, wherever was convenient, including newly constructed camps in various parts of the UK. The American troops came into contact with the local British population in bars, restaurants, and other public spaces. Some troops were even placed in private homes due to lack of space.

Researchers used the locations of almost two thousand military bases across England and Wales where US troops were stationed. They hypothesized that Black troops, through interactions with locals around these bases, could have contributed to a positive shift in attitudes toward Black people.[23] Before the war, most British individuals had no exposure to Black people, and racist attitudes were widespread. As the authors of the study explain:

> In most areas of the U.K. where black G.I.s were stationed, locals would have been seeing and interacting with Black people for the first time. Despite evidence of widespread racial prejudice before the war, the evidence suggests that the British responded to positively to black G.I.s, whilst attitudes towards White soldiers were more mixed. Writing in a biweekly newspaper, George Orwell remarked that 'the general consensus of opinion seems to be that the only American soldiers with decent manners are the Negroes.' . . . a British woman writing to a friend:

> 'Everybody here adores the Negro troops, all the girls go to their dance, but nobody likes white Americans. They swagger about as if they were the only people fighting this war.'[24]

If these improved attitudes are transmitted intergenerationally, then we would expect to see differences in contemporary local populations' attitudes toward minorities based on whether their locations were exposed to Black American troops during World War II.

There are about forty-eight thousand neighborhoods in England and Wales, and analyses showed that the membership rate of the British National Party (BNP) in a given neighborhood was negatively affected by the number of months that neighborhood was exposed to Black troops during World War II. Because the BNP is an openly racist and xenophobic far-right political party known for its nationalist and anti-immigration stance, this finding suggests that areas with greater exposure to Black troops have lower support for antiminority views.

The authors also found that exposure to Black troops during World War II affected recent election outcomes. The BNP's vote share was lower in areas where more Black GIs were stationed. Similarly, an area's exposure to Black GIs reduced the vote share of the Conservative Party. These findings suggest that positive exposure to a minority group can alter racist attitudes.

Poverty and Witch Killings

The previous section highlighted how exposure to others can alter racist attitudes. In this section and the next, I will present evidence demonstrating how economic conditions can shape harmful cultural beliefs, using belief in witches and witchcraft as well as racism and xenophobia as examples.

The belief in the power of witches is still widespread in some parts of the world, particularly in sub-Saharan Africa. It has been reported, for example, that in Tanzania, between 2005 and 2011, three thousand people were reported killed after being accused of being witches.[25] Between 1960 and 2000, forty thousand people were murdered in Tanzania alone for the alleged crime of witchcraft.[26] In the first six months of 2016, almost four hundred people were victims of witch killings in Tanzania.[27] A 2021 UNICEF report titled *Addressing Witchcraft in Tanzania* states: "[In Tanzania] witchcraft has been linked to young girls and boys being raped or injured, sometimes killed. Children living with albinism have been particularly targeted. Witch doctors, or traditional healers, advise adults to bring the blood or a limb of a child, or to rape a child, because it is believed that body parts and blood are needed in witchcraft to bring prosperity, good fortune ad good health."[28]

Witch killings are not limited to Tanzania. There are at least three dozen countries where witch killings routinely take place, including the Democratic Republic of the Congo, Nigeria, Ghana, the Central African Republic, and South Africa.

Amnesty International sent a letter to Nana Akufo-Addo, the president of Ghana, on March 8, 2024, emphasizing that witchcraft accusations, which predominantly target women, constitute human rights violations. The letter outlines several concerns, including the existence of six "camps" that house victims—93 percent of whom are women—banished from their communities after being accused of witchcraft. These accusations often blame them for issues such as illness, accidents, poor harvests, and infertility. It highlights that "fatal incidences of gender-based violence, such as the infamous case of 90-year-old Akua Denteh—accused of being a witch and publicly lynched in the Savannah Region in 2020—should no longer be tolerated. It is a stark reminder of the urgent need to prevent further atrocities and ensure that innocent lives and vulnerable people are protected." The letter also urges the president of Uganda to introduce a bill to Parliament to criminalize the practice of declaring, accusing, naming, or labeling people as witches.[29]

The origins of the belief in witchcraft are complex and linked to various factors, including exploitation by self-proclaimed religious leaders. For instance, as highlighted in an HBO documentary titled *Saving Africa's Witch Children*, a Christian pastor in Nigeria who proclaimed herself "Christendom's first lady apostle" played a significant role in fueling the belief that even infants and toddlers can be witches and warlocks.[30] In some of her publications, she asserted that "if a child under the age of two screams at night, cries often, and experiences continuous fever and declining health, they are a servant of Satan."

Consequently, it has been documented that children are subjected to horrific torture and abuse, "splashed with acid, buried alive, dipped in fire—or abandoned roadside, cast out of their villages because some itinerant preacher called them possessed."[31] According to the Office of the United Nations High Commissioner for Human Rights, the majority of the twenty-five to fifty thousand children who live on the streets of Kinshasa, the capital of the Democratic Republic of the Congo, were abandoned by family members who believed that these children performed witchcraft or were possessed by demons.[32] It wouldn't be surprising to discover that many children who are abandoned by their families due to accusations of witchcraft come from impoverished households. In such situations, the child is scapegoated and expelled because the family lacks food and financial resources, making it challenging to support all its members.

It has been revealed that "young children have become common culprits, and many have been kicked out of their homes or killed by family members following household calamities and negative income shocks."[33] Furthermore, "there are also cases where the community practice is to kill or abandon infant twins or babies born handicapped, female or to large families, as well as old and very sick people, because they are considered to be a burden on the community."[34] There exists no rigorous study, that I know of, analyzing the relationship between family income and the likelihood of abandoning a child for being a witch, although many scholars and analysts have noted a negative correlation between income and witchcraft accusations against children and child murders. There is, however, an important study demonstrating the link between poverty and murder of women as witches, as I describe ahead.

Although there's nothing inherent in the belief in witchcraft and black magic that excludes adult men from being accused as witches, the vast majority of individuals targeted for witchcraft accusations are women. These women are often widowed, impoverished, and elderly. This pattern, combined with instances of young children being abandoned by their families due to suspicions of witchcraft, highlights how this cultural belief is disproportionately focused on the most vulnerable members of society. These individuals are often less capable of defending themselves against physical assaults that may follow accusations of witchcraft.

This suggests that those who accuse others of witchcraft and causing harm are likely to consider the consequences of their actions and tend to target those who they perceive as the safest to attack. To investigate the impact of economic conditions on adult witch killing, an important study analyzed detailed data collected from sixty-seven villages in Tanzania to explore the economic factors behind adult witch killings.[35] In addition to 1,300 households from these villages, the village council members were also surveyed to obtain insights into violent crimes and instances of witch killings. This endeavor yielded comprehensive data on village characteristics, ranging from average education levels to population size and from ethnic and religious compositions to consumption expenditures and incidences of human or cattle diseases. Furthermore, information on each murder was gathered, including the victim's attributes, like age, gender, and ownership of household items such as radios and bicycles, as well as livestock and land ownership. These data were complemented by details on rainfall, weather events like droughts and floods, and other environmental factors.

Analyses of witch murders over a ten-year period revealed that nearly all (96 percent) of the victims of witch killings were female, with an average age of fifty-eight. In these Tanzanian villages, people live near the subsistence level. Although food is plentiful from August to January following the summer harvest, household surveys indicate that the period from January to July is the "hungry season," when food supplies dwindle and households rely on their savings or sell their livestock to survive. Two-thirds of witch murders occur during this hungry season, suggesting that the elimination of an elderly person from the household on accusation of being a witch is correlated with decreased household income.

The study offers further compelling evidence linking economic conditions to witch killings. It demonstrates that extreme weather events, which negatively impact farm production and income, result in an increase in witch killings. An analysis of murder dynamics in these sixty-seven villages over eleven years, while controlling for village demographics and socioeconomic attributes, reveals that the occurrence of a drought or flood in a given year leads to twice as many witch murders compared to other years.

These findings indicate that economic conditions influence the beliefs and behaviors that are part of a society's culture. The frequency of witch killings responds to economic conditions, with a deteriorating economic condition leading to an increase in this violent practice.

Economic Conditions, Racism, Xenophobia, and Hate Crime

The impact of economic conditions is also evident on other persistent cultural beliefs and attitudes, such as racism and xenophobia. For example, as discussed earlier in this chapter, by analyzing surveys conducted in Germany, my coauthor and I detected significant negative feelings among Germans toward Jews, foreigners, and ethnic Germans.[36] Twenty percent of Germans agreed with the statement, "Foreigners living in Germany should choose their spouses among people of their own nationality." Eleven percent agreed, "It is okay for a restaurant owner to refuse to serve foreigners," and 17 percent agreed, "It would be unpleasant if an Italian person married into my family."

In the same research project, we found that people's propensity to agree with these statements decreases when they feel optimistic about their own economic conditions or when they feel that the economic conditions of the country are in good shape. Conversely, these feelings intensify when individuals perceive that their economic well-being is at risk or that the country's economic outlook is uncertain.

Other researchers analyzing a different dataset from Germany reported that an increase in local (state-level) unemployment leads to a rise in *right-wing extremist crime*, defined as crimes with a racist, xenophobic, and/or anti-Semitic background.[37] A similar pattern was observed in the United States before and after the Great Recession of 2008. In states that are hit harder by the recession (based on the employment share in the manufacturing and real estate sectors), internet searches for a racial slur (the N word) increased significantly in comparison to states less affected by the recession. Similarly, hate crimes against Black individuals rose more in states that were more negatively impacted by the Great Recession.[38]

If the majority of the population views minorities as outsiders competing for jobs and economic opportunities, then economic hardship is likely to generate a rise in the intensity of negative feelings toward these minorities. The impact of economic hardship on racist feelings and hate crimes has been documented in other countries as well. For instance, the United Kingdom implemented changes to its welfare system as part of an austerity program. Starting in 2010, spending on various government programs, including injury-incapacity benefits, housing allowance, and child benefits, were cut at different times and by different amounts. The UK is divided into 313 Community Safety Partnership areas, where records of government agencies are linked. Researchers analyzing data from these areas between 2007 and 2015 found that regions that saw greater reductions in benefits due to these austerity measures experienced greater increases in racially or religiously motivated crimes afterward.[39]

These research findings reveal that racist sentiments and hate crimes are influenced by economic fluctuations. Although these conclusions are based on short-term analyses and do not necessarily indicate a lasting change in racism and xenophobia following economic downturns or upswings, the implications are important. As will be discussed in the next chapter, undesirable behaviors such as dishonesty and rule-breaking can be contagious. Therefore, any short-term surge in racism or race-based violence may similarly lead to further strengthening of these feelings in society.

Technological Innovations

As discussed in chapter 3, there are significant differences in women's labor market participation across countries, and these differences are largely determined by societal attitudes toward women's work. In other words, cultural beliefs about women's roles in society play a crucial role in determining the extent to which women engage in paid work outside the home. Consequently, female labor force participation rates tend to remain relatively stable over time. For example, in Morocco and Egypt, the labor force participation rate for women remained between 15 and 20 percent from 1990 to 2023. In Turkey and Guatemala, the rate ranged from 35 to 40 percent during this period, while in Italy and Romania, it increased modestly from 45 to 55 percent over the same timeframe.

In the United States, the female labor force participation rate has remained around 70 percent since the early 1990s. However, it was significantly lower in previous decades. In 1960, the rate was only about 42 percent, but it went up steadily, reaching 50 percent in 1970, 60 percent in 1980, and 70 percent by 1990. Nobel laureate economist Claudia Goldin has demonstrated that this rise in women's labor force participation in the US is largely driven by a technological innovation: the development of the birth control pill.[40]

In the mid-1950s, Margaret Sanger—a nurse, birth control activist, and founder of Planned Parenthood—persuaded philanthropist Katharine McCormick to fund research on oral contraception for women. The ensuing efforts led to the development of the birth control pill, which was approved by the US Food and Drug Administration in 1960. As Goldin discusses in detail, the use of the birth control pill spread rapidly among married women. However, its full impact emerged after most states lowered the age of majority, around the time the Twenty-Sixth Amendment to the US Constitution was adopted in 1971, reducing the voting age to eighteen. This allowed young, single women to have access to the birth control pill.

In 1971, the age of majority was lowered to eighteen in fifteen states, and by 1974, forty states had recognized eighteen-year-olds as legal adults.

Access to contraception expanded significantly during this period. In 1969, only three states—California, Georgia, and Mississippi—allowed fourteen- and fifteen-year-olds to obtain contraceptives without parental consent. By 1971, eleven states permitted access for this age group without parental consent, and twenty-nine states extended access to those eighteen or younger. By 1974, forty-seven states allowed individuals eighteen or younger to obtain contraception without parental consent.

As was acknowledged widely, this dramatic and rapid shift in recognizing eighteen-year-olds as legal adults stemmed largely from the repercussions of the Vietnam War. Of the fifty-eight thousand US casualties, about eleven thousand were eighteen-year-olds, and nearly 60 percent were twenty-one or younger, intensifying demands to lower the age of majority and acknowledge young people as legal adults.

The medical innovation that made birth control easier, coupled with legal changes permitting young single women access to it, had profound effects. Women began delaying marriage, pursuing more education, and entering the workforce in greater numbers.

In 1960, for every woman who earned a bachelor's degree, 1.8 men did the same. Over the next two decades, this gender gap not only closed but reversed. By 1980, men and women were earning four-year college degrees at equal rates, and by 2020, 1.3 women graduated for every man.[41] In other words, after 1960, American women enrolled in and completed college at increasing rates, paralleling their growing participation in paid employment.

It should be recognized that around 1960, American gender norms and societal attitudes toward women's roles were largely traditional. However, the medical innovation of the birth control pill, along with institutional changes that expanded access for young women, set the stage for a cultural shift. This transformation gained momentum with the emergence of female role models like Gloria Steinem, who cofounded *Ms. Magazine* in 1972—a groundbreaking publication that challenged societal norms and provided a platform for women's issues. The Supreme Court's 1973 *Roe v. Wade* decision, which legalized abortion nationwide, further contributed to increasing female education and workforce participation by allowing young women to avoid unwanted pregnancies.[42]

Another factor that likely contributed to the steady rise in women's labor force participation was women's influence as role models for their children. As more women joined the workforce, more children grew up in households with working mothers. Research suggests that this experience influenced men's perspectives on women's roles in society and their attitudes toward working women. In turn, the presence of such men made it more appealing for women to invest in education, develop marketable skills, and pursue careers. US data support this pattern, showing that men raised by working mothers are significantly more likely to have wives who also work.[43] This aspect of cultural change, via the influence of role models, will be discussed in detail in chapter 11.

Economists have also shown that technological advances that changed time allocation in household production have influenced women's decisions to work outside the home. Time-saving innovations, such as home appliances, have played a key role in shaping female labor force participation rates. An analysis of OECD countries reveals that, even after accounting for factors such as income growth, government spending as a share of GDP, average male income, and urbanization rates, a decline in the relative cost of home appliances compared to other consumer goods has a positive effect on women's participation in the labor force.[44] In other words, as appliances become less expensive over time in a country relative to others, the female labor force participation rate increases more rapidly in that country, even when economic conditions are similar between countries.

Along the same lines, research has demonstrated that the introduction of electricity into homes results in time savings in household production, which in turn increases the likelihood of women working outside the home for pay. A recent study analyzed South Africa, where in 1993, a year before the end of apartheid, over two-thirds of South African households were without electricity, and more than 80 percent relied on wood for home production. Following the new government's commitment to universal electrification, two million households—almost a quarter of all households nationwide—were connected to the grid by 2001.[45] Careful statistical analyses revealed that after electrification, more women entered the workforce and worked more hours per week for pay. Communities that gained access to electricity transitioned away from using wood for cooking, heating, and lighting, opting for electricity instead. This shift suggests that electrification reduced the time required for household tasks, enabling women to reallocate their time toward labor market participation.

Research findings like these support the prediction made by Thomas Edison in a 1912 interview, in which he foresaw the transformative impact of electricity on daily life: "The housewife of the future will be neither a slave to servants nor herself a drudge. She will give less attention to the home, because the home will need less; she will be rather a domestic engineer than a domestic labourer, with the greatest of all handmaidens, electricity, at her service. This and other mechanical forces will so revolutionize woman's world that a large portion of the aggregate of woman's energy will be conserved for use in broader, more constructive fields."[46] It is, however, crucial to emphasize that the impact of innovations and new technologies on cultural attitudes and behaviors—whether it's a medical breakthrough like the birth control pill or a time-saving advancement like the washing machine—depends heavily on the existing cultural and institutional framework. For instance, the birth control pill would have little effect on women's behavior if societal norms strongly condemned contraception as immoral or sinful or if laws criminalized its use. In other words, much like the example in chapter 6 that illustrated how an institutional reform in Indian hospitals failed due to deeply rooted cultural attitudes, new technologies may not lead to significant behavioral shifts or drive cultural change if prevailing institutional and cultural norms strongly resist such changes.

10 How Culture Changes: Contagion and Control of Dishonesty

You are an honest student who would never cheat on an exam. You would never receive outside help from anybody when writing a term paper or doing a homework assignment. Whatever grade you receive is the true reflection of your intelligence and the amount of effort and time you put into studying. Some of your classmates, on the other hand, do not behave this way. They cheat on exams and on other assignments. Meanwhile, teachers are either oblivious or they don't care if their students cheat. As a result, cheaters graduate effortlessly, and because of their cheating, they achieve high grade point averages.

Suppose employers place significant importance on grades, which results in cheaters having a higher chance of finding employment. In such a scenario, honesty becomes costly, putting honest individuals at a disadvantage. The cost of honesty is reflected in the lower grades honest students receive compared to cheaters and the less favorable job opportunities they encounter. After observing that cheating is rewarded, will you continue to insist on honesty, or will you also start cheating? Is honesty sustainable in this society?

Consider another scenario. Imagine you always pay your taxes properly and do not engage in tax evasion. But suppose your peers, who own similar businesses and have similar tax obligations, cheat and avoid paying their taxes. As a result, they become significantly wealthier than you. Observing this, would you still teach your children the value of honesty, or would you advise them that honesty is not rewarded but is penalized in society and that it would be foolish not to cheat on tax payments like others?

Even if people perceive themselves as honest, exposure to dishonesty can alter their perception of societal standards regarding honesty. Witnessing dishonest and illicit acts can reshape individuals' perspectives on cheating and the norms of honesty, potentially inducing them to engage in dishonest behavior themselves. In other words, dishonest actions of others signal the acceptability of dishonesty as a social norm and influence one's own behavior.

A substantial body of research in psychology and economics has demonstrated this effect. When people observe others behaving dishonestly, they are more likely to engage in dishonest behavior themselves. Laboratory experiments conducted with both college students and older adults as subjects have consistently shown that the proclivity for cheating and stealing increases when individuals witness others—particularly those who appear to be part of the same group as the subjects—engaging in dishonest behavior.[1]

For example, a study combining experimental methods with real-world data utilized a household survey conducted with 4,200 adults in Costa Rica. At the end of a survey, participants were asked about their willingness to bribe a police officer to avoid a traffic ticket. The experimental component involved embedding informational flyers in the middle of the survey. One-third of the respondents, selected randomly, received a flyer featuring the headline: "Did you know that corruption in Costa Rica has increased?" Beneath the headline, a bar graph illustrated an increase in the percentage of Costa Ricans who had personally witnessed acts of corruption, rising from 16 to 24 percent over the past five years. The second group, comprising another randomly selected one-third of respondents, received a flyer highlighting the inefficiency of the legal system in handling cases of assault with a deadly weapon. This flyer featured the headline: "In 2011, 6,812 cases of assault with a deadly weapon entered the judicial system. However, only 47 individuals were sent to jail for this crime." Below the headline, a bar graph illustrated that over six thousand cases were filed, 333 judicial decisions were made, and only forty-seven people were incarcerated. This served as the placebo treatment as the information was unrelated to corruption. The final one-third of participants received no flyers, serving as the control group.[2]

Statistical analyses revealed that the willingness to bribe a police officer was significantly higher among participants exposed to information about the rising corruption rate in the country. This indicates that being informed about increasing corruption made individuals more likely to consider engaging in corrupt behavior themselves. In contrast, there was no significant difference in the willingness to bribe between the control group and those who received the placebo treatment about judicial inefficiency. This suggests that the increase in the proclivity of survey participants to bribe a police officer was specifically triggered by information about rising corruption in the country, rather than by general exposure to negative information about the inefficiency of the Costa Rican state, indicating that information about the prevalence of dishonesty in a society serves as a motivation for others to also engage in dishonest behavior.

There is ample evidence supporting the contagious nature of dishonesty. Beyond laboratory studies and those combining experiments with field data, one of which was just described, various real-world data sources reveal the ripple effects of cheating. For instance, an analysis of data from over two thousand graduates of the major US military service academies (Air Force, Army, and Navy) found that higher levels of peer cheating significantly increased the likelihood of individual students cheating. It has been shown that each cheater leads to the creation of two additional cheaters in a cohort.[3]

It has also been documented that political corruption sets a precedent for the public, leading to increased cheating and corruption in a society. Of course, the extent of corruption among politicians is shaped by the cultural attributes of a society. As discussed earlier in the book, in a society where illicit behavior is tolerated, rule-breaking and misconduct, including corruption among politicians, tend to proliferate. However, regardless of the prevalence of corruption, would revelations about the dishonest conduct of politicians spur dishonesty within the broader society? An analysis of Mexican middle school students sheds light on this question.

Students in Mexico must take a mandatory national standardized test, conducted by the Ministry of Education, in the spring of each year, covering mathematics, Spanish, and one other subject. The administrators of the test employ various strategies to thwart cheating during the test. To identify students who still manage to cheat, answers are analyzed using specialized software engineered to detect cheating. This software discovers excessively similar patterns of incorrect answers across all test pairs within each classroom, enabling the determination of the prevalence of cheating in each classroom within every school.

The study of Mexican students analyzed the impact of audits of public officials in Mexican municipalities on student cheating. Mexico has nearly 2,500 municipalities, and these municipalities are audited for the proper use of public funds. A typical audit takes one year to complete, and the audit reports are released in February of the following year. These audit results are widely anticipated by the public, and they receive significant media coverage.

The study, based on the analyses of tests taken by students over eight years in about seventeen schools from each municipality, revealed that if an audit report uncovered corruption in a given municipality, then student cheating in the schools of that municipality increased by about 10 percent during that same year.[4] Furthermore, the incidence of cheating rose more significantly if the amount of malfeasance exposed in the audit report was more substantial. This finding indicates that the revelation of corruption at the local level provides a signal to the members of that community about the prevalence of misconduct. This new information impacts the perception of the acceptability of dishonesty, leading to a rise in incidence of cheating.

The effect on cheating was more pronounced if corruption was revealed in a municipality previously considered to be free of corruption. The discovery of malfeasance in a previously trusted local government represents a more significant deviation from the social norm of honesty compared to uncovering corruption in a place already known to be corrupt. Therefore, this larger shift in honesty norms appears to elicit a stronger reaction in terms of increased student cheating.

The study also utilized a national household survey conducted during the same time frame. The survey included questions aimed at assessing individuals' self-perceptions of their honesty and ethical values. Respondents were asked to indicate their level of agreement with statements such as "Cheating is necessary to get ahead" and "Rules are meant to be broken," and to answer questions such as "How likely are you to steal electricity from public lines?" and "How likely are you to return a wallet containing 500 pesos?" Because the survey was administered at different times, some individuals answered these questions shortly before the release of an audit report in their municipality, while others answered the same questions shortly after the audit reports were made public.

Analysis of responses from over nine thousand individuals, adjusted for personal attributes (such as age, education, and employment status), revealed that exposure to an audit report disclosing corruption in their municipality influenced the intrinsic values of those living in the area. More specifically, those who received news about local corruption exhibited a greater inclination toward rule-breaking, corrupt behavior, and illicit tendencies.

A different study from a different country provided a similar insight, demonstrating that exposure to corruption news motivates individuals to engage in dishonest behavior themselves. A team of researchers analyzed customer purchases in an Italian grocery store chain with self-service scanners.[5] These scanners enable customers to scan and bag the items they would like to purchase without any oversight. Researchers utilized data consisting of 280,000 random audits performed on shoppers over a one-year period in two Italian provinces: Modena and Ferrara.

These audits are conducted by the grocery store company, and each audit provided details of what the customer paid for the items in their shopping cart versus the actual value of those items. It's important to note that in this context, underreporting the value of purchases carries no consequences for the customers. There were no fines or legal actions imposed on customers who were found to have paid less than the total value of items in their cart.

Researchers merged these data with information from the archives of two local newspapers regarding corruption scandals involving municipal public administrators. Analyses showed that if a corruption scandal about local politicians in a given municipality makes the news on a particular day, then stealing from a supermarket in that municipality goes up by about 16 percent. The effect starts the day after the corruption news breaks and lasts for about a month. Similar to the result obtained from Mexican students, the impact on theft is bigger following more important and visible corruption news. Detailed analyses confirm that these results are not due to some confounding, an artifact of another factor such as price movements in the stores, or just random errors of customers.

Why Is Dishonesty Contagious?

Psychologists, sociologists, and philosophers have theorized about why people adhere to a cultural norm such as honesty. One theory proposes that individuals see themselves as honest, but when they realize dishonesty can be rewarding, they begin to act dishonestly while still maintaining an illusion of their own integrity.[6] An important mechanism, which is supported by experiments, centers on expectations. It has been argued that two types of expectations may motivate individuals' decision for whether to obey a norm. The first one is what an individual expects others to do. Research indicates that people often act in ways they believe other individuals like them would behave in similar circumstances.[7] The second component influencing a person's conformity to a norm is his perception of what others believe he should do.

When a norm is widely followed by society, one's expectations about other people's behaviors typically align with what one believes others think he should do. For example, following philosopher and psychologist Christian Bicchieri's extensive work on this subject, consider this scenario: If I observe that most of my neighbors adhere to a rule or a norm, such as not throwing garbage on the street, I develop the expectation that most people do not litter. Simultaneously, the fact that most individuals do not litter leads me to believe that others think I should not litter either.

If a norm is frequently violated in society, an inconsistency may emerge between these two types of expectations. For instance, if fraud and bribery are prevalent, this may lead me to believe that most people are dishonest, yet I may still hold the belief that most people disapprove of dishonesty. However, clever laboratory experiments have shown that even in such cases, one's belief about what others do is the primary force driving conformity to a norm.[8] Stated differently, it's not so much what others think I should do that matters; rather, my perception of how others actually behave is what drives my behavior.

This explains the findings about student cheating in Mexico and shoplifting in Italy. Students are well aware that society expects them not to cheat, as evident from the heavy proctoring of the exams and computer analysis of the answers to detect cheating. However, widespread news about local corruption changes students' perceptions of others' dishonesty, leading them to cheat. Shoplifting is not condoned, and Italian customers couldn't have changed their beliefs about societal disapproval of stealing within just a few days around the corruption scandals. However, news about a corruption scandal alters shoplifting behavior in just one day because it changes customers' perceptions of how common misconduct is in society.[9]

In summary, research shows that individuals are influenced by the actions of those around them. Exposure to incidents of cheating, corruption, and dishonesty signals the existence and possibly the prevalence of such behaviors. This leads people to update their beliefs about social norms regarding such behaviors and prompts them to engage in these behaviors themselves. Over time, dishonesty breeds further dishonesty and, if left unchecked, it can evolve into a cultural norm of society.

In the next section, I will discuss a study that highlights three insights: (1) Corruption is a cultural trait that influences individual behavior even when people relocate to a different society; (2) corruption and rule-breaking are contagious, as individuals often mimic the behavior of those around them; and (3) rule-breaking is sensitive to sanctions, which can effectively reduce individuals' inclination toward corruption and misconduct.

Diplomats in New York City and Persistent Dishonesty

New York City hosts the headquarters of the United Nations (UN), and every nation has diplomats who reside in New York to represent their country in the UN. Because New York is a densely populated urban city, it is difficult to find parking spots for vehicles on the streets. Diplomats of foreign nations are protected from lawsuits and prosecution in the US. This immunity also applied to parking violations in New York City. If diplomats were ticketed for parking their vehicles illegally, they were not obligated to pay the fine. As a result, between 1997 and 2002, foreign diplomats in New York City received 150,000 tickets for parking violations, which resulted in fines totaling $18 million that were unpaid.

Researchers gathered detailed data on these parking violations. They also obtained information on the number of diplomats in each nation's diplomatic mission in New York, as well as the number of license plates registered under each country's UN mission to calculate the intensity of parking violations for each nation's diplomats. Because each parking ticket included information on the time of the violation, researchers discovered that most violations were not work-related. Instead, they occurred during nighttime hours, between 10:00 p.m. and 6:00 a.m., and at locations more than five miles away from the UN headquarters.[10]

Kuwaiti diplomats received 249 parking tickets per diplomat between 1997 and 2002, averaging about one ticket per diplomat each week. Egyptian diplomats came in second with 141 tickets over the same period, averaging twenty-eight tickets per diplomat per year. The top twenty-five in this ranking of rule violations were primarily diplomats from developing countries. This is not surprising, given that parking in New York City is expensive. Diplomats from lower-income countries might find it relatively less affordable to park in garages, resulting in more parking tickets compared to their counterparts from high-income countries. Indeed, high-income-country diplomats were mostly at the bottom of the parking violations ranking. For instance, diplomats from the UK, Switzerland, Canada, Denmark, Japan, the Netherlands, Sweden, Norway, and Australia received fewer than one ticket per diplomat over this five-year period. However, some middle-income nations, such as Greece, Ecuador, Moldova, Guatemala, and Azerbaijan, also had similarly low numbers of parking violations.

Saudi Arabia and France are both high-income countries, yet Saudi diplomats received thirty-four parking tickets per diplomat, while French diplomats received only six tickets per diplomat. Similarly, Uruguayan diplomats received about five tickets per diplomat, whereas their counterparts from Paraguay received thirteen tickets per diplomat, despite both countries having similar levels of economic development. Therefore, income differences across nations are neither the only nor the primary driver of the variation in diplomats' proclivity for rule violations.

The number of parking tickets received by diplomats serves as an indicator of their propensity for rule-breaking when there are no consequences. In other words, although diplomats knew it was illegal to park in certain locations, they did so anyway because the cost of such rule-breaking was zero: They did not have to pay the fines despite being ticketed.

In addition to parking tickets, researchers also compiled information on each country's attributes, such as per capita income, the average salary of government workers, the amount of trade with the US, and other variables. After accounting for these economic factors, it was shown that the most important determinant of diplomats' propensity to violate parking regulations was the extent of corruption in their home countries.[11] Diplomats from countries with higher levels of corruption committed more parking violations in New York City. The impact of home county corruption on diplomats' proclivity for violating parking regulations is substantial. The authors of the study noted that "[the decrease in corruption] associated with going from a highly corrupt country such as Nigeria to a largely uncorrupt country such as Norway is associated with a large drop [approximately 80 percent] in the average rate of diplomatic parking violations."[12]

This finding underscores how the prevalence of corruption in a country affects individuals' tendency to break rules. This influence persists even among highly educated individuals like diplomats, and it remains evident even when they are placed in a different setting, like New York City.

Contagious Rule-Breaking and the Impact of Law Enforcement on Cultural Norms

Researchers of the diplomat study also found that the average monthly number of parking tickets received by diplomats tends to increase over time as their tenure in New York City lengthens. This effect is more pronounced for diplomats from low-corruption countries. This suggests that diplomats who initially have a lower tendency for rule-breaking increasingly conform to the average rule-breaking behavior of their peers at the UN as they spend more time in New York City. This pattern aligns with other evidence indicating that dishonesty is contagious, breeds more dishonesty, and, if unchecked, spreads even further.

Although dishonesty is contagious, it is possible to curb dishonest and illicit behavior. If certain institutional features of a society contribute to dishonest conduct and rule-breaking, then reforming and modifying these features can help decrease dishonesty. One example involves law enforcement, a key institutional component. Another finding of the study on UN diplomats is that parking violations responded to the enforcement of sanctions. After January 2002, the New York City Police Department started enforcing parking regulations for diplomats. This meant that diplomats had to pay fines if they received a parking ticket after that date. This policy modification altered diplomats' behavior dramatically, and parking violations plummeted by 98 percent, signifying the major role legal enforcement plays in impacting illicit behavior.

Any economist would anticipate this reaction of diplomats to the enforcement of penalties. Dozens of research articles in economics have conclusively demonstrated that the proclivity for illicit behavior decreases as the certainty and severity of punishment go up. If the "price" of the behavior rises, people engage less in that behavior. It has been shown, for example, that harsher prison sentences reduce crime. There are two main reasons for this. The first is the incapacitation effect, where imprisoning an offender lowers crime by preventing that person from committing further offenses while in prison. Numerous studies have provided strong evidence for the incapacitation effect of imprisonment.[13]

The second reason behind the effectiveness of harsher penalties is the deterrent effect. Increased punishment raises the cost of engaging in crime, serving as a deterrent and thus discouraging potential offenders from engaging in misconduct and criminal activity. This is true not only for crimes involving financial gain, such as burglary and theft, but also for violent crimes, such as assault and murder. A multitude of studies drawing on data from various countries have repeatedly and conclusively shown that tougher prison sentences act as a deterrent, causing a decrease in criminal behavior.[14]

Prison time is not the only penalty to which individuals respond. Rule-breaking declines in response to other sanctions as well, even when rule-breaking is a cultural attribute and widespread in society. I mentioned in the opening pages of the book that Turks viewed strict adherence to rules as an undesirable trait, seeing it as indicative of a lack of judgment and an inability to adapt to circumstances. This attitude was exemplified by their driving behavior. Traffic regulations were seen as rough guidelines rather than strict mandates. For instance, when encountering a red light late at night on empty streets, most drivers would slow down but proceed through the light, finding it absurd to stop and waste time when there were no other cars or pedestrians around. Similarly, despite the requirement to wear seat belts, taxi drivers often chose not to, claiming that wearing a seat belt all day was uncomfortable and that the risk of injury was minimal as they typically drove at low speeds in the city. Perhaps the most critical traffic violation was driving under the influence of alcohol. As in many Mediterranean countries, social dinners in Turkey last for hours and involve significant alcohol consumption. Despite being illegal, it used to be a common practice to drive intoxicated after such gatherings.

Then, things changed. The government significantly increased the penalties for traffic violations. Fines became substantial, and enforcement was serious and persistent. Drivers reluctantly complied, though initially there were attempts to circumvent the rules and outsmart the enforcement. I recall taxi drivers cleverly placing seat belts across their chests without locking them in place, making it appear to an outside observer that they were wearing seat belts even though the belts were merely loose accessories on their chests.

Eventually, however, people started changing their behavior, and persistent enforcement altered the norm of rule violation. Although the Turkish saying "A new custom in an old village" encapsulates the national sentiment, poking fun at new ideas and proposed alterations of traditional practices, wearing seat belts and stopping at red lights even when the road is empty nevertheless became the new norm in Istanbul. I distinctly remember my surprise when a middle-aged taxi driver, after assisting with my luggage, hopped into his seat and immediately buckled his seat belt as if it had been his habit since he first started driving. Moments later, at a four-way intersection, he stopped at a red light despite the absence of any cars behind us or in sight. It was 5:00 a.m., and we were going to the airport. He patiently waited for about a minute until the light turned green.

Altering drunk driving habits was a slower process. People tried various tactics to evade traffic stops targeting intoxicated drivers. These included strategies like using apps or message groups to share information about sobriety checkpoint locations and times. Despite these efforts, persistent law enforcement has proven to be effective. Some of my friends faced consequences, like having their driver's licenses suspended for six months due to exceeding the legal blood alcohol limit. Ultimately, the risks of breaking the law outweighed any benefits for most individuals. Persistent enforcement led to a significant shift in behavior, although it took time for people to adapt consistently. Nowadays, most people either limit their alcohol intake if they plan to drive later, opt for taxis or public transportation (despite its inconvenience compared to driving), or choose nearby venues to minimize driving and the risk of detection. In essence, rigorous law enforcement established a new standard of acceptable behavior.

My personal observation of how rule enforcement affected driving norms in Istanbul does not constitute scientific evidence of how people's driving behavior responds to sanctions. There are, however, rigorous scientific studies examining extensive datasets and documenting this deterrence effect. For instance, an analysis of over half a million driving-under-the-influence (DUI) police stops, along with detailed information about these drivers in the state of Washington, underscores the importance of penalties in curbing drunk driving.[15]

During DUI inspections, drivers undergo blood alcohol content (BAC) tests. A BAC level above 0.08 classifies a driver as being under the influence of alcohol, while drivers with slightly lower BAC levels, such as 0.07, are not considered violators. The penalties for DUI can include fines of approximately $900, jail time, and license suspension. The author of the study compared drivers who were tested for BAC in the same year and county and who were identical in gender, age, and race. The only difference was their alcohol levels: Some drivers had BAC levels slightly above the legal limit, while others were just below it. These drivers were essentially identical in all aspects, except that some had consumed slightly more alcohol. This small difference determined their treatment by the legal system: Those who exceeded the legal limit faced DUI charges and penalties, while those just under the limit were free to continue on their way.

Analyses have revealed that drivers who had BAC levels slightly above the legal limit and who were consequently penalized were 17 percent less likely to drive drunk again within four years of the initial traffic stop, compared to drivers who were not penalized because their BAC levels were just below the legal limit. In other words, similar individuals who have consumed similar levels of alcohol change their future behavior differently. Those who face sanctions are much less likely to reoffend in the future.

A similar study examining how individuals respond to law enforcement was conducted using data from Ricany, a city near Prague in the Czech Republic. The researchers analyzed driving records for 1.3 million vehicles over four years to assess the impact of penalties for speeding.[16] In the Czech Republic, a speeding ticket results only in a fine, without additional consequences such as increased insurance rates, harsher fines for future offenses, jail time, or license suspension. The fine ranges from approximately forty to eighty dollars, depending on how much the vehicle exceeded the speed limit.

The city installed speed cameras that recorded the speed of every vehicle passing by, along with additional details such as travel time and license plate numbers. Researchers analyzed data from twenty-six million trips involving 1.3 million vehicles. Because every vehicle's speed was automatically recorded upon passing a camera, regardless of how fast it was traveling, researchers could accurately determine each vehicle's speed and whether it received a speeding ticket, along with the time of the violation. The analyses demonstrated that receiving a speeding ticket led to a 33 percent reduction in the average car's speeding rate and a 70 percent decline in reoffending rates. These effects were long-lasting, with the deterrent impact of receiving a speeding ticket persisting for up to two years. This highlights, once again, that individuals modify their behavior in response to heightened penalties for rule-breaking, with the change being sustained over time.

In addition to the severity of punishment, the certainty of punishment is also important in deterring crime. My coauthor Hope Corman and I have demonstrated that increased arrests and a rise in the size of the police force generated a reduction in all types of crime in New York City.[17] Similarly, other researchers have found that increased police presence causes a reduction in crime in other cities, including Buenos Aires, London, Philadelphia, Dallas, and across the US.[18] These findings reveal that law enforcement, as part of the institutional structure of a country, plays a key role in curbing illegal behavior. The presence of the police and application of sanctions provide a signal about the potential consequences of rule-breaking and therefore dissuade individuals from engaging in illicit behavior.

Enforcement Creates Deterrence Spillovers

Enforcing rules and penalizing violators deter all types of offenses, ranging from violent crime to tax evasion to traffic violations. Importantly, it also creates spillover effects by altering the behavior of those who were not direct targets of sanctions.

The phenomenon of enforcement spillover has been demonstrated in several studies. One such example is a study in which researchers partnered with the city of Tilburg, the sixth-largest city in the Netherlands, to conduct a field experiment involving all seventy thousand of its households.[19] The city collects garbage on sixty-five routes, each consisting of about one thousand households. Households are required to separate their waste into garbage and recyclable items and place them in separate containers, identified by different-colored covers, before placing the containers on the curbside. But despite a ninety euro fine for failing to separate waste, compliance was low.

Letters were sent to households notifying them that failing to separate their waste was illegal and could result in fines. Three weeks after the letters were distributed, enforcement officials began conducting random inspections over a month-long period. These inspections were designed to be highly visible, with inspectors attaching brightly colored warning labels to containers, indicating violations. These labels not only increased visibility but also conveyed the message of strict rule enforcement. Households could face fines after receiving a second warning.

The experiment resulted in an immediate increase in the collection of paper, plastic, and organic waste, along with a concurrent decline in residual garbage. There was no decrease in total garbage, indicating that households did not reduce their overall garbage production but began separating organic material from the rest as intended by the program. The response was substantial, with a decline of about 1.3 tons of residual waste per week per route, amounting to eighty-five tons per week for the city. This means that the average household started separating an additional 2.5 pounds of material per week.

This effect was permanent and remained consistent at the end of the eight-month program when data collection stopped. So the enforcement was successful. It changed the behavior of the entire city. Not only those who were directly targeted by inspectors but also their neighbors, who observed the signs of enforcement and compliance, modified their behavior.

A similar example of how enforcement generates behavioral spillovers comes from Austria. Several countries around the world require households to pay a fee for access to TV and radio broadcasts. Each household must pay an annual fee if they own at least one TV set or radio. Examples of countries that impose this broadcasting fee include Switzerland, Germany, Norway, Japan, South Korea, and France, among many others.

Austria is one of the countries where households must register and pay an annual TV and radio license fee of approximately 220 euros. Unlicensed households face fines of more than 2,000 euros. This operation is managed by a specific government agency, which also handles enforcement through its inspectors. These inspectors do not wear uniforms or use official-looking vehicles, making their presence and visits to households inconspicuous to others in the neighborhood.

Researchers examined the records of all new license registrations, all inspections conducted, and the detections of unlicensed households across Austria's approximately 2,400 municipalities over a five-month period.[20] Unlicensed users who are detected by inspectors are required to register after being caught. The interesting finding of the study is that an increase in registrations due to detection and enforcement in a municipality led to a rise in unsolicited registrations within the same municipality. In other words, when some households are detected by inspectors and forced to register (after paying a fine), other previously unregistered households in the same area tend to register, even though they were not inspected themselves. Specifically, if ten households are detected without proper registration despite owning a TV or radio, then four unrelated households in the same municipality register within the same month. This shows that enforcement creates compliance spillovers. People learn through word-of-mouth that some households in the municipality were caught evading the fee, which prompts them to voluntarily comply with the regulation and register to pay their fee.

There's a plethora of evidence, such as the cases mentioned above, to demonstrate that people learn from their neighbors, peers, and members of their community about law enforcement, the likelihood of punishment, and its severity. Numerous examples of these enforcement spillovers exist, with an interesting one coming from a team of researchers who studied data from Finland.

In Scandinavian countries, individuals' personal information—including health and school records, employment details, and all interactions with government agencies—is meticulously recorded and linked through people's unique citizenship numbers. This comprehensive data collection spans from birth to death, allowing for detailed tracking of a person's life. Furthermore, these records can be connected to other individuals and institutions with whom the person has personal or professional affiliations.

This extensive data collection is a treasure trove for researchers studying human behavior. Although the information is highly sensitive and confidential, Scandinavian governments provide access to researchers after anonymizing personal identifiers. This allowed researchers to analyze people's interactions with the criminal justice system, their employment details, and other attributes without compromising privacy.

Now imagine two Finnish individuals who are arrested and tried for the same financial white-collar crime. By chance, one of them encounters a lenient judge, while the other faces a stringent judge. Judges' leniency or strictness is determined by how they ruled in similar past cases. Suppose both defendants are found guilty. Although they both are convicted, the defendant who faced the tougher judge receives a prison sentence, while the one who faced the more lenient judge receives a lighter punishment, such as a fine or probation.

A team of researchers utilized twenty-five years of administrative data from the entire country of Finland.[21] By analyzing every criminal case with sophisticated statistical procedures, they discovered the following: If a financial crime defendant is sentenced to prison, the probability that he commits another crime during the three years after leaving prison decreases by more than 40 percent compared to an otherwise identical defendant who did not go to prison, as this latter person was lucky enough to face a lenient judge. So, consistent with dozens of other research findings, punishment deters *recidivism* (future crimes of the offender).

But in addition, researchers have also uncovered significant spillover effects. Sending a person who has committed a financial crime to prison reduces the likelihood that his coworkers will commit financial crimes in the future. If a colleague received a prison sentence for a financial crime in a given year, the propensity for others working in the same firm, plant, or establishment to commit fraud or financial crimes in the subsequent three years drops to nearly zero. This once again illustrates that enforcement has a ripple effect, leading to increased deterrence among those who witness the consequences for violating norms.

Consider a final example of enforcement spillovers from Brazil, where one of the world's largest welfare programs has been implemented. This program provides financial assistance to poor families on the condition that all school-age children in the family attend school for at least 85 percent of the school days each month. The program supports fourteen million families, reaching approximately sixty million people in need.

The program began in 2003, but the attendance requirement was not enforced until 2007, meaning that families received their stipends regardless of their children's school attendance record. In 2007, the government began rigorous monitoring and enforcement. Families received up to five warnings, with penalties escalating in severity for each subsequent instance of noncompliance. The first instance resulted in a warning letter. By the third instance, families lost benefits for sixty days, and after the fifth instance of noncompliance, the family was removed from the program.

Researchers focused on the northeast region of Brazil, known for its high poverty rates, with more than half of the population living below the poverty line. They randomly selected 10 percent of the households participating in the program between 2008 and 2009, resulting in a sample size of nearly half a million households.[22] The study revealed that an increase in the number of classmates being punished for noncompliance boosts a student's school attendance. This effect extends to penalties received by classmates of the student's siblings in other grades or schools. In other words, when families learn that some students in their children's classrooms are penalized for not attending school, they ensure their own children skip school less frequently. Furthermore, a student's attendance record improves more significantly if the penalties received by their peers are more severe.[23]

The discussion and the examples in this chapter demonstrate that dishonesty and rule-breaking is contagious, and it can lead to a widespread behavioral pattern and a cultural attribute if it is not curbed. On the other hand, people react to the certainty and severity of sanctions for rule-breaking.

Furthermore, enforcement spillovers indicate that penalizing one rule-breaker changes the proclivity of rule-breaking for others. If laws are enforced and fewer people break them, social stigma about law-breaking behavior goes up as well. In other words, deterrence and rule enforcement are strong tools to tackle dishonesty, cheating, violence, and rule-breaking.

People can also be "nudged" to change certain behaviors through the provision of information about what others do, steering them toward a desired behavior. For instance, some studies have shown that when individuals receive letters from an agency comparing their water or energy usage to the average consumption in their area, they tend to reduce their usage if it is above the average. In this case, the nudge is the informational letter, and the goal is to encourage people to conserve water and energy.

Receiving a letter that informs you that you use more electricity than your neighbors may prompt you to reduce your electricity consumption and save money by doing so. However, the effectiveness of similar information-based nudges on significant cultural attributes such as honesty and tendency toward violence is highly questionable. It has been shown that sending letters to taxpayers indicating how the tax revenue will be spent in their community has no impact on compliance. Similarly, a letter with statement such as "Only a small number of people do not pay taxes" has no impact on people's tax compliance. But a letter that describes the fines and penalties of tax evasion increases compliance.[24] Norm-nudging through information provision will not be effective in most other cultural dimensions either. Domestic violence will not be reduced by simply sending informational letters with statistics about its prevalence in the community.

Broken Windows

One reason that law enforcement deters illicit behavior is that it signals to society the unacceptability of such actions and reinforces societal norms. A good example of this is the *broken windows* hypothesis. Originally proposed by criminologist George L. Kelling and political scientist James Q. Wilson, the hypothesis argues that the tolerance of rule-breaking can lead to the spread of more serious crime. If disorder is left unchecked, it escalates into greater and more severe disorder.

The concept is straightforward: Imagine there's an empty building in town. One day, someone throws a stone and breaks one of its windows. If the broken window isn't repaired, it sends a signal to society that no one cares or nobody is in charge. Consequently, more people will break windows; in the end, the building will lose all its windows.

New York City adopted broken windows policing in 1990 when William Bratton became the chief of the New York City Transit Police. This approach was expanded citywide in 1994 when Bratton was appointed police commissioner. The New York Police Department (NYPD) began arresting individuals for misdemeanor offenses that had previously been overlooked, such as public urination, aggressive panhandling, graffiti, and subway fare evasion. The aim was to signal to society that rule-breaking would not be tolerated, thereby helping to curb more serious crimes. Commissioner Bratton called the broken windows strategy *quality of life policing*. He noted: "We wouldn't ignore the little things. Fare evasion and graffiti would no longer be considered too petty to address. In fact, we'd focus on them as vigorously as on serious crimes like robberies, if not more so. Why? Because serious crime was more likely to occur in a lawless environment—and ubiquitous low-level disorder signaled lawlessness even more than serious crime, which was less common."[25]

A test for the broken windows hypothesis involves investigation of whether curbing misdemeanor crimes causes a reduction in more serious crimes. My coauthor Hope Corman and I tested this hypothesis using data from the NYPD on all types of crimes committed in the city, arrests for these crimes, and the number of police officers in uniform for each month from 1974 to 1999. We supplemented these data with socioeconomic determinants of crime, such as the real minimum wage, the city's unemployment rate, and the number of New York City residents in state prisons.[26]

Between 1990 and 1999, when broken windows policing was implemented, several other factors influencing crime also changed. The number of police officers increased by roughly 40 percent, from around twenty-five to thirty-five thousand, directly deterring crime. The unemployment rate in New York City fluctuated during this period, rising from 7 to 21 percent between 1990 and 1992, then declining to around 8 percent between 1994 and 1997 and further dropping to 6 percent by the end of 1999. The nominal minimum wage was raised four times during the 1990s, but its inflation-adjusted value remained relatively constant. The most significant change was in the enforcement of misdemeanor offenses. Arrests for misdemeanor crimes rose by more than 65 percent, from roughly 11,000 to about 18,500 per month.

Detailed analyses have revealed that specific crimes, such as robbery, burglary, and murder, are influenced by economic factors, the size of the police force, and arrests for those particular crimes. However, even after adjusting for these factors, misdemeanor arrests have a separate, independent impact on robberies, motor vehicle thefts, and grand larcenies. Broken windows policing was effective in delivering a signal and creating a deterrent effect for these crimes.

Broken windows theory suggests that it is not only social disorder, such as petty crime, that fosters further crime; the same is true for physical disorder. Abandoned buildings, signs of vandalism, and dirty streets are examples of physical disorder, which can encourage rule-breaking by signaling society's indifference to violations of norms.

Innovative field experiments have provided evidence supporting this phenomenon. An example is the following. Imagine you are in a grocery store parking garage. Customers can bring their purchased merchandise in shopping carts to their cars, but they are expected to return the carts to a designated location before leaving the garage. This expectation is clearly communicated by visible signs stating, "Please return your shopping carts." Suppose you exit the grocery store without a shopping cart, simply carrying your few items in a plastic bag. As you head toward your car, you notice that every car in the parking lot has an advertising flier tucked under their windshield wiper. Would you remove the flier from your windshield and discard it on the floor of the parking garage? Or would you opt to keep it in your car and dispose of it properly later? It turns out that 30 percent of shoppers threw the flier on the floor of the garage and littered. For comparison, the identical experiment was then conducted in the exact same location using the same approach, but with the addition of a sign of disorder: four shopping carts left standing in the middle of the parking garage, indicating a disregard for the "returning the shopping carts" rule. Customers were monitored to see how they would behave in this disorderly environment. It turns out that they were twice as likely to litter. Walking through the parking garage, now cluttered with shopping carts, nearly 60 percent of customers littered by throwing the fliers on their windshield to the ground.[27]

Another experiment provided similar results. In this experiment, conducted in the city of Groningen in the Netherlands, researchers placed a mailing envelope, which was addressed and stamped and had a visible five-euro note inside, so that it was partially hanging out of a mailbox's mailing slot. The envelope was highly noticeable to anyone approaching the mailbox, clearly indicating the presence of money.[28] In one version of the experiment, the area around the mailbox was clean and free of litter. Out of seventy-one people who passed by and saw the envelope with money, 13 percent stole the envelope. The researchers then repeated the experiment with the same setup, but this time they littered the area around the mailbox. Among the seventy-two people who walked by and saw the envelope in this littered environment, 27 percent took the envelope. Finally, in the third version of the experiment, the researchers covered the mailbox with graffiti. In this situation, 25 percent of the sixty passersby stole the envelope. Thus people's inclination to steal doubled when the environment signaled physical disorder through littered garbage and graffiti.

There are many other different types of field experiments in this spirit conducted in different cities around the world, ranging from Athens to Munich, from Bern and Zurich to New York City. They reveal the same insight: People tend to contribute to physical disorder themselves if the environment is disorderly. Similarly, signs of disorder motive people to break rules.[29]

The Impact of Laws on Norms

Enforcing laws against illicit behavior not only reduces misconduct and rule violations through their deterrent effect but also creates spillover effects by influencing others' behavior. But apart from this direct impact, laws also serve as indicators of desirable social norms, which is another channel for their effectiveness. Legal scholars make the point that laws have an "expressive function" because laws make statements about the importance of norms.[30] As articulated by theorists, "Imposing a heavy sentence for some offense or a zero price on certain transactions means both setting material incentives and sending a message about society's values, and hence about the norms according to which different behaviors are likely to be judged."[31]

This means that laws can alter individuals' preferences and behaviors as they provide a new benchmark for what socially acceptable norms are. Recent studies provide evidence on the norm-altering effect of laws, beyond their impact on the costs and benefits of rule-breaking. An example of this occurred in Switzerland. In half of the twenty-six Swiss cantons, voting in elections was mandatory. However, the penalty for failing to vote was merely symbolic: a fine of just one dollar. This meant that while voting was required by law, there was effectively no cost for breaking the law and choosing not to vote. When the law was repealed and voting became nonmandatory, there was a substantial decline in voter turnout in the cantons that abandoned the law. This indicates that the law had signaled voting as a civic duty, and when the law was abolished, people's perception of voting as a social norm changed, leading to much lower voter participation.

Of course, the enactment of a law may reflect changing social attitudes and norms. For example, if there was a general trend in Switzerland toward abstaining from voting and voter turnout had been declining, then legislators might have reacted to this changing norm by repealing the voting mandate. Although this could be true in principle, it is not the case here. Such a nationwide trend against voting would also impact voting behavior in cantons that did not have the voting mandate. However, the findings reveal that the voting rate remained unchanged over time in cantons without the mandate. In contrast, the voting rate declined substantially after the repeal of the law in cantons where voting was mandatory.[32]

The impact of laws on the perception of norms has been reported by other studies as well. For example, a careful study analyzed the impact of the June 2015 US Supreme Court decision legalizing same-sex marriage. By surveying more than one thousand individuals both before and after the court ruling (from March 2015 to July 2015), researchers found that the ruling did not change the personal feelings or attitudes of non-LGBTQ Americans toward gay marriage. However, it did shift their perception of social norms in support of gay marriage.[33]

Individuals seek to understand the collective or dominant opinion of society and societal norms by observing the actions and behaviors of others. This perception of social norms can lead to changes in one's personal opinions. To the extent that laws are seen as reflections of social norms, they can influence attitudes and behaviors through their signaling value. Consequently, laws and their enforcement can shape attitudes and behaviors, even those that are widespread and have become cultural attributes of society.

But it should be emphasized that merely having laws on the books may not be sufficient for changing behavior and altering norms if these laws are not properly enforced. If law enforcement and the judicial system find ways to circumvent these laws and reduce their enforcement, the laws will lose their effectiveness.

For example, in Uganda, individuals accused of witch killing have several defense options. One is the "mistake of fact" defense, which suggests that the defendant mistakenly believed the victim was a witch. This implies that if the victim had indeed been a witch, the killing might have been considered justified. Other defenses include "self-defense," where the defendant claims to have killed the victim to protect themselves from witchcraft, and "provocation by witchcraft," where the defendant argues that they were provoked by the victim's engagement in witchcraft.[34] A Zimbabwean judge declared that "there is little redeeming about African witches who, through sheer malice, either consciously or sub-consciously employ magical means to inflict all manner of evil on their fellow human beings."[35] If the judicial system tends to be lenient toward those who commit murder based on witchcraft accusations, then having a law against murder will not effectively deter such crimes or reduce the belief in witchcraft.

So reforming legal institutions is an important avenue through which cultural norms can be altered, but the success of these reforms is not guaranteed. For instance, though rape is a violent crime and illegal, if judges insist on the view of the "victim wearing provocative clothing" as a mitigating circumstance in the case of a forty-year-old man raping an underaged girl, it signals a lack of proper enforcement and can lead to an increase in such violent acts.

The effectiveness of institutional reforms such as increasing sanctions on illicit behaviors to shift culture in a different direction depends on the existing cultural context. This represents a trap from which it is difficult to escape. One option is to draft laws with minimal human discretion in their application, such as strict sentencing guidelines and mandatory sentences. However, removing judicial discretion entirely is not ideal, and actors within the criminal justice system often find ways to circumvent these limitations anyway. For instance, police may be hesitant to make arrests if they know the punishment will be severe, and the same reluctance can be seen among prosecutors.

One solution to this dilemma is unequivocal support from societal leaders for the laws and the norms they represent. This includes political leaders, intellectual leaders, and prominent media figures. The importance of political leaders in forming public opinion and shifting societal norms is well-known, and there are numerous studies demonstrating this effect. Two examples are provided ahead, and the impact of the media and role models in changing culture will be discussed in detail in chapter 11.

During the COVID-19 pandemic, Brazilian President Jair Bolsonaro exhibited defiance in the face of scientific recommendations related to social distancing, which were aimed at curbing the virus's spread. Although public officials and local governments implemented social distancing regulations, Bolsonaro publicly encouraged citizens to disregard these rules on multiple occasions. In particular, he made two prominent moves against social distancing policies in 2020. On March 15, 2020, he participated in a public demonstration that deliberately broke social distancing rules, full of antics such as fist-bumping people and taking selfies with demonstrators. The second event was on March 24, 2020, where he made an official TV address opposing COVID-19 regulations imposed by local governments and downplaying the severity of the disease. He and his three sons, who are also prominent politicians, followed these events by tweeting heavily against social distancing measures.

Researchers analyzed credit card transactions and geotagged mobile phone data from close to sixty million devices across Brazil.[36] The phone data indicated an increase in mobility and a decrease in social distancing after these acts of the Brazilian president. Researchers were able to differentiate between online and in-person credit card expenses and found that in-person credit card spending, which involves visiting a physical store, also rose after the president's actions.

This example illustrates how a political leader's words and deeds can influence behavioral shifts in society. Here, the Brazilian president's actions were intended to encourage people to disregard rules, a strategy that proved effective. In contrast, the next example ahead showcases a leader who inspired his followers to uphold rules that are often disregarded.

Brazil is a predominantly Catholic nation, with almost 80 percent of its population adhering to Catholicism. During his visit to Brazil in October 1991, Pope John Paul II embarked on a ten-day tour across ten cities, delivering thirty-two speeches. The transcripts of these speeches reflect his discussions on a wide array of topics, spanning from poverty and peace to charity and education. In addition, the pope frequently touched upon themes related to family and children.

In his speeches, the pope also reiterated the Catholic Church's opposition to birth control through contraceptive methods, addressing related issues such as abortion. Although these speeches may not have introduced new teachings to Catholic adherents, the emphasis placed by the pope on the importance of avoiding birth control signaled to his followers the significance of the issue within Catholic doctrine.

Researchers analyzed surveys conducted in Brazil during the weeks prior to, during, and after the pope's visit, revealing that exposure to his speeches led to a 40 percent decrease in women's contraceptive usage and their intentions to use contraceptives.[37] This indicates that the visible presence of the pope and the content of his speeches inspired women to adhere more closely to a specific tenet of the religion, highlighting the influential impact of the pope's messages on people's adherence to rules.

Furthermore, when researchers analyzed Brazilian births, they discovered a notable increase in births in July 1992, nine months after the pope's visit. Statistical analyses revealed that, for the approximately 29.3 million women aged fifteen to forty-nine in 1991, the papal visit resulted in an additional fifty-two thousand births among the 3.3 million births in that cohort. Thus, the pope's message contributed to an increase in births by nearly 2 percent, aligning with the Catholic doctrine's emphasis on larger families.

In summary, dishonesty and rule-breaking are contagious and can become ingrained cultural attributes. Enactment of laws against such behaviors helps curb these acts and promotes behaviors that align with human well-being. Laws also signal societal values to the community.

However, the effectiveness of laws depends on the credibility of their enforcement as well as on the commitment of societal leaders to uphold the norms represented by these laws.

11 Cultural Change: Institutions, Education, Media

Chapter 6 emphasized the role of institutions in shaping cultural behaviors and beliefs, highlighting how institutions create cultural differences between societies. Chapter 10 discussed the importance of laws and legal institutions in altering norms. In this chapter, I will discuss education and the media, two other key mechanisms shown to influence the cultural attributes of societies.

Education's Impact on Culture Through Brain Anatomy

As discussed in chapter 7, recent research in cognitive neuroimaging has provided fascinating insights into how the anatomy of the brain changes in response to learning a second language. The studies discussed in that chapter, as well as other similar research that will be discussed ahead, demonstrate how the brain's structure adapts to the acquisition of new skills and highlight the profound influence of education on culture.

To start, consider a study that examined the brain images of male London taxi drivers who had an average of fourteen years of experience. The images were compared to those obtained from a group of men who did not drive taxis. Analyses revealed significant differences between the two groups in the gray matter volume in the hippocampus region of the brain. *Gray matter* is a type of brain tissue primarily composed of *nerve cell bodies* (the main part of nerve cells, which contain the nucleus, the cell's control center).[1] The gray matter in the posterior hippocampus, which is involved in contextual memory, spatial memory, and navigation, was significantly larger in the brains of taxi drivers, suggesting that the brain adapts to environmental stimuli.[2] In response to the demands of navigation, the brains of taxi drivers have allocated more space to the region responsible for navigation (the posterior hippocampus) compared to the brains of individuals who do not rely on navigation as extensively.

It could be argued that individuals with genetically larger posterior hippocampi, which make them better navigators, are more likely to have chosen to become taxi drivers. However, the analyses also revealed a positive correlation between the number of years spent as a taxi driver and the volume of the posterior hippocampi. In other words, taxi drivers had larger hippocampi, and those with more years of experience as a driver had even bigger hippocampi. This suggests that, much like muscles growing with increased exercise, the brain region involved in navigation expands with more experience in tasks that require it.

Another neuroscience study in this vein introduced an experimental component. Researchers divided participants into two groups, neither of which had prior juggling experience at the time of their initial brain scan, which was taken using three-dimensional structural MRI imaging. This first MRI scan revealed no regional differences in brain structure between the groups.

The first group was then given three months to learn a three-ball cascade juggling routine. After mastering the skill over this time period—demonstrated by juggling three balls for at least sixty seconds—a second brain scan was conducted. Subsequently, participants stopped practicing juggling, and a third brain scan was performed three months later.[3] The results from the second scan showed significant differences between the groups in terms of gray matter volume. Nonjugglers showed no change in gray matter over this three-month period, whereas the volume of gray matter in the brain's midtemporal area (hMT/V5) had increased for those who learned juggling. This region is responsible for processing the direction and speed of moving objects, playing a central role in motion perception, helping the eyes track moving objects, and supporting the ability to predict their trajectories. This finding indicates that learning to juggle altered the brain's anatomical structure, enlarging the area essential for performing this activity. Because the jugglers stopped practicing after the second scan, most were no longer proficient in juggling by the time of the third scan three months later. As a result, the extent of the expansion in the jugglers' hMT/V5 area decreased, illustrating the principle that "you lose it if you don't use it."

More importantly, the study also revealed that the left posterior intraparietal sulcus (IPS) increased in size for those who learned juggling. This area of the brain is primarily associated with symbolic numerical tasks, such as understanding symbols, performing mathematical operations, and processing numerical information, including counting and arithmetic. It also supports the concept of magnitude (e.g., comparing sizes or quantities) and links abstract symbols (e.g., numbers or letters) to their meanings. Damage to the left posterior IPS can impair several cognitive and perceptual abilities, such as performing mathematical operations (e.g., addition, subtraction), understanding numerical symbols, and comparing or estimating quantities and magnitudes.[4]

This finding demonstrates that learning a new task, such as juggling, not only increases the volume of the gray matter in the specific brain region required for mastering that task but also provides the additional benefit of strengthening areas linked to broader cognitive functions. Other studies have also yielded similar findings, highlighting the benefits of learning a new skill, whether it is mastering judo, learning to play golf, or practicing simultaneous translation.[5]

In summary, research in neuroscience demonstrates the collateral advantage to the brain from training to acquire a new skill. This is similar to how cardiovascular exercise, such as running, enhances lung capacity and circulation while simultaneously strengthening leg muscles. This important discovery will play a central role in our discussion ahead on the link between education and cognition.

Education, Intelligence, and Culture

Psychologists define *intelligence* as consisting of two components: fluid intelligence and crystallized intelligence. *Fluid intelligence* includes skills that are parts of executive functions, such as working memory, cognitive flexibility, and problem-solving, as well as other abilities like abstract reasoning, pattern recognition, logical thinking, and the capacity to adapt to new or complex situations. *Crystallized intelligence*, on the other hand, refers to the ability to use acquired knowledge and general facts.[6]

Acquiring new knowledge through education, such as learning historical facts and studying geography, enhances crystallized intelligence. Learning skills such as mathematics and language through education alters the brain's structure by increasing gray matter volume in specific regions, boosting fluid intelligence and improving cognitive abilities like memory, attention, and executive functions.[7]

This is directly related to culture because improved cognitive skills enable individuals to think more analytically, critically, and independently, potentially shaping their preferences, beliefs, and attitudes. To put it differently, education strengthens fluid intelligence, leading to changes in thought process and preferences, and thus generating behavioral and cultural change.

One clear implication of this research is that societies with higher education levels are likely to exhibit greater average cognitive abilities. As a result, some of the observed cultural differences between countries may stem from differences in the average cognition levels of their populations if these countries have significantly different education levels. These cultural differences may arise directly from education's influence on crystallized intelligence and indirectly through its effects on fluid intelligence, which is shaped by changes in brain biology.

It is important to emphasize that the structural changes in the brain resulting from education are unrelated to individuals' genetic makeup. The findings of neuroscience suggest, for instance, that genetically identical twins would have different brain anatomies and intelligence levels if they acquired different levels of education or engaged in different intensities of brain stimulation.

Biological change in the brain, independent of genetic makeup, is similar to the change in human height over time in different societies. There are significant differences in people's average height across countries. In places like Scandinavia, it is impossible not to notice how tall the average person is. The average height of an eighteen-year-old man is about 181 cm (5′9″) in Denmark, Finland, Norway, and Sweden. In contrast, men in South Korea average 175 cm, (5′7″), while the average height is 171 cm in Japan (5′6″) and 169 cm, 167 cm, and 165 cm in Mexico, Egypt, and Tanzania, respectively.

There is no doubt that genetic differences between societies are responsible for some of these height differences, but genetics is not the whole story. A few years ago, I was invited to give a seminar at Aarhus University in Denmark. While there, I visited an area of the city dedicated to preserving houses, barns, and other structures, along with their furniture and artifacts from the past few centuries. I was surprised when I entered one of these farmhouses, where peasants lived centuries ago, because it was evident that Danish people were short during the seventeenth and eighteenth centuries. The door heights were low, and the beds were designed for people no taller than 160–165 cm. So despite Hollywood's portrayal of towering Vikings in movies,

Danes a few centuries ago were not tall by today's standards. (Of course, they were likely taller than people from other parts of the world at the time.) The point is that the average height of a Danish man appears to have increased by around 20 cm (about eight inches) over the past three or four centuries. Women are shorter than men in every society, but the same increase has also been observed in women's height over time.

This means that while the genetic makeup of Danes remained the same or very similar to what it was three hundred years ago, their biology has changed dramatically. The same is true in other countries. In the early twentieth century, the average height of Japanese men was 156 cm (5′1″), while Egyptian men averaged 159 cm (5′2″). At the time, both were shorter than Danes, and they are shorter today, primarily due to genetic factors. However, the average height of Japanese men has since increased to 171 cm (5′6″), whereas Egyptian men have experienced a more modest rise to 167 cm.[8]

The upshot is that human height does have a genetic, heritable component, but height is also shaped by factors such as nutrition and exposure to disease during fetal development, childhood, and adolescence. Therefore, a given society with a particular genetic makeup experiences a faster or slower height growth over the years based on these nongenetic, economic and environmental factors. Similarly, the average intelligence of a society may increase at a faster or slower rate over time, depending on the extent of education and other cognition-developing activities that are prevalent in that society.

How to Identify the Impact of Education on Culture

Education has also an indirect effect on culture. By increasing individuals' productivity, education alters the opportunities and constraints faced by them. An increase in educational attainment leads to higher wages, which affects people's inclination to participate in the labor market. This in turn influences preferences and behaviors for several reasons. For instance, working in the labor market typically exposes individuals to a wider range of ideas and viewpoints as well as different groups of people. It can also enhance women's financial power and autonomy and shift the bargaining power between men and women within the household.

Determining the causal impact of education on people's behaviors, beliefs, and attitudes is complex. Comparing groups with different education levels is problematic, as individuals with more education may systematically differ from those with less education in ways beyond their educational attainment. Let's say, for example, that we want to investigate whether education causes people to read more books. Suppose we find that individuals with a high school education read an average of four books per year, while those without a high school education read two books per year. It would be incorrect to conclude that high school education directly motivates people to read more books because the difference in the number of books read by the two groups could be due to other factors. For instance, because education leads to higher earnings power, individuals with a high school diploma typically have higher incomes than those without. As a result, the desire to read books may be the same between the two groups, but more educated individuals read more because they can more easily afford to buy books. In this example, education does not change people's preferences for reading books but indirectly impacts book reading through its influence on income.

There are additional complications to consider. An individual's level of education might be influenced by her interest in books. If more curious people are inclined to read books and also pursue more education (because they have a greater desire to learn), then the difference in the number of books read by more educated and less educated groups is not due to education itself, but rather to differences in their inherent curiosity.

Various scientific methods have been developed to address these complications and isolate the direct causal impact of education on preferences and behaviors. Consider the following hypothetical example: Suppose we take all six-year-olds in a country and randomly divide them into four groups. We prevent the first group from receiving any education. We educate the second group for exactly eight years, the third group for twelve years, and the fourth group for sixteen years. Each group will include children from both poor and rich families as well as children with educated and uneducated parents. The kids will also vary in intelligence, willingness to work hard, and other characteristics. In this scenario, neither the children nor their families decide how many years of education they receive. Consequently, no family or child characteristic is correlated with the education imposed on these kids. As a result, in this fictional experiment, any differences in the propensity to read books among these four groups, once the children become adults, can be attributed to the differences in education they received.

Education, Religiosity, and Superstition

The hypothetical experiment just described cannot be conducted, but there are instances where it can be approximated in real life. One example is when a country increases its compulsory years of education. For instance, in Turkey, the mandatory number of years of education was initially five, covering only elementary school. In the summer of 1997, the government unexpectedly raised it to eight years. This change meant that children who completed the fifth grade and received their elementary school diploma in the summer of 1997 were not required to continue their education (although of course some did). Meanwhile, those who completed the fourth grade that same summer were required to stay in school and complete at least eight years of education to receive a middle school diploma.

This means that two cohorts of students, born one year apart, faced different mandates. One cohort was forced to obtain three more years of education than the other cohort. To the extent that children who are one year different in age are not different from each other in a systematic way, the behaviors of these two cohorts (those who received five years of education and those who were forced to receive eight years of education) can be compared.

In a research study, my coauthor and I did this type of analysis utilizing the Turkish education reform just mentioned, which revealed a substantial impact on women.[9] Among women in their mid-twenties, the reform increased the share who have at least a middle school diploma (at least eight years of education) from about 55 percent to close to 85 percent. Statistical analyses revealed that these women, who received three additional years of education and obtained a middle school diploma, were about 45 percent less likely to identify themselves as religious in comparison to otherwise similar women who had three fewer years of education and received only an elementary school diploma. We also found that women who were mandated to receive more education were nearly 70 percent less likely to wear a religious head cover (head scarf, turban, or burka). They were also more likely to self-identify as "modern" rather than "traditional conservative" or "religious conservative." Furthermore, they were much less likely to vote for Islamic political parties.[10]

The reform increased men's educational attainment as well. Among men in their mid-twenties, the reform increased the share with at least a middle school diploma from 77 percent to about 94 percent. Interestingly, however, receiving three additional years of education had no significant influence on men's behaviors and beliefs. Neither their religiosity nor their likelihood of voting for an Islamic party is influenced by more education. This finding, that an increase in education at a low level (from five years to eight years of schooling) has no effect on men, is noteworthy and has been observed in other studies—a topic I will revisit later in this chapter.

The same impact of education on religiosity has been documented in various countries and time periods. For example, in several Canadian provinces, the minimum school-leaving age was raised at different times during the twentieth century. A study comparing adults who were influenced by these changes in school-leaving-age laws found that an additional year of education significantly reduced the likelihood of an individual identifying with any religion.[11] Similarly, increased school enrollment in German cities during the late nineteenth and early twentieth centuries led to a decline in church attendance.[12]

In a separate project, a colleague and I examined fourteen European countries that enacted compulsory schooling reforms, mostly during the 1960s and 1970s.[13] For instance, France extended mandatory education from eight to ten years in 1959, while Greece increased it from six to nine years in 1976. Belgium raised the compulsory years of education from eight to twelve in 1983. This means that some individuals who were school-age children in the 1970s and 1980s were exposed to these reforms and, bound by their mandate, received more education compared to slightly older children in the same country during that period.

Using data from surveys conducted in these countries in early-to-mid 2000s, we compared individuals who are citizens of the same country and who are otherwise similar, but who differ in their years of education due to varying exposure to mandatory schooling reforms, depending on the year they started school. Statistical analyses revealed negative effects of schooling on religiosity, attendance at religious services, and frequency of prayer. In addition, when we examined the impact of education on superstitious beliefs, we found that an increase in mandatory schooling years reduced individuals' tendency to believe in the power of lucky charms and to consider horoscopes in daily life.

So the evidence shows that education has a causal impact on both religiosity and superstitious beliefs. An increase in educational attainment makes individuals less likely to be religious and superstitious.[14]

Education and Consanguineous Marriage

Consanguinity refers to marriages between couples who are second cousins or closer.[15] These marriages can lead to significant health issues for the offspring. Babies born to consanguineous parents have a higher risk of premature birth and prenatal mortality. Medical research has shown that the mutation of recessive genes inherited from a common ancestor increases the likelihood of serious genetic disorders in offspring. Consequently, a range of congenital anomalies and conditions are more common among children of blood-related parents. Specifically, these children are more likely to experience stunting and severe intellectual disabilities. Other health issues include hearing or vision impairments, childhood glaucoma, congenital heart defects, and cerebral palsy.

Consanguineous marriages are more widespread among countries with majority-Muslim populations. However, this practice is not exclusive to Muslim nations nor solely a product of Islam. In fact, Islamic marriage rules share similarities with those in Judaism, though notable differences exist. For example, while Islam forbids uncle-niece marriages, they are permitted in Judaism. Cousin marriage is also generally permissible in Protestantism, while in Catholicism, it is not allowed without a diocesan dispensation.

Until the early twentieth century, the practice of first-cousin marriage was accepted in Europe, and it was particularly common among the elites. For example, Queen Victoria of England married Prince Albert, her father's brother's son. Before that, George IV married his aunt's daughter. Similarly, George V married a second cousin once removed in 1893, and Queen Elizabeth II and Prince Philip, who were third cousins through Queen Victoria and second cousins once removed through King Christian IX, married in 1947.

In many countries across the Middle East, North Africa, and West Asia, the rate of consanguineous marriages ranges from 10 to 40 percent, while in certain regions of China, Afghanistan, India, Saudi Arabia, and Syria, it rises to 45–50 percent.[16] Despite the significant health issues associated with consanguineous marriages, over 10 percent of the global population is married to a second cousin or closer, indicating that these unions may offer certain advantages. These marriages may serve as a strategy for consolidating, retaining, and transmitting wealth across generations within families related by blood. Furthermore, they facilitate network creation, which improves economic and social well-being in societies where in-group favoritism and distrust of out-groups are prevalent.[17]

Cousin marriages are more common in collectivist societies and help maintain certain attributes of such societies, such as in-group favoritism and nepotism. Put differently, these marriages help perpetuate kinship relations, which can be detrimental to intergroup cooperation and economic development.

Strengthened by consanguineous marriage, kin networks can hinder the development of democratic, participatory institutions. It has been argued that Europe's economic progress was facilitated by a shift from closed kinship systems to a system in which knowledge was transmitted across individuals—in contrast to other parts of the world, where extended families or clans remained the dominant structures.[18]

In a study, my coauthor Pelin Akyol and I examined the impact of the same Turkish education reform, mentioned earlier, on individuals' likelihood of entering into a consanguineous marriage.[19] Twenty percent of marriages in Turkey are consanguineous. Analyzing women's marriage decisions as well as their responses to survey questions about marriage, we found that women who were exposed to the Turkish education reform were less likely to find consanguineous marriage as an acceptable practice. Furthermore, the reform reduced women's propensity to marry a first cousin or a blood relative. Women who were exposed to the education reform were less likely to be in a marriage arranged by their families. The reform also reduced women's propensity for being in a marriage into which they were forced by their families, indicating that the reform reduced the likelihood of women getting married without their consent. Moreover, the reform made women significantly less likely to agree with the statement, "Only a son can ensure the continuation of the family blood line."

These results show that the education reform, which extended the duration of compulsory schooling, significantly influenced women's preferences regarding consanguineous marriage. Given the strong cultural basis of such marriages, these findings highlight the powerful role of education in transforming preferences and behaviors that are deeply rooted in culture.

As discussed in chapter 9, preferences are transmitted intergenerationally, from parents to children. This vertical transmission is a key aspect of the persistence of cultural attributes. The research summarized in this chapter so far reveals that acquiring more education alters the preferences of those who receive it. This implies that if parents' preferences change due to gaining more education, then their children's preferences would likely also change, as parents would transmit their changed preferences to their kids.

To provide evidence of this mechanism, my doctoral student Nur Orak and I examined how education influences the traits adults want to instill in children.[20] Using the same education reforms in Europe discussed earlier in this chapter, we analyzed survey data from over twenty-five thousand adults across nineteen European countries. The survey asked, "Which qualities do you consider especially important for children to learn at home?" The possible answers were independence, hard work, responsibility, imagination, tolerance and respect, determination/perseverance, religious faith, unselfishness, and obedience.

The respondents were, on average, forty-four years old during the survey, with an average of twelve years of education. Comparing individuals of similar age within the same country who completed different years of schooling, due to exposure to the education reform in their country, revealed the following: Women who gained additional education as a result of these reforms are more likely to prioritize traits such as imagination, determination, perseverance, and a sense of responsibility to instill in children. Conversely, they are less inclined to view religiosity, obedience, and unselfishness as essential qualities for children to learn at home.[21] In other words, acquiring more years of schooling changes people's views of the attributes they consider important for children, highlighting education's role in altering the pattern of vertical cultural transmission.

Education and Acceptability of Violence

Sierra Leone is one of the poorest countries in the world, with a per capita income of $500. About 60 percent of females and 45 percent of males in the country are illiterate. The decade-long civil war in Sierra Leone that ended in 2001 severely impacted education, with widespread destruction of schools and disruptions to educational services. Even before the war, school attendance was low, partly due to parents bearing the costs of tuition, school fees, teaching materials, textbooks, and exam fees.

After the conclusion of the war, Sierra Leone started implementing a program to provide free primary education in public schools. The program was financed by domestic public funds, donor contributions from international financial institutions, and foreign governments. The government restored and renovated old school buildings and built new ones, committing almost 20 percent of its spending to education.

By design, the program increased access to education for primary-school-age children but did not benefit children who were older. During that time, the population of the country was about 5.5 million, and the number of students doubled from 0.6 million to 1.3 million between 2001 and 2004.

In a study, Colin Cannonier and I made use of data on the variation in children's access to the program, generated by birthdates and by the differences in resources among the fourteen districts of the country. The analyses investigated whether the increase in educational attainment due to the program had an impact on women's attitudes on various issues when they became young adults.[22]

We found that the increase in schooling facilitated by the program influenced women's attitudes toward matters regarding women's health and attitudes toward violence against women. Specifically, each additional year of schooling made women more inclined to support a wife's right to refuse sex when tired or when the husband has a sexually transmitted disease. Likewise, higher schooling levels made women more likely to oppose wife beating and increased their propensity to advocate for an end to the practice of female genital mutilation. So the findings demonstrate that increased education alters women's preferences and reduces acceptance of violence directed toward them. This indicates that education empowers women as an increase in education makes women more intolerant of practices that conflict with their well-being.

On the other hand, increased education had no impact on men's attitudes toward women's well-being. Men who were exposed to the same education reform were no different from men who did not benefit from the reform regarding their propensity to agree with the statements about violence toward women. This finding is consistent with the ones obtained from Turkey, where an increase in educational attainment does not alter the attitudes of men regarding religiosity.

It is important to note that the increase in educational attainment examined in these studies involves approximately three additional years of schooling, starting from an already low baseline. Providing more years of education, such as achieving a high school diploma, may influence men's preferences and behaviors. Still, the contrast between men and women remains striking.

This difference in how men and women respond to increased education may help explain why certain groups that seek to preserve traditional cultural patterns, especially in developing countries, oppose efforts to expand women's education.

Curriculum

In addition to the number of years of education, what is being taught in the classroom is also vital in influencing attitudes, preferences, and behaviors. A school curriculum plays a crucial role in enhancing students' cognitive ability and exposes them to diverse subjects such as modern science, history, arts, and literature. Studies have shown that state-mandated mathematics courses in high school lead to increased investment income and better credit management in the future for students who took these courses. Financial education during high school results in fewer debt defaults and higher credit scores when students become young adults. Moreover, high school curricula that include algebra and geometry classes contribute to higher earnings for students even ten years after graduation.[23]

Of course, curricula can also be designed to promote specific beliefs and preferences, including particular religious or ideological viewpoints. This is especially evident in autocracies and dictatorships, where those in power often tailor school curricula and textbooks to inculcate their desired religious and ideological perspectives.

For an example of how a school curriculum can influence students' political attitudes and beliefs, consider a study that investigated the impact of a recent Chinese high school curriculum reform.[24] The Chinese Communist Party introduced a new curriculum between 2004 and 2010 with the explicit intention of shaping students' political ideology. The goal of the reform was clear. As stated by the authors of the study, the Chinese State Council and the Ministry of Education issued documents outlining the government's objectives for the new curriculum. These goals included emphasizing adherence to the Chinese government's rules of law, teaching students about Chinese socialist institutions, educating them on China's unique economic institutions and development path, and fostering a traditional national identity in students.

The study surveyed two thousand Peking University students to investigate the influence of this curriculum overhaul, which changed the textbooks and significantly modified the way in which classes are taught. As part of this effort, teachers underwent training for the new curriculum.

Because the new curriculum was introduced in different provinces of China at different times, researchers were able to compare the attitudes of students who were from the same province and studying the same subject at the same university but had different exposures to the curriculum reform while in high school. Some students graduated from high school and entered the university under the old curriculum, while others were in high school when the new curriculum was implemented.

The results showed that the new curriculum was successful in changing students' attitudes in the direction intended by the Chinese government. Students exposed to the new curriculum demonstrated greater trust in Chinese government officials, viewed them as more civic-minded, and perceived bribery as less prevalent compared to students who studied under the old curriculum. Furthermore, students who were exposed to the new curriculum perceived China as more democratic and were more skeptical of "unconstrained democracy," aligning with the government's goal of promoting a "socialist democracy." They were also more likely to oppose Western free-market institutions.

These findings reveal that classroom instruction and course content can be vehicles through which students can be indoctrinated and through which their worldviews can be shaped.

The Impact of the Media

Studies analyzing various countries and time periods repeatedly documented that exposure to the views promoted by the media changes individuals' attitudes and preferences. In this section, I present examples from a broad range of literature on the impact of the media—encompassing film, radio, and television—across various countries and time periods. I begin with its impact on political views.

Movies

The 1915 film *The Birth of a Nation* offered a fictionalized portrayal of the white supremacist group the KKK. The film was a major hit, attracting around ten million American viewers—approximately 20 percent of the adult white population at the time. It has long been argued that this film's racist depiction of Black people, propagation of racial stereotypes, and its glorification of the KKK fueled racial tension and bolstered support for the group.

Unlike today, movies in the early twentieth century were not released simultaneously everywhere. The film industry was still developing, and fewer than 60 percent of counties in America had movie theaters. *The Birth of a Nation* was distributed across the country between 1915 and 1920 in a manner similar to a concert tour, with showings in various locations at different times.

Economist Desmond Ang analyzed detailed historical data, including the locations and seating capacities of movie theaters that screened *The Birth of a Nation* and the dates of these showings, to examine the relationship between each county's exposure to the film's premiere and the subsequent changes in racism and race-related violence in those counties between 1915 and 1920.[25]

The analyses revealed that a county was four times more likely to experience a lynching of a Black person in the month following the film's arrival. Similarly, state-level murders of minorities, but not of white people, increased after the movie's screening. In addition, the film's release in a county was associated with a higher likelihood of that county having a KKK chapter in the future and an increase in KKK membership.

These results demonstrate that media is a powerful tool for shaping public opinion and spreading ideologies. In this particular case, *The Birth of a Nation* propagated violence, and as the author the analysis stated: "A fictionalized version of the Klan was introduced to millions of Americans across the country, leading to the rebirth of the KKK on a scale far larger than had ever existed before."[26]

Radio

In the late 1920s, an American Roman Catholic priest named Charles Coughlin began broadcasting religious sermons. During the Great Depression, he expanded his broadcasts to comment on economic and social issues, portraying America as being ruled by tycoons, atheist Marxists, and Jewish bankers. Coughlin's radio program was picked up by CBS in 1930, which allowed him to reach a broad audience due to the rapidly rising radio ownership rate among American households. Although CBS dropped him a year later, he established his own radio network, and his weekly show was heard by approximately one in four Americans, or about thirty million listeners.

As described in a recent study, even though Coughlin supported Roosevelt in the 1932 presidential election, he later became a staunch critic of Roosevelt labeling him "'anti-God' and a 'great betrayer and liar' controlled by both international bankers and communists."[27] The author of the study explains that Coughlin also became overtly anti-Semitic and he openly advocated Nazism by the late 1930s. He blamed Jews for inciting violence in Europe and supported pro-Nazi organizations in America, such as German American Bund. He also published a weekly newspaper called *Protocols of the Elders of Zion*, which promoted Nazi views to the extent that some of his writings in that publication were directly copied from Hitler's minister of propaganda, Joseph Goebbels.[28] As described in the study, Coughlin labeled Roosevelt as "the world's chief warmonger" and opposed America's involvement in World War II.

The study examined whether exposure to Coughlin's radio broadcasts influenced political preferences and voting behavior between the 1932 and 1936 elections. The author collected comprehensive data, including information on all radio stations that aired Coughlin's weekly program. The signal strength of each station was used to identify counties that received the broadcasts and those that did not. In addition, data from 1930 on county characteristics—such as demographics, employment statistics, religious composition, literacy rates, and radio ownership—were gathered for the analysis.

The results revealed that counties with exposure to the radio signal of the program experienced a decrease in Roosevelt's vote share from 1932 to 1936, with the effect being more pronounced in counties with higher Catholic populations. This negative impact of Coughlin's broadcasts persisted and continued to be evident until the 1952 presidential election. Furthermore, the radio program negatively affected the extent of support for World War II among the population. In counties with greater exposure to the program, due to stronger signal reception, per capita bond sales for the war were lower. Moreover, Coughlin's anti-Semitic views exacerbated anti-Semitism. Counties exposed to his program were more likely to have a local branch of the German American Bund organization.

Television

Switching to more recent years, numerous studies have demonstrated the impact of political views propagated by certain media outlets on voter behavior. An insightful study analyzed the influence of Fox News, which was launched in March 1996.[29] Before that time, news constituted only a small part of the Fox Broadcasting Corporation's operations, and its prime-time broadcasts did not cover news. The creation of Fox News introduced a twenty-four-hour cable news channel with a political orientation that was more right-leaning than other major television news sources, such as ABC, CBS, NBC, and CNN.

By 2000, Fox News was available in 20 percent of US towns with cable services. Analyses have shown that Fox News did not target specific areas based on that area's political orientation. The towns that gained access to Fox News between 1996 and 2000 were similar in demographic attributes and political orientation to those that did not receive Fox News.

Researchers analyzed how the Republican vote share changed between the 1996 and 2000 presidential elections in response to Fox News entering a cable market. The results indicated that exposure to Fox News, adjusting for other determinants that can influence voting behavior, shifted two hundred thousand votes from the Democratic candidate, Al Gore, to the Republican candidate, George W. Bush, emphasizing the media's role in shaping political views.

In summary, the media plays a crucial role in shaping viewers' beliefs and political preferences through persuasion. Politicians have long understood this influence and have sought to mold public perceptions, political opinions, and beliefs through media content. Vladimir Putin is reported to have said, "Contrary to a common perception, mass media is an instrument, rather than an institution."[30]

Role Models

Role models can be defined as individuals who can "influence role aspirant's achievements, motivation and goals by acting as behavioral models, representation of the possible, and/or inspirations."[31] Individuals identify with those who they perceive as role models, whether in real life or through the media. Extensive literature in economics highlights the impact of role models on people's attitudes, preferences, and behaviors. For example, a randomized experiment demonstrated that exposing female freshmen to successful women who majored in economics at the same university increased their likelihood of choosing economics as their major.[32] In the spring of 2016, researchers at Southern Methodist University conducted an experiment in which they invited two successful female alumni to speak about their experiences as economics majors, their careers, and how their education in economics had benefitted them. Both individuals spoke in each of the four randomly selected classes in the spring. Because students choose to register for specific sections of a class (e.g., morning or afternoon), researchers compared students who were exposed to the role models' visits and speeches to students who took the same class, from the same instructor, in the same time slot the previous year, in spring 2015. The latter group of students was not exposed to this role model treatment.

The results revealed that exposure to these female role models had a significant impact on female students. The proportion of female students who subsequently enrolled in additional economics classes doubled compared to those who were not exposed to the role models, and the percentage of female students majoring in economics increased by 100 percent. Economics is a field predominantly dominated by men, with women receiving only 30 percent of bachelor's degrees in the discipline. Therefore, this is a significant impact in terms of increasing female presence in the discipline. Conversely, there was no noticeable impact on male students, arguably because female alumni did not constitute appropriate role models for male students.

Another recent study investigated the impact of a role model on secondary school students in Uganda.[33] In this study, 1,500 fourth- and twelfth-grade students in Kampala were randomly assigned to watch either a movie featuring a female role model or a placebo movie. The role model movie, *Queen of Katwe,* features a female character who excels in mathematics. IMDb describes the film as follows: "Living in the slum of Katwe in Kampala, Uganda, is a constant struggle for 10-year-old Phiona and her family. Her world changes one day when she meets Robert Katende, a missionary who teaches children how to play chess."[34] Phiona is "striving to become a chess master through hard work and perseverance. Along the way, she must overcome many obstacles to achieving her dream, including learning to read and write and getting into the top school in Uganda in order to play chess."[35]

After watching the movies, all students took an important national exam. Fourth graders took their exam one week after the screening, while twelfth graders took theirs one month later. Analyses of the exam results revealed that exposure to the role model in the movie led to better performance compared to students who watched the placebo movie. The impact was particularly significant in mathematics and was more pronounced for female students. Furthermore, female students exposed to the role models were less likely to drop out of school in the following years.

These examples from students in America and Uganda are just two among dozens of scientific studies illustrating how individuals react to what they perceive as role models. Ahead, we will examine additional examples of how adults respond to role models and situations depicted on television.

Television Shows and Cultural Preferences

Television soap operas, known as *novelas*, have been highly popular in Brazil. Their primary broadcaster, Globo, held a near monopoly for the production of these widely watched shows, which often featured themes of love, intrigue, and social issues. The novelas portrayed lifestyles and family structures that were not representative of typical Brazilian society. Female characters were predominantly depicted as young, unmarried, and childless. Nearly three-quarters of these characters had no children, and another 20 percent had only one child. Only one-quarter of these female characters were married, often portraying smaller, nontraditional families.[36]

The Globo network was established in 1965, but less than 1 percent of Brazil received its signal by 1970. Coverage increased to 36 percent in 1980 and 86 percent in 1991. The Globo signal reached various municipalities in Brazil at different times during this expansion. This timing variation allowed for a comparison between areas with similar socioeconomic attributes but different years of exposure to novelas. Using data from the 1991 Brazilian Census, the authors of a study constructed a retrospective history of each Brazilian woman, determining where and when each woman gave birth over the previous twelve years. Analyses revealed that women living in municipalities that received the Globo signal had lower fertility rates compared to those in similar municipalities that had not yet received the signal. In other words, the portrayal of female characters without children in novelas influenced the fertility preferences of women by providing new role models for women on TV.[37]

Further analyses confirmed that the fertility decline was specifically due to the influence of novelas and not just television access. The decline was more pronounced among women of similar age to the novela characters. Moreover, fertility reductions were greater following storylines featuring childless women achieving upward social mobility. Finally, parents in areas with Globo signal access were significantly more likely to name their newborns after novela characters during the year in which those novelas were broadcast, underscoring the role model effect of these TV shows.

A separate study examined the impact of Brazilian novelas on divorce rates using data from the 1970, 1980, and 1991 Brazilian Censuses. The staggered rollout of the Globo network allowed for a comparison between areas with similar socioeconomic attributes but different years of novela exposure. The analysis discovered a significant increase in the proportion of separated or divorced women following the introduction of the Globo signal, suggesting that exposure to these soap operas influenced marital dissolution rates in the affected areas.[38] Thus, these studies have shown that the female characters on television served as role models and influenced the preferences of Brazilian women regarding marriage and fertility.

The impact of TV shows on attitudes and behaviors has also been observed in India's rural and remote villages. Researchers tracked individuals from 180 villages across five states of India over three years, during which cable TV was introduced in some of these villages. The aim of the study was to investigate the influence of exposure to cable TV programming, which is quite different from government-broadcast TV channels. The most popular programs on cable TV are game shows and soap operas. For example, as stated by the authors, among the most popular shows, based on the Indian Nielsen ratings, "is *Kyunki Saas Bhi Kabhi Bahu Thi* (*Because a Mother-in-Law Was Once a Daughter-in-Law, Also*), a show based around the life of a wealthy industrial family in the large city of Mumbai. As can be seen from the title, the main themes and plots of the show revolve around issues of family and gender."[39]

Analyses revealed that exposure to cable TV programs significantly impacted women's attitudes and behaviors.[40] After cable TV was introduced to a village, women were less likely to accept wife beating as permissible and were less likely to express a preference for sons over daughters. In addition, women's autonomy has increased after access to cable TV. They were more likely to go out without permission and were more likely to participate in household decisions.

It can be argued that changes in women's attitudes were influenced by other factors, such as rising incomes. If higher incomes were the driving force in women's changing attitudes, and if cable TV penetration took place in villages with higher incomes, we would incorrectly attribute the change in women's attitudes to cable TV when in fact it was driven by income. However, this is not the case. First, there were no socioeconomic differences between villages with and without cable TV. Second, women's attitudes changed shortly after the introduction of cable TV. Each woman in each village was surveyed in three consecutive years, and the findings showed that regardless of a woman's personal characteristics (age education, household income, etc.), her attitudes and preferences changed after having access to cable TV.

Role Models from the "Glory Days" of the Past

Having traveled to Turkey frequently, I have observed a very noticeable cultural shift over the years, related to young Turkish men. An extremely popular TV series titled *The Magnificent Century* (*Muhteşem Yüzyıl*) began airing in 2011 and continued for almost five years. This historical drama, which has become a TV phenomenon, revolved around the reign of Sultan Suleiman the Magnificent, the tenth and longest-reigning sultan of the Ottoman Empire. The series offered a dramatized portrayal of his life, focusing on his personal and political actions, his court, and his harem. It was designed to evoke a sense of nostalgia for the powerful era of the Ottoman Empire by highlighting influential political and military figures of an empire that, at the time, controlled Anatolia, the Middle East, North Africa, Cyprus, the Arabian Peninsula, parts of the Caucasus, the Balkans, and parts of Eastern Europe.

Most of the powerful characters in this series were men, all of whom wore beards. This reflected the historical practice of Ottoman Turks, who typically wore beards as a tradition inspired by their imitation of Prophet Muhammad, who was known to have a beard. The powerful Ottoman male characters, who seem to have become role models for many younger Turkish men today, appear to have influenced the fashion of facial hair among these young men. Having facial hair was once seen as a symbol of religiosity and religious commitment, typically worn by middle-aged and older men, but now it has become a very noticeable popular trend among young men since the series began airing and has remained in fashion.

This particular role model hypothesis—that a TV series glorifying powerful Ottoman figures with beards has motivated young Turkish men to grow facial hair—is challenging to test scientifically. This is because such a study would require one group of Turks exposed to this TV series and another group with similar personal attributes, but not exposed. The preferences for facial hair could then be compared between the two groups before and after the airing of the series. However, it is difficult to find anyone who hasn't seen this widely popular show, and survey data to measure preferences for facial hair or the tendency for men to grow beards are not available in Turkey.

Growing beards to emulate historical figures who are considered as role models is harmless unless it aligns with undesirable shifts in men's attitudes, such as hypermasculinity, machismo, and increased aggression, including disrespect toward women. However, a recent study examined a similar exposure to a TV series in India and identified its influence on people's beliefs and preferences, with clear consequences shown.

A group of economists analyzed the impact of a TV series consisting of seventy-eight episodes, which was broadcast in 1987–1988 in India. The series was named *Ramayan*, after one of Hinduism's most revered religious texts. Written in Sanskrit, this epic describes the life of Ram, an avatar of the god Vishnu. As noted by the authors of the study, "India came to a standstill every Sunday morning [when the show was on air]. Streets emptied, shops closed, and families gathered around television sets, often sharing with neighbors. . . . Viewers often treated the broadcast as a religious event, adorning their TV sets with flowers and performing rituals before each episode (Mitra, 1993)."[41]

It has been argued that this religious TV series played a key role in standardizing and spreading a specific version of Hindu mythology across India's diverse population. Although various versions of this religious epic existed across different regions of India in multiple languages and dialects, this TV series established a unified narrative. That is, the series brought Hindus together in a shared experience, much like a congregation in a religious setting, where individuals participate in the same activity at the same time. It arguably created a sense of unity or collective participation in a religious practice.

The researchers of the study took advantage of random variations in TV signal quality across regions, related to differences in the topography. Areas that had higher exposure to the TV series *Ramayan*, due to the signal strength, developed a stronger religious identity. For example, Hindu parents became more likely to give their newborn sons common Hindu names, and lower-caste households increased their adherence to orthodox Hindu dietary practices, including a substantial rise in vegetarianism. Importantly, higher exposure to *Ramayan* lead to a short-term increase in Hindu-Muslim communal violence in the years following the series' conclusion. In addition, areas with greater exposure saw an increase in Hindi nationalism, with the Hindu nationalist Bharatiya Janata Party (BJP) having a higher probability of winning state assembly elections.

In summary, cultural beliefs and attitudes are malleable, and education and media are powerful tools for shaping culture. Education influences culture through several mechanisms: enhancing intelligence and driving biological changes in the brain that improve cognition; increasing earning power and the opportunities that come with it; and exposing individuals to diverse environments, such as new labor markets and social circles.

Media is also a powerful tool for shaping culture. Exposure to various forms of media, from TV series to podcasts, influences individuals' preferences and beliefs across many dimensions, including political views, fertility decisions, national and religious identity, and norms of personal conduct, including language use. Role models in the media have been shown to be particularly influential in shaping attitudes, preferences, and behaviors. The rise of social media "influencers" is a prime example of how perceived role models impact culture.

Of course, both education and the media can be used to shape beliefs and preferences in undesirable ways. The content of education plays a crucial role in shaping students' views, and the same applies to media, including social media. Studies have shown that curricula can be designed to strongly influence students' political views, serving as a tool for indoctrination toward harmful objectives. Similarly, negative behavioral changes can be induced by exposing individuals to harmful role models through media; these role models are imitated because they appear to embody success.

12 Conclusion

There are notable cultural differences between societies in terms of preferences, beliefs, and behaviors. These differences are revealed in a variety of forms. Language, for instance, serves as a marker of society's cultural traits. Its structure reveals aspects such as tendencies to avoid responsibility, respect for hierarchy, perspectives on the present versus the future, and the degree of connection speakers feel toward their in-group versus outsiders.

As an example, the nature of insults and curse words reflects the distinction between collectivist and individualistic attitudes in a society. Whether a typical insult is directed at the individual or their family reveals the relative emphasis placed on the individual identity versus the community. Similarly, the prevalence of common first names and the tradition of naming children after religious figures are indicators of collectivist values. The way people address each other in a society, particularly through the use of the second-person pronoun, offers insights into that society's social hierarchy.

A nation's folk stories also carry cultural symbolism and insights. A recent study examined oral folk stories and tales from hundreds of societies. Stories are classified into categories, such as those portraying men as dominant and women as submissive, whether protagonists succeed or fail in challenges, and how tricksters—characters who deceive others—are rewarded or punished. The study showed that the prevalence of certain character archetypes in stories predicts cultural attributes of societies. For instance, in societies where tricksters are successful in folk stories, there tends to be lower levels of trust among people. In societies where stories depict women as submissive and confined to domestic roles, women often hold subordinate societal positions in the present day.[1]

Cultural differences between societies are visible to a casual observer who travels around the world. One might notice, for instance, that in some countries the streets of major cities are named after scientists, writers, and artists, with their statues placed throughout the city, while cities in other countries may honor politicians, war heroes, and military or religious leaders through their street names and monuments.

The Panthéon in Paris is an impressive building, constructed as a grand church dedicated to Saint Genevieve, the patron saint of Paris. But after the French revolution, it was converted into a public mausoleum, where important French figures, mostly scientists, philosophers, artists, writers, and poets, are buried—including Voltaire, Marie Curie, Joseph Fourier, Victor Hugo, Émile Zola, Alexandre Dumas, and Jean-Jacques Rousseau. In contrast, in some countries, even the suggestion of converting a temple into another use, such as a school, can provoke accusations of blasphemy and lead to riots.

There are scientific ways to quantify many dimensions of cultural differences across societies. Culture encompasses a wide array of elements, such as how people in different societies think about the present versus the future, their general risk aversion or risk-taking tendencies, level of trust in others, intrinsic proclivity for dishonesty and cheating, willingness to work for pay versus enjoying leisure, inclination toward violence, proclivity for cousin marriage, tolerance of corruption, and others. These attributes can be measured using surveys contained in internationally comparable datasets, as demonstrated throughout the book.

Cultural characteristics play a significant role in explaining differences in individual well-being and variations in prosperity across societies. Although cultural traits are persistent over time, they are not immutable; they can be influenced and reshaped by various factors and incentives. Consequently, if a society finds itself in an unfavorable equilibrium—with undesirable cultural attributes and detrimental outcomes generated by these attributes—then an adjustment to transition toward a more favorable equilibrium would improve overall welfare.

In economics, *equilibrium* refers to a steady state where there is no tendency to deviate from the current outcome. The underlying forces or factors are in balance, so minor changes in these forces do not disrupt the outcome. A useful analogy is a small marble resting at the bottom of a bowl: Its position is determined by factors like its size, the bowl's shape and curvature, and the force of gravity. If given a small push, the marble will move but quickly return to its original position, restoring equilibrium.

The book has provided numerous examples of bad states of equilibria, where societies remain stuck in undesirable circumstances. Two aspects of this statement require clarification. First, when I mention what is *desirable* for a society, I am referring to factors that objectively promote human well-being, as determined through scientific criteria. In contrast, *undesirable circumstances* are those that detract from or harm human well-being. For example, good health is desirable, while illness is not. Wealth is preferable to poverty. Experiencing assault, torture, mutilation, or suffering from domestic violence are undesirable. Living in a violent environment is bad, whereas a physically safe environment is good. Freedom of thought and speech is desirable, whereas being punished for one's ideas or expressions is not. Rule of law is preferable to the law of the jungle.[2]

Second, although people may voluntarily choose or inherit certain beliefs and behavioral patterns, the widespread adoption of these beliefs and behaviors can create a bad equilibrium, resulting in society being trapped in an undesirable state. An example is the practice of open defecation in India, mentioned in chapter 2. Nobody forces people to defecate in the open; they choose to do so themselves. However, the situation is a representation of *being stuck in a bad equilibrium*. The society is *stuck* in this equilibrium as the prevalence of this harmful cultural practice has not changed appreciably over a very long period of time. And it is a *bad* equilibrium because scientific evidence shows that open defecation is detrimental to human well-being as it causes disease, stunting, and death in children, resulting in a terrible loss of human capital.

No sensible person can disagree that good health is preferable to disease, cleanliness to filth, physical safety to exposure to violence and torture. No reasonable person can deny that a society where honesty is the norm should be preferable to one where cheating and dishonesty are rampant. However, cultural differences between societies in terms of the prevalence of harmful attributes prevent some scholars from acknowledging the detrimental nature of these attributes. As surprising as this may sound, this perspective is the guiding principle of *cultural relativism*, propagated primarily by anthropologists since the 1950s. This view argues that each cultural practice should be evaluated within its own context and by the people who practice it. It has been claimed that no one has the right to judge the cultural beliefs and practices of another society, regardless of how much those practices seem to conflict with the viewpoints of outside evaluators.

A stunning example of this position is detailed by Sam Harris in his book *The Moral Landscape*. He recounts an exchange at a conference panel between himself and a scientist who subsequently has been appointed to the US President's Commission for the Study of Bioethical Issues. When the scientist argued that no one has the right to judge the cultural practices of another society, Harris posed the following scenario: "What if we found a culture that ritually blinded every third child by literally plucking out his or her eyes at birth, would you then agree that we have found a culture that was needlessly diminishing human well-being?" Her answer was: "It would depend on why they are doing it." Sam Harris continued—after slowly returning his eyebrows from the back of his head, as he described in the book: "Let's say they were doing it on the basis of religious superstition. In their scripture, God says, 'Every third must walk in darkness.'" Her response: "Then you could never say that they were wrong."[3]

The underlying reason for her astounding response could be the fear that acknowledging the harmful and undesirable nature of some cultural practices might lead to condescension toward the societies that practice them, and even to racism. There is a concern that comparing cultural practices across societies might result in labeling some societies as having poor cultural attributes and could be perceived as cultural imperialism by promoting "Western cultural practices" over others.

This cultural relativism argument is unconvincing, and it is counterproductive for human well-being. As demonstrated in this book, beneficial and detrimental cultural beliefs and practices are not confined to any one country, group of countries, or region of the world. There are harmful cultural attributes in some developed nations as well, with racism being a notable example. Identifying cultural beliefs and practices that are harmful to human well-being and prosperity is a fundamental responsibility of science. Based on evidence provided by rigorous scientific research, scientists must recommend methods and procedures to change these practices.

Female genital mutilation, discussed in chapter 3, is a violent cultural practice that is often performed without anesthetics. Its brutality is so severe that I was advised against describing its details in this book. Although the World Health Organization has declared female genital mutilation a human rights violation, some scholars and policymakers advocate the "cultural autonomy" of societies that practice it. Some even argue that efforts to eliminate this practice by those outside these societies might represent a form of "postcolonial imperialism."

The concern over offending communities that practice female genital mutilation has even prompted efforts to downplay its undeniable violence by using the term "cutting" instead of "mutilation." An interagency statement issued by multiple international organizations declared: "Some United Nations agencies use the term 'female genital mutilation/cutting' wherein the additional term 'cutting' is intended to reflect the importance of using non-judgemental terminology with practising communities," and "The preference for [the term cutting] was partly due to dissatisfaction with the negative association attached to the term 'mutilation,' and some evidence that the use of that word was estranging practising communities."[4]

Meanwhile, more than 230 million women worldwide are living with the consequences of this violent practice—and because female genital mutilation is often performed in unsanitary conditions, complications such as hemorrhage and infection result in more than forty-four thousand deaths annually.[5] This is one of the prime examples of a cultural practice that is detrimental to human well-being and should be abandoned. The notion that advocating for the elimination of this practice is a "moral judgment" about the countries where the practice is prevalent is both misguided and counterproductive.

It has also been argued that certain traditional beliefs and practices, despite appearing harmful to outsiders, must provide a benefit; otherwise, they would have been abandoned. This view, seemingly grounded in the concept of evolutionary adaptiveness, posits that the very existence of these practices implies that they have served a purpose throughout evolution, thereby justifying their ongoing presence.

Cultural evolution has been studied by evolutionary biologists through theoretical models and the interpretation of empirical patterns. They make the case of culture-gene coevolution and describe how individuals learn from one another, and how this learning can lead to adaptive behaviors that enhance survival and reproductive success, often referred to as *fitness* by biologists.[6] But these scholars also acknowledge the existence of cultural beliefs and behaviors that are maladaptive. Robert Boyd, a prominent scholar of human evolution, stated:

> There are many, many examples of maladaptive culturally transmitted traits. . . . Systems of folk medicine seem to contain a lot of useless or harmful nostrums. In many places disease and misfortune are attributed to the malicious actions of friends and neighbors, and such beliefs often lead to very costly actions. For example, among the Gebusi, a group living in the Fly River region of Papua New

> Guinea, all deaths are thought to be the result of sorcery. When someone dies, a homicide inquest is held, and in a substantial fraction of cases someone is found guilty and executed. . . . The list of plausibly maladaptive behaviors is long.[7]

The upshot is that the mere continuation of a cultural practice does not prove that it enhances human well-being. Furthermore, defenders of harmful cultural practices often neglect the concept of the *counterfactual*, a cornerstone of scientific analysis to determine causal effects. The counterfactual question here is, "What would have happened to the society engaging in a particular cultural practice if that society had not engaged in that practice?"

Although conducting counterfactual analyses in general are challenging because it is difficult to emulate the unobserved "what if" conditions, the answers are quite obvious when the "what if" counterfactual is applied to detrimental beliefs and practices. For instance, an acquaintance of mine, who is a medical doctor, recounted a case where a man was brought to the emergency room with a burst appendix, needing immediate surgery. However, the patient refused surgery or any medical treatment because he insisted that his astrological sign reading indicated a terrible outcome if he had any medical intervention that day. As any rational person would predict, he almost died from septic shock and had to be operated on under difficult conditions to save his life.

There is no need to conduct a scientific experiment to investigate whether a group of people who reject medical treatment due to superstitious beliefs will experience worse health outcomes compared to another group that has no such beliefs and follows the advice of medical science. We already know the counterfactual: The group adhering to medical science will have better health outcomes.

Imagine a society where individuals make daily decisions based on the guidance they believe the stars and planets provide. Similarly, picture a society where prayer or witchcraft is relied upon more than modern medicine for healing diseases. Consider also societies where young girls undergo genital mutilation as part of cultural traditions or where people defecate in the streets. As discussed in the book, we understand the origins of and initial reasons for these practices. However, their persistence over time and their continued use do not imply any current benefit. Rather, it suggests that these societies are trapped in a detrimental equilibrium, unable to move away from these practices. With the insights provided by twenty-first-century science, we can easily infer the counterfactual outcomes: Individual well-being would have improved had these societies abandoned such beliefs and practices.

As noted by scholars in various fields, research on nonhuman primates as well as analyses of small-scale societies indicate that throughout much of humans' evolutionary past, interactions beyond one's immediate community, and particularly beyond one's linguistic or ethnic groups, were often dangerous. Those who were outsiders of the group were mistrusted and viewed with suspicion. As discussed in chapter 7, evolutionary biology appears to have shaped the tendency to trust and prefer those who are familiar while treating "others" less favorably. However, even though evolutionary biology and primitive economic transactions may have created the conditions to favor those who are kin or part of the in-group, such as the local community and the tribe, the evolution of this attribute has been dramatically different across societies. More specifically, there are significant differences between countries in their degree of individualistic versus collectivist tendencies and in the level of trust they place in their in-group (e.g., family, neighbors, those of the same religion) compared to outsiders. Related to this, there are also substantial differences in ethics and morality. Some societies treat others by the same standards with which they treat in-group members, whereas other societies provide favoritism and preferential treatment to those who are part of the in-group. Consequently, the extent of nepotism and corruption as well as the concept of fairness differ between societies.

At first glance, moral differences across societies may not appear to have substantial impacts on individual well-being or economic outcomes. For instance, what harm comes from a strong preference for the in-group over the out-group in a community? What's wrong with hiring my less-qualified nephew over a more capable candidate simply because he belongs to my in-group, while the other candidate is a stranger? After all, isn't one person's loss another's gain, balancing out in the end?

Arguments like these fail to recognize the broader societal consequences of in-group favoritism. Modern economic systems rely heavily on cooperation among individuals who are not related to each other. Consequently, favoring one's in-group at the expense of others creates significant barriers to economic development. Nepotism and in-group favoritism lead to misallocation of talent and resources in the economy. Widespread in-group favoritism encourages discrimination and stifles competition. These factors also hinder economic growth by limiting innovation and investment in human capital. It has been shown, for instance, that 40 percent of the productivity growth in the US between 1960 and 2010 is attributable to a better allocation of talent across occupations. This was driven by a decrease in discrimination against Black people and women, changes in cultural norms that previously discouraged these people from working in high-skill occupations, and an increase in educational attainment, which is also partly due to changes in norms.[8]

Also, applying different moral and ethical standards to different groups results in unwarranted disparities in economic and social outcomes. As a result, preferential treatment of in-group members, particularly in education, criminal justice, and the legal systems, fosters resentment and social discord. Moreover, by constraining people's ability to extend empathy to everyone equally, in-group favoritism deepens social inequalities. A simple example is politicians and civil servants providing preferential treatment for those who belong to their in-group and depriving others of services that they need and are entitled to.

Tribalism and loyalty-based favoritism can impose substantial costs on society in other ways as well. For instance, in some countries, wholesale dismissal of government employees after the election of a new government and the installation of loyalists in their place results in substantial loss of expertise. And appointment of unqualified individuals to critical roles in the government because they are in-group members undermines institutional quality and effectiveness.

Is there any downside to corruption, cheating, and dishonesty being a cultural norm in society? What is wrong about bribing a police officer to avoid a traffic ticket? Isn't it true that this transaction involves only two parties, and if it is voluntary, then both parties benefit? I save twenty dollars by paying a thirty-dollar bribe instead of a fifty-dollar fine, and the officer receives thirty dollars in the process. Some analysts have actually made this type of argument, suggesting that corruption can "grease the wheels" of the economy. The general idea is that bribery may help offset the inefficiencies of bad governance, bureaucratic red tape, and slow administrative processes. Furthermore, some have argued that bribing government workers and public officials serves as an informal fee, supplementing their low salaries while providing people a more efficient way to access government services.

However, numerous studies over the past three decades have consistently shown that corruption undermines public trust, stifles entrepreneurship, and negatively affects a country's economic development. In addition, corruption directly affects people's well-being. In societies where corruption is widespread, public officials responsible for enforcing health and safety regulations can pose significant risks to public health. For instance, research has shown that in such societies, inspectors often accept bribes and ignore emission violations, leading to severe pollution and serious public health consequences.[9]

Corruption can also result in death and widespread devastation, such as excessive loss of life and destruction caused by natural disasters in nations with high levels of corruption. Earthquakes have a significantly greater impact in such countries. It has been calculated that between 1980 and 2010, 83 percent of all deaths from building collapses during earthquakes occurred in highly corrupt nations.[10] In these countries, earthquakes claim thousands of lives, whereas an earthquake of the same magnitude in a nation with low level of corruption may result in no casualties at all. Earthquake-related deaths are, of course, influenced by a country's level of economic development: Wealthier nations have greater resources for emergency response and rescue services as well as high-quality medical care. However, the primary issue is not deaths caused by poor disaster management after an earthquake, but rather the collapse of buildings constructed through corrupt practices.[11]

Corruption, as a cultural trait, tends to be persistent. But, as discussed in chapter 10, there are mechanisms to deter corruption and illicit activities, which can pave the way to change the culture of corruption. Achieving this change, however, requires a concerted and deliberate effort from both political and social leaders.

There are many other examples, some of which are tongue-in-cheek observations about cultural differences between societies. A prominent Turkish novelist, Aziz Nesin, once attributed the underdevelopment of Islamic countries to Muslims' avoidance of eating pork. He humorously argued that the resulting protein deficiency caused lower cognitive development, which led to social, political, and economic debacles. Of course, protein can be obtained from many other sources, and this argument doesn't explain the relative success of Jewish communities, who not only avoid pork but also follow a much more restricted diet compared to Muslims. However, our concern isn't with dietary differences between societies. We are not worried about who eats pork, who does not eat shellfish, and who considers monkey brain a delicacy. What we are primarily concerned about are the systematic and persistent acts, as well as the beliefs and preferences that lead to these acts, that are unequivocally harmful to human well-being. For example, killing people based on the belief that they are witches is a harmful cultural practice wherever it occurs. Violence against women also reduces welfare.

Corruption, criminal behavior, and dishonesty are similarly detrimental to human prosperity.

Although some cultural differences between societies do impact economic well-being, they are difficult to change, and therefore it can reasonably be argued that there is little reason to focus on those attributes regardless of their impact on economic success. An example is time preference. As discussed in chapter 3, individuals who are more patient and value future rewards more than immediate gratification tend to be more successful. Countries where people are more future oriented have higher education levels, invest more, and are healthier and wealthier. However, it is difficult to alter time preferences (although there is evidence that education is one means through which people become more future oriented).

Culture is transmitted vertically across generations. It is also transmitted horizontally via interactions between individuals or groups, through socialization processes that lead to imitation and learning, as described in some economic models of cultural transmission and models in evolutionary biology that emphasize gene-culture coevolution. One of the key points of these models is that cultural change can take place because individuals are influenced by their environment and that people react to changes in that environment.

Consistent with this insight, research has shown that media is a powerful tool to influence culture. Educational and entertainment programs can shape individuals' preferences, as people are influenced by what they see on screens, whether it's characters in soap operas or prominent figures on social media. As discussed in chapter 11, numerous scientific studies have demonstrated how exposure to TV programming can affect a wide range of preferences and behaviors, including religiosity, political views, fertility, and divorce. Media role models can significantly alter preferences and behaviors because they project images of success in areas crucial for survival and well-being, such as dating, wealth accumulation, and access to power. The impact of role models on behavior is further evident in the rise of the "influencer" occupation, which explicitly focuses on influencing and changing the preferences of those exposed to their actions and ideas.

The influence of the media has long been recognized by politicians, with authoritarian regimes using it not only to control the information flow, but also to shape preferences. Similarly, the actions and speeches of social leaders, such as politicians, TV commentators, and opinion writers, play a crucial role in shaping cultural attitudes, preferences, behaviors, and even the use of language. This aspect of cultural change will become quite important with extended influence of social media and artificial intelligence–created algorithms that can easily create new cultural beliefs and attitudes and propagate their transmission in society.

At the beginning of this chapter, I mentioned how the language of a society reflects certain attributes of that society. However, as explored in chapter 7, language not only reflects culture but also can shape it. The way language is used by role models and influential individuals in society can influence not just everyday language usage but also behavioral norms. For example, when politicians, TV personalities, and social media influencers use crude language, profanities, and slang, it can normalize this type of language, leading to a shift in cultural communication and behavior styles.

Similarly, the complexity of language can be altered, either intentionally or unintentionally. In his 1949 novel *Nineteen Eighty-Four*, George Orwell portrays a society where the rulers create a new form of language with a limited vocabulary, aimed at restricting freedom of thought and preventing dissent. The simplification of language, or the creation of words with vague or no meaning, can undermine both communication and the sophistication of society. With a restricted vocabulary, engaging in meaningful debates and exchanging ideas becomes more challenging. Moreover, as explored in detail in chapter 7, research has shown that language and cognition are intertwined. The structure of a language shapes how its users think, process information, and perceive concepts, which in turn can influence cultural preferences, beliefs, and behaviors.

The persistence of cultural attributes on the one hand and their responsiveness to a variety of influences on the other is not a contradiction. Both these properties coexist, and whether culture remains unchanged or shifts depends on the strength of the forces driving change. Describing both these effects, in the year 1900, Mark Twain wrote:

> The outside influences are always pouring in upon us, and we are always obeying their orders and accepting their verdicts. . . . Morals, religion, politics, get their following from surrounding influences and atmospheres, almost entirely; not from study, not from thinking. . . . . . Mohammedans are Mohammedans because they are born and reared among that sect, not because they have thought it out and can furnish sound reasons for being Mohammedans; we know why Catholics are Catholics; why Presbyterians are Presbyterians; why Baptists are Baptists; why

> Mormons are Mormons; why thieves are thieves; why monarchists re monarchists; why Republicans are Republicans and Democrats are Democrats. We know it is a matter of association and sympathy, not reasoning and examination; that hardly a man in the world has an opinion upon morals, politics, or religion which he got otherwise than through his associations and sympathies.[12]

The "outside influences" mentioned in Mark Twain's passage can take various forms, as explored in the book, ranging from the media to peers and social networks. Education is a particularly significant one. Education can alter culture through several mechanisms. For instance, it has been demonstrated that education increases cognition. This effect works through two channels. As discussed in chapter 11, *crystallized intelligence*, as it is called by psychologists, rises as individuals accumulate more factual knowledge, such as history, geography, or other learned information. Education also enhances fluid intelligence, which is linked to abstract thinking, analytical ability, memory, and executive functions such as planning, reasoning, ignoring irrelevant information, and problem-solving.

When individuals acquire a new skill and challenge their brain by processing new information—such as learning mathematics or a new language—the regions of the brain responsible for these tasks expand in gray matter volume. Importantly, other areas of the brain also grow in gray matter and cortical thickness. These anatomical changes enhance abstract thinking, problem-solving, cognitive flexibility, and adaptability to new or complex situations. So education strengthens both crystallized and fluid intelligence, improving overall cognitive abilities. This means that societies with higher levels of education will, on average, demonstrate greater cognitive capacity.

Imagine a society where education and learning are deeply valued as cultural attributes. In this society, individuals pursue formal education for many years, acquiring new skills while continuously challenging their brains. They learn foreign languages and develop lifelong habits of reading and learning. Contrast this with another society where a lack of education is seen as a virtue. Here, schooling ends after only a few years, people do not learn any language beyond their own, and their reading is limited to a single book they consider sacred. Neuroscience research indicates that the average level of cognition will be higher in the former society. This means that the former society will likely be more creative, innovative, and productive, achieving higher economic growth. Moreover, enhanced analytical and critical-thinking skills will positively impact individual well-being across various domains, including health and overall quality of life.

Education also indirectly impacts culture by increasing individuals' productivity, thereby altering the opportunities and constraints they face. Additional years of education result in higher wages, which affect people's likelihood of participating in the labor market. This participation, in turn, influences preferences and behaviors for several reasons. For example, being part of the labor market often exposes individuals to a broader range of ideas and perspectives. It can also enhance women's financial independence and autonomy, shifting the balance of bargaining power within households between men and women.

As discussed in chapter 11, even an additional two to three years of education can alter people's preferences. This effect is particularly evident among women, for whom more schooling leads to decisions that better align with their own well-being. When education reforms increase the mandatory years of schooling, women with a few extra years of education are significantly less likely to approve of the practice of cousin marriage, less likely to marry a blood relative, and less likely to view domestic abuse by a spouse as acceptable. This aspect of education is understood by certain "culturally conservative" politicians and religious figures in some developing nations, who therefore oppose women's education, advocating for the early marriage of girls instead of schooling.

The substance of education is also important. The content of the school curriculum has been shown to influence both cognitive ability and students' beliefs, including political views. This means that a society's cultural values and preferences, ranging from religiosity to attitudes toward "others," can be shaped by both the amount and the content of education.

Vladimir Lenin is often quoted as saying, "Give me four years to teach the children, and the seed I have sown will never be uprooted." In the early 1920s, the average number of years of education in Russia was fewer than two, making Lenin's goal of indoctrinating children for four years a substantial time commitment. In today's context, this is a relatively short period of time for successful indoctrination, especially considering the influence of social media and other external sources that can shape children's beliefs and values outside of the classroom. However, as revealed by the evidence discussed in chapter 11, the impact of high school curricula on students' beliefs and attitudes is well established. Therefore, children's exposure to a specific curriculum during primary and secondary education, aimed at altering cultural beliefs and preferences, would be effective. This tool of cultural change can, of course, also be exploited for destructive purposes. For instance, indoctrinating students in schools with harmful beliefs, even ridiculous ones, such as the notion that their society is the one favored by their deity among all societies on the planet or that "certain other people" are less valuable as human beings, would likely be effective in shaping and transforming their beliefs.

Evidence of politicians' conviction that this is a successful strategy for cultural change can be seen globally in some governments' efforts to implement curriculum reforms that reflect their political and religious ideologies. In the US, the ongoing debates over the content of science textbooks in high schools and the types of books allowed in public libraries further illustrate the belief in the power of education to shape culture.

Institutional change is another avenue for fostering cultural transformation, with legal institutions playing a crucial role. Detrimental behaviors such as cheating, corruption, and other illicit acts are contagious, as discussed in chapter 10. Thus, increasing sanctions, along with effective law enforcement and efficient legal institutions, is critical for incentivizing individuals to change these behaviors and steer society toward a more desirable cultural equilibrium. Because people calibrate their beliefs and behaviors based on what they observe in their environment, sanctions are effective in creating spillovers in behavioral change. Chapter 10 provides scientific evidence of the impact of legal sanctions.

However, as highlighted in various chapters of the book, the efficacy of institutions is influenced by cultural attributes—and cultural tendencies may lead individuals to resist changes initiated by institutional reforms. As mentioned by Bisin and Verdier, Niccolo Machiavelli wrote in 1531, "This was a good institutional order when citizens were good . . . but when citizens became bad the system turned into a horrible order."[13] The example in chapter 6 about the failure of reforms in Indian hospitals demonstrates that institutional change cannot be effective without considering the interplay between culture and institutions. Therefore, the credibility of institutional reform and the commitment of political leaders to these reforms are essential for generating permanent behavioral change.

In summary, cultural differences have emerged and persisted for various reasons, including historical events, ecological factors, and economic conditions. Some beliefs are deliberately created to serve specific purposes. Cultural beliefs and practices have a direct impact on human welfare, either promoting or undermining individual well-being. Most cultural attributes influence the prosperity of a society, both directly and indirectly. But, as mentioned in chapter 1, this book's goal is not to label societies as having "good" or "bad" cultures. Instead, I have attempted to describe cultural beliefs and behaviors, examining their origins and their impact on human well-being and prosperity. Although discussing cultural change has often been taboo in academic circles, I believe it's crucial to address various policy tools that can promote a pathway to such change.

Acknowledgements

I would like to express my sincere thanks to the team at the MIT Press for their enthusiasm and support throughout this project. Executive Editor Catherine Woods, Senior Editor Kathleen Caruso, and copyeditor Melinda Rankin were exemplary in their efficiency, professionalism, and attention to detail. I am grateful to former Acquisitions Editor Emily Taber, who encouraged me to write this book. The reviewers for the MIT Press provided insightful comments and suggestions. I also thank Thao Bui for her valuable research assistance. Nur Orak provided exceptional research support throughout the writing of this book.

Notes

Chapter 1

1. Although I imply here that the grading scale was from 0 to 100, it was actually from 0 to 10 in Turkey, where 10 was the highest grade. The standard grading scale is from 10 to 0 in German, with 0 being the highest and 10 being the lowest grade.

2. I remember my surprise when I experienced this during a two-week visit to Germany at age fifteen.

3. Haerpfer et al., "World Values Survey Trend File"; and EVS, "EVS Trend File 1981–2017."

4. Arrow, "Gifts and Exchanges," 357.

5. Guiso et al., "Cultural Biases in Economic Exchange."

6. These fifteen countries were Austria, Belgium, the UK, Denmark, Netherlands, Finland, France, Germany, Greece, Ireland, Italy, Norway, Portugal, Spain, and Sweden.

7. Germans trust Germans the most, followed by the Swedes and Austrians. Those who are least trusted by Germans are Italians, Portuguese, and Greeks. Italians trust Swedes more than they trust themselves; and they trust Portuguese and the Irish the least. Greeks trust Greeks the most, followed by French and Spanish. Greeks trust Austrians the least, followed by Italians and the citizens of the UK. These differences in bilateral trust are impacted by a number of factors, such as differences in religion and the extent of historical wars and conflict between countries.

8. See Guiso et al., "Trusting the Stock Market"; Bottazzi et al., "Importance of Trust for Investment"; Aghion et al., "Regulation and Distrust"; Zak and Knack, "Trust and Growth"; and Algan and Cahuc, "Inherited Trust and Growth."

9. OECD, "Average Annual Hours Actually Worked."

10. Imagine that for each hour of work you earn twenty dollars, and you pay 20 percent of that wage as income tax and retain the remaining sixteen dollars. Now

assume that your boss asks you to work overtime hours on the weekend, for which you would get paid twenty-five dollars per hour for the extra work—but suppose the tax rate for such overtime income is 40 percent. This means that out of each twenty-five dollars earned, you would pay ten dollars in tax and keep fifteen dollars. In this case, the incentive to work would be diminished in comparison to the situation where the tax rate is lower because the reward for the work goes down when the tax rate goes up.

11. As I discuss later in this chapter, economic policy decisions such as the amount of support provided to unemployed workers, the tax rates, the level of the minimum wage, and other economic policy variables do not vary randomly between countries. Rather, they also reflect certain attributes of societies.

12. Let Y represent total production, H stand for total hours worked in the economy, and N be the total number of workers. The equation $Y = (Y/H) \times (H/N) \times NY$ breaks the total output down into three components. The first term on the right-hand side, (Y/H), represents average worker productivity. The second term, (H/N), indicates the average hours worked per worker, and N is the total number of workers in the economy. It could be argued that when workers work fewer hours, their productivity might increase during the hours when they do work. In other words, working fewer hours might lead to higher productivity per hour. Consequently, total output may not suffer from reduced working hours because each hour of work would produce more output. In other words, in the preceding equation, when (H/N) goes down, it will raise (Y/H); as a result, Y would remain about the same.

Although this is possible in theory, it does not hold in practice. For instance, worker productivity in the US is higher than in Italy, France, and Sweden, even though US workers work significantly longer hours. In other words, the US has a larger total output Y because both (Y/H) and (H/N) are higher. (One reason for this is higher capital intensity and better technology in production.)

13. Mocan, "Taxes and Culture of Leisure."

14. Behaviors may be considered to belong to a different category than beliefs, values, and preferences. This is because behaviors are shaped by beliefs, preferences, and values, but they are also influenced by socioeconomic variables and constraints. For example, labor force participation of women is a behavior that is impacted by values and beliefs about women's role in society. In a country where a cultural belief restricts women from working outside of the home, female labor force participation will be low in comparison to another country where cultural attitudes do not put restrictions on women's work. As a behavior, however, labor force participation is also impacted by economic factors, such as the wage rates women can receive in the labor market. To tease out the cultural component, therefore, one would filter out the impact of wages on labor force participation by using statistical methods. So values, beliefs, and preferences are more direct ways of gauging culture, but the advantage of

relying on behaviors is that they are readily observed. Throughout this book, I will attribute behavioral differences between groups to culture only when these groups face similar socioeconomic variables and constraints related to the behavior.

15. Bisin and Verdier, "Economics of Cultural Transmission and Socialization."

16. Boyd and Richerson, *Origin and Evolution of Cultures.*

17. North, *Institutions, Institutional Change and Economic Performance*, 3.

18. North and Weingast, "Constitutions and Commitment."

19. The work of Daron Acemoglu, James Robinson, and Simon Johnson, which was recognized with a Nobel Prize, suggests that the key driver of a nation's sustained economic growth is the nature of its institutions. Specifically, it emphasizes the distinction between *inclusive institutions*, which promote innovation and the active participation of a broad segment of society in economic and political decision-making, and *extractive institutions*, which concentrate power and resources in the hands of a few.

20. In Belgium, unemployed individuals are eligible to receive 80 percent of the income they earned before job loss as unemployment benefits. After five years of unemployment, they are still eligible to receive sixth percent of their previous income. In the US, the typical unemployment benefit is around half of the unemployed person's last salary (not to exceed about $1,800 per month), and it only lasts for a maximum of twenty-six weeks in an average state.

21. Agüero and Beleche, "Health Shocks."

22. United Nations Children's Fund and World Health Organization, *State of the World's Hand Hygiene*, 37.

23. De Kraker et al., "Implementation of Hand Hygiene."

24. World Health Organization and WHO Patient Safety, *WHO Guidelines on Hand Hygiene*, 79–80.

25. Kuran, "Behavioral Norms."

26. Glock and Stark, *Religion and Society in Tension.*

27. Greif and Iyigun, "Social Organizations, Violence, and Modern Growth"; Greif et al., "Social Organizations, Risk-Sharing Institutions, and Economic Development."

Chapter 2

1. Shiller et al., "Popular Attitudes Toward Free Markets."

2. In fact, if these individuals swap places, everyone else would probably spend a bit less time in line, because the person who is in a hurry and who is willing to pay ten

dollars to swap places with the first customer has only one item to pay for, and she most likely would check out very quickly. In other words, the amount of time that would have been spent during checkout is the same or shorter for all other customers who were not involved in the transaction.

3. In the same survey, survey respondents in Moscow were asked, "Do you think that those who try to make a lot of money will often turn out to be not very honest people?" Almost 60 percent of the respondents in Moscow agreed with that statement, whereas less than 40 percent of Americans agreed with it.

4. Oosterbeek et al., "Cultural Differences in Ultimatum Game Experiments."

5. There is also substantial evidence that the propensity to punish free riders, in situations where cooperation enhances social benefits, varies across societies. For example, see Herrmann et al., "Antisocial Punishment Across Societies."

6. Mocan et al., "Quality of Judicial Institutions, Crimes, Misdemeanors, and Dishonesty."

7. Of course, illegal behavior depends, in part, on the economic circumstances of individuals, such as their income, wealth, and employment status. Enhanced probability of apprehension faced by potential lawbreakers and the severity of punishment serve as deterrents to criminal proclivity. In other words, differences between countries in their economic conditions as well as in the intensity of law enforcement can explain some, but not all, of the differences in criminal activity between them.

8. Mocan, "What Determines Corruption?"

9. Cohn et al., "Civic Honesty Around the Globe."

10. This definition is from Hofstede et al., *Cultures and Organizations*, 92.

11. Hofstede worked for the IBM corporation, and he surveyed IBM employees around the globe to study differences in corporate environment between countries. He created measures that gauge various attributes of IBM employees; these employees were uniform in many ways as they all worked for IBM, had the same level of education, and did the same type of work. Hofstede created indices that measured key attributes, one of which is individualism. The index of country individualism, as well as other indices of Hofstede, have been validated by other researchers and have been widely used.

12. See Gorodnichenko and Roland, "Which Dimensions of Culture Matter for Long-Run Growth?"; Alesina and Giuliano, "Power of the Family"; Gorodnichenko and Roland, "Culture, Institutions and Democratization"; and Gorodnichenko and Roland, "Culture, Institutions, and the Wealth of Nations."

13. Labor force participation rates for men in these countries are much less dispersed, ranging from 70 to 90 percent. World Bank Open Data, "Labor Force Participation Rate, Male"; and World Bank Open Data, Labor Force Participation Rate, Female."

14. Hamamy et al., "Consanguineous Marriages, Pearls and Perils."

15. The question, due to its wording, focuses on domestic violence among married heterosexual couples.

16. Haerpfer et al., "World Values Survey: Round Seven."

17. Roos, "Human Sacrifice."

18. United Nations, *Sustainable Development Goals Report 2017*; Coffey et al., "Open Defecation."

19. Lakshminarayanan and Jayalakshymy, "Diarrheal Diseases Among Children in India"; and World Bank Open Data, "Mortality Rate, Under-5."

20. Children are identified as *stunted* if their height-for-age is more than two standard deviations below the World Health Organization's Child Growth Standards median.

21. B. S. and Guddattu, "Understanding the Change in the Prevalence"; Gupta and Santhya, "Proximal and Contextual Correlates."

22. Ramanan Laxminarayan, a vice president of Public Health Foundation of India, stated that "India's stunting problem represents the largest loss of human potential in any country in history, and it affects 20 times more people in India alone than H.I.V./AIDS does around the world." See Harris, "Poor Sanitation in India."

23. Subramanyam et al., "Socioeconomic Inequalities in Childhood Undernutrition."

In India, the infant mortality rate is significantly lower among minority Muslims in comparison to Hindus, although Muslims are poorer and have less education and less access to government services. But Indian Muslims are much less likely to defecate in the open, and the sanitation environment is different between Muslim and Hindu neighborhoods. See Geruso and Spears, "Neighborhood Sanitation and Infant Mortality."

Similarly, open defecation rates are lower in most Asian and African countries, even though they are poorer compared to India. See Coffey and Spears, *Where India Goes*, 10.

24. In comparison, the population density is sixty-six people per square kilometer in Mexico. It is 107/km^2 in Turkey, 148/km^2 in China, 240/km^2 in Germany, 347/km^2 in Japan, 529/km^2 in South Korea, and 1,264/km^2 in Bangladesh.

Mahatma Gandhi recognized this problem when he reportedly wrote the following in 1925: "The cause of many of our diseases is the condition of our lavatories and our bad habit of disposing of excreta anywhere and everywhere." See Harris, "Poor Sanitation in India."

25. Coffey et al., "Open Defecation."

26. Dinnoo, "Millions of Indians Defecate in the Open."

27. Harris, "Poor Sanitation in India."

28. Mocan and Yu, "Self-Fulfilling Prophecy."

29. Kuo and Li, "Year of the Dragon Baby Boom."

30. Bastian, *Die Deutsche Expedition an der Loango-Küste*, quoted in Sumner, *Folkways*, 24.

31. Tuchman and Levine, "New York Jews and Chinese Food."

32. Malinowski, *Magic, Science and Religion*, as cited in Nunn and Sanchez de la Sierra, "Why Being Wrong Can Be Right."

33. Guiso et al., "Does Culture Affect Economic Outcomes?"

34. Nunn and Sanchez de la Sierra, "Why Being Wrong Can Be Right."

35. Sinding Bentzen, "Acts of God?"

36. Sinding Bentzen, "In Crisis, We Pray"; and Sahgal and Connaughton, "More Americans Say COVID-19 Has Strengthened Religious Faith."

37. Cesur et al., "War, Traumatic Health Shocks, and Religiosity."

Chapter 3

1. World Bank Open Data, "Labor Force Participation Rate, Male."

2. World Bank Open Data, "Labor Force Participation Rate, Female."

3. Harmon et al., "Returns to Education: Microeconomics"; Montenegro and Patrinos, "Comparable Estimates of Returns to Schooling."

4. Barro-Lee Dataset, "Education Attainment."

5. That women acquire much more education in these particular Muslim-majority countries compared to other Islamic countries can be attributed to the Soviet regime's emphasis on education. Because they were part of the Soviet Union for about seven decades, these countries experienced a regime that—despite its failures in many dimensions, ranging from economics to human rights—arguably played a key role in cultivating a lasting legacy of high female education in these nations.

6. Although women's labor force participation rates evolve gradually over several decades, they don't experience abrupt and drastic fluctuations. For instance, it is unlikely to see a sudden drop in the labor force participation rate—say, from 50 percent to 20 percent within a span of two years—followed by a rapid rebound—such as to 40 percent within a year. As a result, variations in female labor force participation rates among different countries tend to remain relatively stable over time.

7. In other words, this regularity exists among countries that adhere to the same religion, be it Catholicism, Protestantism, Islam, or East Asian religions. As an example,

Turkey and Tunisia are both countries where the majority of the population is Muslim. In Tunisia, 65 percent of the population believes that men should have priority over women in having jobs, and fewer than one-third of Tunisian women work outside the home. In Turkey, the proportion of people who think that men should have job priority is 52 percent, which is lower than the rate in Tunisia. Consequently, a higher proportion of Turkish women, at 40 percent, participate in the labor market compared to Tunisian women.

8. Of course, there is not a perfect inverse relationship between these two rates around the world. For example, in Puerto Rico, the support for the idea that men should have job priority over women is very low: Only 10 percent of the population agrees that men should have job priority. But female labor force participation is still not very high in Puerto Rico, where less than half of working-age women participate in the labor market. In Japan, female labor force participation is quite high (73 percent of Japanese women participate in the labor force), but the agreement with the idea that men should have priority in employment is not very low: More than a quarter of the Japanese population agree with the suggestion that men should have job priority.

9. Alesina et al., "On the Origins of Gender Roles."

10. Boserup, *Women's Role in Economic Development.*

11. Alesina et al., "On the Origins of Gender Roles."

12. Fredriksson and Gupta, "Irrigation and Gender Roles."

13. Becker, "Crime and Punishment."

14. Examples of this research include the following: Helland and Tabarrok, "Does Three Strikes Deter?"; Levitt, "Juvenile Crime and Punishment"; Drago et al., "Deterrent Effects of Prison"; Corman and Mocan, "Time-Series Analysis of Crime"; Di Tella and Schargrodsky, "Do Police Reduce Crime?"; Draca et al., "Panic on the Streets of London"; Weisburd, "Police Presence"; Raphael and Winter-Ebmer, "Identifying the Effect of Unemployment"; Corman and Mocan, "Carrots, Sticks, and Broken Windows"; and Mocan and Unel, "Skill-Biased Technological Change."

15. World Bank Open Data, "Intentional Homicides."

16. Hackney, "Southern Violence"; and Lottier, "Distribution of Criminal Offenses."

17. The southern states, based on the classification of the US Census, are Alabama, Arkansas, Delaware, Florida, Georgia, Kentucky, Mississippi, North Carolina, Tennessee, Texas, Virginia, West Virginia, Louisiana, Maryland, Oklahoma, and South Carolina.

18. Author's own calculations using data from FBI, "Crime/Law Enforcement Stats."

19. Gastil, "Homicide and a Regional Culture of Violence."

20. Nisbett and Cohen, *Culture of Honor.*

21. For a detailed and colorful depiction of this history, see chapter 1 of *Honor Bound* by Ryan Brown.

22. Grosjean, "History of Violence."

23. Schell et al., *State-Level Estimates of Household Firearm Ownership*.

24. Cao et al., "Herding, Warfare, and a Culture of Honor."

25. This is a standard statistical problem in the same vein as detecting a positive relationship between ambient air temperature and ice cream sales: Although air temperature and ice cream sales are positively correlated and go hand in hand, this does not mean that an increase in ice cream consumption generates a rise in air temperature. Rather, the causality runs from temperature to ice cream sales, where a change in temperature results in a change in ice cream sales.

26. Cao et al., "Herding, Warfare, and a Culture of Honor."

27. Nisbett and Cohen, *Culture of Honor*, 5.

28. Goldschmidt, "Introduction: The Theory of Cultural Adaptation," 6.

29. These differences were identified using a variety of methods. One procedure was to show hand-drawn pictures to respondents to elicit their responses to what is happening in the picture and what should happen. These pictures included such scenes as cattle damaging a farmer's maize field, a woman passing by a man hiding behind a bush, a man watching what could be construed as a sexual act, and so on. One of these pictures depicts a scene in which a number of spear-waving warriors are rushing toward some cattle being protected by three small boys. The respondents were asked what they think the outcome of this situation would be. Potential answers were "The enemy will steal the cattle and escape," "The enemy will be repulsed, or pursued and killed," "Don't know," or no answer. About 125 people from each tribe evaluated this picture. In each tribe, the proportion that indicated that the enemy will steal the cattle and escape was larger among the farmers, and the proportion that indicated that the enemy will be repulsed or pursued and killed was larger among the pastoralists.

30. Edgerton, *Individual in Cultural Adaptation*, 280.

31. Buss, *Dangerous Passion*; Buss et al., "Sex Differences in Jealousy"; and Platek and Shackelford, "Introduction to Anti-Cuckoldry Tactics."

32. See Becker, "Origins of Restricting Women's Promiscuity," and the literature she cites therein.

33. UN Women, "FAQs on Female Genital Mutilation"; and United Nations Population Fund, "Female Genital Mutilation."

34. UNICEF, "Female Genital Mutilation (FGM)."

35. Mackie, "Ending Footbinding and Infibulation."

36. Becker, "Origins of Restricting Women's Promiscuity."

Chapter 4

1. Akyol and Mocan, "Education and Consanguineous Marriage."

2. See https://www.pewresearch.org/religion/2022/08/23/sidebar-sex-ratios-around-the-world/.

3. Almond and Edlund, "Son-Biased Sex Ratios."

4. Almond et al., "Son Preference and the Persistence of Culture."

5. Blau et al., "Son Preference in the United States."

6. Khera et al., "Gender Bias in Child Care."

7. Jayachandran and Kuziemko, "Mothers Breastfeed Girls Less than Boys"; Ramakrishnan et al., "Gender Differences in Surgery"; and Jayachandran, "Ten Facts About Son Preference."

8. United Nations Population Fund, *State of World Population 2020.*

9. Alesina et al., "Traditional Agricultural Practices."

10. Carranza, "Soil Endowments."

11. Grosjean and Khattar, "It's Raining Men!"

12. In Charles Darwin's book *The Descent of Man, and Selection in Relation to Sex*, the male-female sex ratio plays an important role in the discussion of sexual selection. Darwin theorizes that differences in the numbers of males and females can influence mating competition.

13. Baranov et al., "Men."

14. Teso, "Long-Term Effect of Demographic Shocks."

15. For example, see Falk et al., "Global Evidence on Economic Preferences."

16. Of course, the time span of the "future" is important too. If you know that you have a genetic disease that increases your chances of dying to 50 percent before you reach the age of forty, you will discount the future more heavily.

17. See Chabris et al., "Individual Laboratory-Measured Discount Rates"; Kirby et al., "Heroin Addicts Have Higher Discount Rates"; Ashraf et al., "Tying Odysseus to the Mast"; Meier and Sprenger, "Present-Biased Preferences"; Figlio et al., "Long-Term Orientation"; Golsteyn et al., "Adolescent Time Preferences"; and Hanushek et al., "Patience, Risk-Taking, and Human Capital."

18. Burro et al., "Patience Decreases with Age."

19. Sunde et al., "Patience and Comparative Development."

20. Sutter et al., "Language Group Differences."

21. Martín et al., "Appropriate Response of Spanish Gitanos."

22. This does not imply that both Romani and non-Romani Spaniards face identical economic and institutional constraints. It is possible, for example, that Romani people face discrimination in the labor market that would adversely impact their job prospects and wages. However, this does not change the central point, which is that different groups of people exhibit different time preferences that are common within the group, regardless of the particular reasons. In fact, historical discrimination could be a reason for the development of short-term orientation as a cultural attribute. A related example will be given in chapter 5, in which exposure of Black Americans to violence and its effect on cultural behavior is discussed.

23. Rosati et al., "Evolutionary Origins of Human Patience."

24. Stevens et al., "Ecology and Evolution of Patience."

25. Aiello and Wheeler, "Expensive-Tissue Hypothesis"; Fish and Lockwood, "Dietary Constraints on Encephalization in Primates."

26. Galor and Ozak, "Agricultural Origins of Time Preference."

27. The *ancestral crops* of a geographical location are those that can grow naturally without extensive human intervention, such as irrigation.

28. Fouka and Schlapfer, "Agricultural Returns to Labour."

29. Talhelm et al., "Large-Scale Psychological Differences."

30. That wheat farming is not labor-intensive does not imply that wheat farming is not difficult. Consider a one-acre field of tall grass and weed. The grass can be cut using a hand-pushed manual mower with one person pushing it, or the same job can be done by three people working side by side, each with a sickle. The former scenario represents a production technology that is less labor-intensive than the latter one, but it does not imply that the person in that production spends less effort. In fact, in this example, pushing the hand mower through a field of tall grass and weed may be more difficult than cutting the grass with a sickle.

31. Talhelm et al., "Large-Scale Psychological Differences."

32. Ang, "Agricultural Legacy and Individualistic Culture."

33. The research considered the historical attributes of countries that may be related to both their historical farming environment and their collectivist tendencies. For example, they considered the length of the time the country existed as a nation, the

historical affluence and population density of the society, its religious composition, the legal tradition, and the prevalence of the disease environment, just to name a few.

34. Twenge et al., "Fitting in or Standing Out"; and Schonberg and Murphy, "Relationship Between Name and Personality."

35. Bazzi et al., "Frontier Culture"; and Varnum and Kitayama, "What's in a Name?"

36. Some immigrants in the US change their first names to common American names. This may partly be a practical decision to make their names easier for the average American to pronounce, but it can also signal a desire to integrate into the new community. Former Louisiana Governor Bobby Jindal, born Piyush Jindal to Indian parents, changed his name to Bobby as a child. It is impossible to know whether his political career would have been as successful if he had kept his original name, Piyush.

37. Martin Fiszbein et al., "Agrarian Origins."

Chapter 5

1. For a nontechnical paper on this view, see Sachs et al., "Geography of Poverty and Wealth."

2. Diamond, *Guns, Germs, and Steel.*

3. To the south of this region lies the Arabian Peninsula, which suffers from arid and sandy soil and high temperatures, but it contains valuable natural resources, including some of the world's largest petroleum reserves.

4. An analogy from medicine can be presented for a similar idea. Medical science has determined that smoking is a serious risk factor for heart disease and that smokers are more likely to have heart attacks. An observation such as, "My uncle has smoked a pack of cigarettes for his entire life, but never had any heart disease" is not evidence for falsification of the claim that smoking causes heart disease. There are other factors, ranging from genetics to food diet, that also influence heart disease. The relative importance of these factors for a given person and the interplay between them may reduce the risk of heart attack despite heavy smoking, but this does not prove that smoking is unrelated to heart disease.

5. United States Census Bureau, "Historical Reported Voting Rates."

6. United States Census Bureau, "New Educational Attainment Data."

7. Guzman and Kollar, "Income in the United States: 2022."

8. There is a current debate about whether some states are deliberately attempting to restrict voter registration of Black Americans by raising eligibility standards, such as strict voter ID laws. However, the point made in this section precedes these recent developments in voter registration.

9. See Williams, "Historical Lynchings," and the references cited therein.

10. Dickerson, *Reconstruction Era.*

11. Garrow, *Protest at Selma.*

12. These six states are Alabama, Florida, Georgia, Louisiana, North Carolina, and South Carolina.

13. Greenberg et al., "Intergenerational Transmission of Occupation."

14. Dal Bó et al., "Political Dynasties"; Querubin, "Family and Politics"; Lindquist et al., "Entrepreneurial Parents"; and Dunn and Holtz-Eakin, "Financial Capital."

15. Leeds and Rockoff, "Jim Crow in the Saddle."

16. Teo, "Kentucky Derby's Forgotten Black Past"; Walker, "Black Jockeys"; Menderski, "Trailblazing Black Jockeys."

17. As discussed in Leeds and Rockoff, "Jim Crow in the Saddle."

18. The data are obtained from Leeds and Rockoff, "Jim Crow in the Saddle."

19. Nunn and Wantchekon, "Slave Trade and Mistrust in Africa"; and Charles Piot, "Of Slaves and the Gift."

20. Miguel et al., "Civil War Exposure and Violence."

21. Couttenier et al., "Violent Legacy of Conflict."

22. Aleshka et al., "Crimean Tatars."

23. During the deportation, a large number of Tatar soldiers of the Russian Red Army were actually fighting Germans at the front line. When the war ended, they too were treated as Nazi collaborators, and nine thousand Tatar veterans were sent to Eastern Asia to meet their deported families, as described in Williams, *Crimean Tatars.*

24. In 1992, the Crimean Parliament declared the autonomy of Crimea within Ukraine. In 1996, Ukraine adopted a new constitution, which granted Crimea some self-governance rights while maintaining its status as part of Ukraine.

25. Lupu and Peisakhin, "Legacy of Political Violence."

Chapter 6

1. Becker et al., "Empire Is Dead."

2. Ingrao, *Habsburg Monarchy, 1618–1815.*

3. Sieghart, *Die Letzten Jahrzehnte Einer Großmacht,* as cited in Becker et al., "Empire Is Dead."

4. İnalcık, *Ottomon Empire*; Imber, *Ottomon Empire, 1300–1650.*

5. Becker et al., "Empire Is Dead."

6. Corneo and Grüner, "Individual Preferences for Political Redistribution."

7. Although East Germans were no different from West Germans when Germany was divided into two countries at the end of World War II, there were some differences between the East and the West. The population living in the areas that subsequently came under the jurisdiction of East Germany had a higher proportion of Protestants in comparison to West Germany. The share of workers in the manufacturing sector was higher and the share in agriculture lower in the East before World War II (see Becker et al., "Separation and Reunification of Germany"). Therefore, the manufacturing base was stronger in the East—but the Soviets dismantled East Germany's industrial plants and moved them to other Soviet Union countries. This, and a variety of other reasons related to the operation of the communist economic system, created a significant divergence in economic performance between East and West Germany. By the time East Germany collapsed, the per capita income in West Germany was twice the per capita income in East Germany. Because people who are less affluent benefit more from government redistribution and social welfare programs, they are more likely to favor the government's involvement in different areas of social security. Hence, when comparing the perspectives of individuals who experienced life under the East or West German regimes, it is imperative to consider disparities in their income levels, which is recognized by researchers.

8. Alesina and Fuchs-Schündeln, "Good-bye Lenin (or Not?)."

9. The wedge between East and West Germans in the strength of pro-government preferences was biggest among those born before 1945. This is because East Germans who were born before 1945 lived most of their lives under the communist regime. Those who were born in East Germany between 1945 and 1960 also have stronger pro-government preferences compared to West Germans born during the same period, but the difference is smaller as this cohort of East Germans experienced communism for only thirty to forty-five years. Finally, those born in East Germany after 1960 experienced communism for a maximum of thirty years. This group of East Germans also prefers government redistribution more strongly in comparison to their West German counterparts who are the same age, but the difference between East and West is smaller in this cohort because their exposure to communism was shorter.

10. Mocan et al., "Quality of Judicial Institutions."

11. Gachter and Schulz, "Intrinsic Honesty."

12. Bau, "Can Policy Change Culture?"

13. The lack of government protection for landowners' property rights, allowing individuals to occupy private property, is a prime example of dysfunctional institutions.

14. Di Tella et al., "Formation of Beliefs."

15. These were not the first instances of anti-Jewish violence. The earliest recorded pogroms occurred in 1096 in the Rhineland (modern-day Germany), when crusaders, on their way to the Middle East during the First Crusade, launched brutal attacks on Jewish communities.

16. Becker and Pascali, "Religion, Division of Labor, and Conflict."

17. See the press release about their work on the Nobel Prize website: https://www.nobelprize.org/prizes/economic-sciences/2024/press-release/.

18. McCloskey, "Max U Versus Humanomics." 10.

19. Acemoglu and Robinson, *Why Nations Fail*, 449–450.

20. McCloskey, "Max U Versus Humanomics."

21. Much like the acceptability of driving a vehicle after a few drinks during and after important football games and during Mardi Gras in some Southern states.

22. Acemoglu and Robinson, *Why Nations Fail*, 79–80.

23. Acemoglu and Robinson, *Why Nations Fail*, 83.

24. World Bank Group, "World Bank in DRC."

25. It is difficult to pin down the source of this sentiment. As highlighted in this book, countries differ in their hierarchical orientation, deference to power, and collectivist tendencies, all of which can impact people's attitudes regarding their individual rights and power in relation to those in a position of authority.

26. Benabou and Ok, "Social Mobility."

27. John Steinbeck, "America and Americans," *Saturday Evening Post*, July 2, 1966, as cited in Alesina, Stantcheva, and Teso, "Intergenerational Mobility and Preferences for Redistribution."

28. Alesina and La Ferrara, "Preferences for Redistribution"; and Alesina et al., "Intergenerational Mobility."

29. Greif, "Cultural Beliefs and the Organization of Society."

30. Greif, "Cultural Beliefs and the Organization of Society," 922–923.

Chapter 7

1. Hofstede et al., *Cultures and Organizations*.

2. Kashima and Kashima, "Culture and Language."

3. Licht et al., "Culture Rules."

4. Semin and Rubini, "Person by Verbal Abuse."

5. Davis and Abdurazokzoda, "Language, Culture and Institutions."

6. Coffey and Spears, *Where India Goes*, 54.

7. One exception is when someone threatens to cause physical harm to the president. In such cases, the language used may be subject to investigation in order to assess its credibility and determine the level of danger the speaker poses to the president.

8. Licht et al., "Culture Rules."

9. Gorodnichenko and Roland, "Which Dimensions of Culture Matter." Economic research has also shown that individuals whose ethnicities are associated with more individualistic cultures are more likely to work in research-oriented occupations within the same country. This suggests that a cultural heritage that puts emphasis on individualism may lead to a greater inclination for scientific inquiry, compared to a collectivist cultural heritage. See Gorodnichenko and Roland, "Culture, Institutions, and the Wealth of Nations."

10. Burro et al., "Patience Decreases with Age."

11. Chen, "Effect of Language on Economic Behavior."

12. In German, *Ich werde das machen* can also be used to say, "I will do that." That formulation is more formal and stricter. It is similar to "I will do," as it emphasizes the future.

13. Chen, "Effect of Language on Economic Behavior."

14. Keenan, "Norm-Makers, Norm-Breakers."

15. Keenan, "Norm-Makers, Norm-Breakers."

16. This point, which is relevant not only for Turkish but also some other languages, such as Spanish, is also highlighted by cognitive scientist Lera Boroditsky.

17. Fausey and Boroditsky, "Who Dunnit?", 150.

18. Fausey and Boroditsky, "Who Dunnit?"

19. Fausey et al., "Constructing Agency."

20. Pinker, *Language Instinct*; and Chomsky, *Logical Structure of Linguistic Theory*.

21. MacLaury, "From Brightness to Hue"; and Marian, *Power of Language*, 48.

22. Reinforcing this conclusion, when researchers distorted the subjects' ability to use language by making them repeat numbers during the experiment, the

discrepancy in the speed with which Russian and English speakers identified colors was eliminated. Winawer et al., "Effects of Language on Color Discrimination."

23. Boroditsky and Schmidt, "Sex, Syntax, and Semantics."

24. Boysen and Berntson, "Responses to Quantity"; Boysen et al., "Quantity-Based Inference."

25. Marian, *Power of Language*, 50.

26. As in many languages, Chinese Mandarin uses spatial terms that describe horizontal time movements (*good times are ahead of us*; *the worst is behind us*; etc.). But Mandarin speakers also frequently use vertical metaphors to talk about time and to order events over time. Earlier events are labeled as *up* (*shàng*), and later events are labeled as *down* (*xià*). For example, "Cat goes up the tree" is *māo shàng shu* in Mandarin, where *shang* means up. "Last month" is *shàng gè yuè*, where *shang* stands for *last* (or *previous*). "Cat goes down the tree" is *māo xià shu*, where *xia* means *down*. "Next month" is *xià gè yuè*, where *xia* stands for *next*. This means that in Mandarin, time flows from up to down. Now, lift your left arm until it is horizontal to the ground and make a fist with your left hand. Imagine that the location of your left fist in the air represents the lunch time. Show with your right hand where breakfast is and where dinner is in comparison to the lunch time. If you are an English speaker, you will most likely indicate that breakfast, which comes before lunch, is below your fist, and that dinner is above your fist. But if you are a Mandarin speaker, you will denote that the location of breakfast is above your fist, and that dinner is below your fist. This is because in the structure of the Mandarin language, time flows vertically from up to down. Boroditsky, "Does Language Shape Thought?"

27. Li et al., "Neuroplasticity as a Function of Second Language Learning."

28. Lee and Kim, "Bilingualism and Creative Potential"; Leikin and Tovli, "Bilingualism and Creativity"; Ricciardelli, "Creativity and Bilingualism"; and Van Dijk et al., "Bilingualism and Creativity."

29. Adi-Japha et al., "Cognitive Flexibility"; Costa et al., "Bilingualism Aids Conflict Resolution"; Bialystok et al., "Bilingualism as a Protection"; Alladi et al., "Bilingualism Delays Age"; and Grant et al., "Cognitive Control."

30. Diamond, "Executive Functions."

31. Diamond, "Executive Functions," 136.

32. De Cat et al., "Identifying a Threshold"; Bialystok, "Bilingual Adaptation"; Bialystok et al., "Bilingualism, Aging, and Cognitive Control"; and Barac et al., "Young Dual Language Learners."

Although some researchers have questioned the existence of a bilingual advantage in executive function (e.g., Paap et al., "Bilingual Advantages Dependent upon Specific Tasks"; and Paap et al., "Bilingual Advantages in Executive Functioning"), compelling counterarguments have been presented, and numerous studies have validated these findings (e.g., Bak, "Impact of Bilingualism"; Bak, "Beyond a Simple 'Yes' and 'No'"; Grundy, "Effects of Bilingualism on Executive Functions"; and Bialystok, *Where Language Meets Thought*).

33. Calvo and Bialystok, "Independent Effects of Bilingualism"; Kovács and Mehler, "Cognitive Gains"; Blom et al., "Benefits of Being Bilingual"; Brito and Barr, "Influence of Bilingualism"; and Barac et al., "Young Dual Language Learners."

34. Della Rosa et al., "Neural Interactive Location"; Martensson et al., "Growth of Language-Related Brain Areas"; and Mechelli et al., "Structural Plasticity in the Bilingual Brain."

35. Federico et al., "Cortical Thickness Mediates Technical-Reasoning Skills."

36. Yuan et al., "Fluid Intelligence"; Burzynska et al., "Cortical Thickness Linked to Executive Functioning"; Colom et al., "Gray Matter Correlates"; and Choi et al., "Multiple Bases of Human Intelligence."

37. Hopkins et al., "More Intelligent Chimpanzees"; and Mulholland et al., "Age- and Cognition-Related Differences."

38. Pliatsikas et al., "Effect of Bilingualism on Brain Development"; DeLuca et al., "Linguistic Immersion"; Klein et al., "Language Learning Shapes Brain Structure"; Li et al., "Neuroplasticity as a Function of Second Language Learning."

39. Anthropologist Joseph Henrich, who studies culture and human evolution, argues that WEIRD societies are psychologically different from others. He states:

> Literacy changes people's biology and psychology without altering the underlying genetic code. A society in which 95 percent of adults are highly literate would have, on average, thicker corpus callosa and worse facial recognition than a society in which only 5 percent of people are highly literate. These biological differences between population will emerge even if the two groups were genetically indistinguishable. Literacy thus provides an example of how culture can change people biologically independent of gene differences. Culture can and does alter our brains, hormones, and anatomy, along with our perceptions, motivations, personalities, emotions, and many other aspects of our minds. (*WEIRDest People in the World*, 7)

40. Lawn, "Tu and Twitter."

41. Another example is the impact of the 1960s youth movement on the use of second-person pronouns in terms of politeness in Europe, particularly in Scandinavian countries. The movement's emphasis on equality and breaking down social barriers led young people to use the "familiar you" instead of the "polite you," reducing the usage of the latter, although not eliminating it entirely.

42. Boroditsky and Gaby, "Remembrances of Times East."

43. Orwell, *Nineteen Eighty-Four*, 389.

Chapter 8

1. Parks, *Italian Ways*, 8.

2. McCloskey, "Max U Versus Humanomics."

3. Haidt and Joseph, "Intuitive Ethics"; and Graham et al., "Moral Foundations Theory."

4. De Waal, *Good Natured*.

5. Bielen et al., "Racial Bias and In-Group Bias"; Mocan and Osborne-Christenson, "In-Group Favoritism and Peer Effects"; Shayo and Zussman, "Judicial Ingroup Bias"; and Bar and Zussman, "Identity and Bias."

6. See Kelly et al., "Three-Month-Olds, but Not Newborns, Prefer Own-Race Faces"; Kelly et al., "Cross-Race Preferences"; Bar-Haim et al., "Nature and Nurture"; and Mahajan and Wynn, "Origins of 'Us' Versus 'Them.'" See also Dunham et al., "'Minimal' Group Affiliations in Children," and the literature they cite therein.

7. Bloom, *Just Babies*, 108.

8. See Tajfel et al., "Social Categorization and Intergroup Behaviour," and Sherif et al., *Intergroup Conflict and Cooperation*, for the origin of social identity theory, which emerged following early experiments in minimal grouping.

9. Jordan et al., "Development of In-Group Favoritism."

10. Billig and Tajfel, "Social Categorization and Similarity"; Mullen et al., "Ingroup Bias as a Function of Salience"; Tajfel et al., "Social Categorization and Intergroup Behaviour"; Bernhard et al., "Group Affiliation and Altruistic Norm Enforcement"; Goette et al., "Impact of Group Membership"; and Chen and Li, "Group Identity and Social Preferences."

11. Banfield, *Moral Basis*.

12. Haerpfer et al., "World Values Survey: Round Seven"; and EVS, "European Values Study 2017."

13. Each individual's average response to these questions can take the value of 0, 1/3, 2/3, or 1. Averaging everybody's response in the same country would provide a value ranging from 0 to 1, which can be rescaled to range from 0 to 100.

14. Luttmer, "Group Loyalty."

15. Cappelen et al., "Universalism." These researchers also analyzed whether the responses changed when the questions included language underlining morals: "If you were to do what you think is *morally right*, how much of the $1,000 would you give you to [Person 1], if the rest goes to [Person 2]." Respondents made very similar allocation decisions when they were asked just to allocate the money as they did

when they were asked to do "what is morally correct" when allocating the money. This means that altruism, measured by how people allocate money between different individuals, is a reflection of the differences in people's understanding of what is morally right.

16. D'Acunto et al., "How Costly Are Cultural Biases?"

17. A key and innovative aspect of the study is its next phase, which involves evaluating loan applications using an algorithmic robo-advising tool. This tool provides an independent recommendation for each application regarding whether it should be approved or rejected, and the results are then shared with loan officers. It has been observed that loan officers tend to accept the tool's approval recommendations for out-group applicants they had initially rejected, rather than overriding them. This suggests that cultural biases against out-group members, such as distrust and reluctance to engage in economic transactions, are associated with economic costs—but also that these biases may be mitigated if the potential economic losses from such biases are made visible to decisionmakers.

18. Herrmann et al., "Antisocial Punishment Across Societies."

19. World Bank DataBank, "World Development Indicators (Rule of Law)."

20. Country-level per-capita income data is from World Bank DataBank, "World Development Indicators (GNI per Capita)."

21. Le Rossignol and Lowes, "Ancestral Livelihoods."

22. Moscona et al., "Keeping It in the Family."

Chapter 9

1. In a study in this genre, researchers examined young Australians, aged sixteen to twenty-five, and their parents. More than three thousand parent-offspring pairs were surveyed to assess their levels of patience and risk tolerance. The survey included questions about individuals' willingness to take financial risks and their time horizon for saving and spending. The analyses revealed that risk-averse parents are more likely to have risk-averse children. In addition, children's levels of patience are influenced by their parents' patience. Although sons are equally impacted by both parents, daughters are more likely to be influenced by their mothers. Brown and Van der Pol, "Intergenerational Transfer."

Another study was conducted using a sample of more than 3,750 German parent-child pairs, with children averaging twenty-five years old. The study measured the willingness to take risks in various domains, including financial matters, career, health, and sports and leisure. It also gauged individuals' propensity to trust others through questions about whether one can trust people and whether it's better to be cautious before trusting strangers. The findings indicated that both mothers' and fathers' willingness to take risks significantly influence their children's willingness to take risks. Similarly, parents' trust in others is shown to have a strong impact on their children's inclination to trust others. Dohmen et al., "Intergenerational Transmission of Risk."

2. Hjalmarsson and Lindquist, "Origins of Intergenerational Associations."

3. Björklund et al., "Origins of Intergenerational Associations."

4. Luttmer and Singhal, "Culture, Context, and Taste for Redistribution."

5. Mocan, "Taxes and Culture of Leisure."

6. Giavazzi et al., "Culture."

7. Gershman, "Witchcraft Beliefs."

8. Gershman, "Witchcraft Beliefs."

9. These countries are Argentina, Bolivia, Brazil, Colombia, Costa Rica, Dominican Republic, Ecuador, El Salvador, Guatemala, Honduras, Mexico, Nicaragua, Panama, Paraguay, Peru, Uruguay, and Venezuela.

10. Gershman, "Witchcraft Beliefs."

11. Davidson et al., "Power of Dragon Babies."

12. Mocan and Yu, "Self-Fulfilling Prophecy."

13. Voigtländer and Voth, "Persecution Perpetuated."

14. Mocan and Raschke, "Economic Well-Being."

15. Barlow et al., "Contact Caveat."

16. Dhont and Van Hiel, "Intergroup Contact Buffers."

17. Carrell et al., "Impact of College Diversity."

18. Dahl et al., "Does Integration Change Gender Attitudes?"

19. Rao. "Familiarity Does Not Breed Contempt."

20. Students participated in a "dictator game" in the lab, in which they were randomly paired. One student in each pair, designated as the "dictator," was given ten rupees and asked to decide how to split it with the other player. The second player, the recipient, had no input and had to accept whatever the dictator chose to give. Although the players remained anonymous, the dictators were shown photographs and the name of the recipient's school, clearly indicating whether it was an elite private school catering to wealthy children or a school serving poor children.

21. Marble et al., "Exposure to Celebrities."

22. Mohamed Salah songs that Liverpool fans sing in stadiums, pubs, and at various other gatherings can be found on YouTube. Examples include the following:

https://www.youtube.com/watch?v=5L4V2rD19SE&list=RD5L4V2rD19SE&start_radio=1
https://www.youtube.com/watch?v=b-icmPutQDk
https://www.youtube.com/watch?v=angfhBLxcvw
https://www.youtube.com/shorts/9TqeW302HZU
https://www.youtube.com/watch?v=5Ct6R-pnTUw
https://www.youtube.com/watch?v=1IK6dIcb2gc

23. Schindler and Westcott, "Shocking Racial Attitudes."

24. Schindler and Westcott, "Shocking Racial Attitudes," 495.

25. *BBC News*, "Tanzania Arrests 23."

26. Müller and Sanderson, "Witch Hunts."

27. Migiro, "Tanzania's 'Witches' Fight for Land."

28. UNICEF, *Addressing Witchcraft in Tanzania.*

29. Amnesty International, "Rights of Women Accused of Witchcraft."

30. This documentary can be accessed via paid media. A follow-up documentary, titled *Return to Africa's Witch Children* can be found on Youtube: https://www.youtube.com/watch?v=5Y06sKAg9Do&t=684s.

31. Oppenheimer, "Nigerian Witch-Hunter Explains Herself."

32. Horowitz, "Persecution of Witches."

33. Miguel, "Poverty and Witch Killing," 1156.

34. Van Cott, "Legal Pluralism in Bolivia and Colombia," 222.

35. Miguel, "Poverty and Witch Killing."

36. Mocan and Raschke, "Economic Well-Being."

37. Falk et al., "Unemployment and Extremist Crime."

38. Anderson et al., "Downturns Fuel Racial Animus."

39. Bray et al., "Welfare Cuts and Hate Crime."

40. Goldin and Katz, "Power of the Pill."

41. National Center for Education Statistics, "Table 318.10."

42. See Joyce and Mocan, "Impact of Legalized Abortion," for the effect of *Roe v. Wade* on teenage births in New York City.

43. Fernández et al., "Mothers and Sons."

44. De V. Cavalcanti and Tavares, "'Engines of Liberation.'"

45. Dinkelman, "Effects of Rural Electrification."

46. As cited in Greenwood et al., "Engines of Liberation."

Chapter 10

1. Innes and Mitra, "Is Dishonesty Contagious?"; and Vives et al., "Following Your Group."

2. Corbacho et al., "Corruption as a Self-Fulfilling Prophecy."

3. Carrell et al., "Peer Effects in Academic Cheating."

4. Ajzenman, "Power of Example."

5. Gulino and Masera, "Contagious Dishonesty."

6. Mazar et al., "Dishonesty of Honest People."

7. Cialdini et al., "Focus Theory of Normative Conduct."

8. Bicchieri and Xiao, "Do the Right Thing."

9. Bicchieri, *Norms in the Wild*"; and Bicchieri and Xiao, "Do the Right Thing."

10. Fisman and Miguel, "Corruption, Norms, and Legal Enforcement."

11. Country-level corruption is measured using well-established and validated metrics created by other researchers or independent institutions, such as Transparency International, and based on assessments by country experts, investors, and various surveys.

12. Fisman and Miguel, "Corruption, Norms, and Legal Enforcement," 1036.

13. Examples include Owens, "More Time, Less Crime?"; Buonanno and Raphael, "Incarceration and Incapacitation"; and Barbarino and Mastrobuoni, "Incapacitation Effect of Incarceration."

14. Vollaard, "Preventing Crime"; Helland and Tabarrok, "Does Three Strikes Deter?"; Kessler and Levitt, "Using Sentence Enhancements"; Levitt, "Juvenile Crime and Punishment"; and Drago et al., "Deterrent Effects of Prison."

15. Hansen, "Punishment and Deterrence."

16. Dušek and Traxler, "Learning from Law Enforcement."

17. Corman and Mocan, "Time-Series Analysis of Crime."

18. For Buenos Aires, see Di Tella and Schargrodsky, "Do Police Reduce Crime?" For London, see Klick and Tabarrok, "Using Terror Alert Levels"; and Draca et al., "Panic

on the Streets." For Philadelphia, see MacDonald et al., "Effect of Private Police." For Dallas, see Weisburd, "Police Presence." For a nationwide study, see Mello, "More COPS, Less Crime."

19. Vollaard and van Soest, "Punishment to Promote Prosocial Behavior."

20. Rincke and Traxler, "Enforcement Spillovers."

21. Huttunen et al., "Punishing Financial Crimes."

22. A family consisting of two parents and three children was categorized as *extremely poor* if their monthly family income was 300 Brazilian real (approximately $120 based on the exchange rate at that time). Such families would receive a government transfer of 120 real if all their children complied with the school attendance policy.

23. Brollo et al., "Learning Spillovers."

24. Castro and Scartascini, "Tax Compliance and Enforcement."

25. Bratton, "Broken Windows," 1–2.

26. Corman and Mocan, "Carrots, Sticks, and Broken Windows."

27. Keizer et al., "Spreading of Disorder."

28. Keizer et al., "Spreading of Disorder."

29. Keuschnigg and Wolbring, "Disorder, Social Capital, and Norm Violation"; Keizer et al., "Importance of Demonstratively Restoring Order"; and Berger and Hevenstone, "Norm Enforcement in the City."

30. Sunstein, "Expressive Function of Law."

31. Benabou and Tirole, "Laws and Norms," 2.

32. Funk, "Expressive Function of Law."

33. Tankard and Paluck, "Effect of a Supreme Court Decision."

34. Rukundo, "Witch-Killings and the Law."

35. Statement during *The State v. Shingirai Hamunakwad* (2015) (HH 323-15 CRB No. 58/15) [2015] ZWHHC 323, as cited in Rukundo, "Witch-Killings and the Law."

36. Ajzenman et al., "More Than Words."

37. Bassi and Rasul, "Persuasion."

Chapter 11

1. Other parts of gray matter consist of *dendrites* (branches that receive messages from other cells), *unmyelinated axons* (nerve fibers without a protective covering),

glial cells (support cells that help maintain the brain's environment), and tiny blood vessels (which supply nutrients and oxygen).

2. Maguire et al., "Navigation-Related Structural Change."

3. Draganski et al., "Changes in Grey Matter."

4. The neuroplasticity of the brain in response to learning juggling has been confirmed by another study, in which jugglers were given seven scans over four months to investigate potential changes in their brain anatomy. Supporting the finding of the original study, the results demonstrated that jugglers' hMT/V5 region of the brain increased in size when they practiced juggling, and the gain was lost when juggling exercise stopped. Researchers also detected a significant increase in gray matter volume in the frontal and temporal lobes and in the cingulate cortex. These regions are involved in various critical brain functions. The frontal lobe is responsible for executive functions such as planning, decision-making, problem-solving, working memory, and impulse control. The temporal lobe primarily handles auditory processing, including interpreting sound and speech. The cingulate cortex contributes to executive functions, emotional regulation, and the integration of cognitive and emotional responses. Driemeyer et al., "Changes in Gray Matter."

5. Hervais-Adelman et al., "Cortical Thickness Increases"; Jacini et al., "Can Exercise Shape Your Brain?"; and Bezzola et al., "Training-Induced Neural Plasticity."

6. Cattell, *Intelligence*; and Deary and Caryl, "Neuroscience and Human Intelligence Differences."

7. Yao et al., "Sulcal Depth in Prefrontal Cortex"; Kuhl et al., "Early Cortical Surface Plasticity"; Tadayon et al., "Differential Contribution of Cortical Thickness"; Chen et al., "Fluid Intelligence Associated with Cortical Volume"; Cox et al., "Structural Brain Imaging Correlates"; Yuan et al., "Fluid Intelligence in Older Adults"; Basten et al., "Smart Brains Are Different"; and Karama et al., "Cortical Thickness Correlates."

8. See NCD Risk Factor Collaboration (NCD-RisC), "Century of Trends in Height," and the articles cited therein.

9. Cesur and Mocan, "Education, Religion, and Voter Preference."

10. When the survey used in the study was administrated, the Islamic political parties in Turkey were the Justice and Development Party (AKP), the Felicity Party (SP), and the People's Voice Party (HAS).

11. Hungerman, "Effect of Education on Religion."

12. Becker et al., "Education and Religious Participation."

13. Mocan and Pogorelova, "Compulsory Schooling Laws." The countries in the study are Austria, Belgium, Denmark, France, Germany, Greece, Hungary, Ireland,

Italy, Poland, Portugal, Spain, Sweden, and the United Kingdom; different regions of the United Kingdom and Germany implemented changes in different years.

14. However, this does not mean that every highly educated person will be non-religious, or that all less-educated people will be religious. As discussed earlier in the book, such findings reflect average effects. This is similar to scientific studies showing that smoking is a major risk factor for heart attacks, which does not imply that all smokers will have heart attacks, nor does it mean that nonsmokers have no heart attack risk, as other factors also contribute to heart disease. The same applies to education: While it is a major determinant of religiosity, it is not the only one.

15. This corresponds to an inbreeding coefficient (*F*), which is equal to 0.0156 or higher. This, in turn, signifies that parental couples share 1/32 of their genes inherited from common ancestors and that their offspring has a probability of 1/64 (or 0.0156) of having identical gene copies of all loci, inherited from both parents. In cases of first cousin marriage, *F* goes up 0.0625, and in case of uncle-niece marriages, practiced in South India, *F* becomes 0.125. Hamamy, "Consanguineous Marriages."

16. Hamamy et al., "Consanguineous Marriages, Pearls and Perils." See the global consanguinity website at https://consang.net for detailed information on the variation in consanguinity rates within countries.

17. The prevalence of this cultural practice, partially shaped by economic factors, has evolved over time in response to changing institutional constraints. For example, evidence suggests that the Catholic Church's restrictions on cousin marriage contributed to the breakdown of kin-based networks in Europe, facilitating the rise of democratic political institutions; see Schulz, "Kin Networks and Institutional Development." In addition, these regulations, which encouraged the formation of smaller nuclear families, have been linked to the development of a distinct psychological profile that influenced behavior and paved the way for strong economic growth. See de la Croix et al., "Clans, Guilds, and Markets."

18. De la Croix et al., "Clans, Guilds, and Markets"; and Schulz, "Kin Networks and Institutional Development."

19. Akyol and Mocan. "Education and Consanguineous Marriage."

20. Mocan and Orak. "Education and Preferences."

21. This effect of education was stronger among Catholic women. Although it is not obvious why this is the case, Catholicism has a highly structured hierarchy, with the pope at the top, followed by cardinals, archbishops, bishops, priests, and other clergy. The church's authority and traditional biblical interpretations are central to its teachings. Compared to Protestantism and Judaism, Catholicism's centralized doctrine and organized structure are more strict. Therefore, this fading may suggest that education shifts preferences toward independence and individualism, moving

away from obedience, hierarchy, and collectivism in societies with more rigid, hierarchical cultural frameworks.

22. Cannonier and Mocan, "Impact of Education."

23. Rose and Betts, "Effect of High School Courses"; Brown et al., "Financial Education"; and Urban et al., "Effects of High School Policies."

24. Cantoni et al., "Curriculum and Ideology."

25. Ang, "Birth of a Nation."

26. Ang, "Birth of a Nation," 1458.

27. Wang, "Media, Pulpit, and Populist Persuasion," 3069.

28. Warren, *Radio Priest.*

29. DellaVigna and Kaplan, "Fox News Effect."

30. As cited in Enikolopov et al., "Media and Political Persuasion."

31. Morgenroth et al., "Motivational Theory of Role Modeling," 4, as cited in Porter and Serra, "Gender Differences in Choice of Major."

32. Porter and Serra, "Gender Differences in Choice of Major."

33. Riley, "Role Models in Movies."

34. IMDb, "Queen of Katwe."

35. IMDb, "Queen of Katwe."

36. La Ferrara, "Mass Media and Social Change."

37. La Ferrara et al., "Soap Operas and Fertility."

38. Chong and La Ferrara, "Television and Divorce."

39. Jensen and Oster, "Power of TV," 1062.

40. Jensen and Oster, "Power of TV."

41. Ahmed et al., "Ancient Epics in the Television Age."

Chapter 12

1. Michalopoulos and Xue, "Folklore."

2. A typical naive reaction to these statements is to object to some of the listed items being definitively good or bad. For example, objections to the notion that "being wealthy is better than being poor" often include arguments such as "Income is not everything; per capita national income is not a good indicator of national

well-being; there are plenty of poor societies where people are happy with their lives; high income creates negative outcomes such as environmental pollution," and so on. Although each of these objections may have merit, they are peripheral issues and do not negate the reality that being rich is better than being poor. The objection to the statement "being wealthy is no better than being poor" is so unconvincing that it hardly warrants discussion.

Although no sensible person can defend poverty as a desirable state of humankind, it is not uncommon to observe in some societies a cultural tendency to almost encourage poverty. This is often done in the form of articulating the supposed spiritual benefits of poverty and convincing the poor that their state of poverty is a blessing rather than an undesirable situation. Religious arguments are made that support fatalism and that argue that poverty will be rewarded in the afterlife, whereas being rich will have disadvantages.

Lionel Sosa, for instance, has famously argued that glorification of poverty as a means to enter Heaven in Catholicism is a key factor that has kept Mexican Americans, who are predominantly Catholic, from being economically successful in America. A Turkish cleric, who is also a TV personality, has lectured that being poor is preferable to being rich because poor individuals will enter heaven five hundred years before the rich. (Of course, given the notion that afterlife in heaven will last forever, even if that claim were true, then entering heaven five hundred years before someone else is akin to being entitled to an additional grain of sand on a sandy beach that runs forever. Nevertheless, the sheer fact that he made such a statement suggests that there is a market for this type of rhetoric.)

3. Harris, *Moral Landscape*, 44.

4. World Health Organization, *Eliminating Female Genital Mutilation*, 3, 22.

5. Ghosh et al., "Estimating Excess Mortality."

6. Richerson and Boyd, *Not by Genes Alone*; and Henrich, *Secret of Our Success*.

7. Boyd, *Different Kind of Animal*.

8. Hsieh et al., "Allocation of Talent."

9. Lisciandra and Migliardo, "Impact of Corruption"; Zhou et al., "Air Pollution in China"; and Varvarigos, "Cultural Persistence in Corruption."

10. Ambraseys and Bilham, "Corruption Kills."

11. Civil engineering has long established guidelines for building safe structures, and this knowledge is widely available. There is no significant difference in the technology used to produce concrete or iron rods across countries. The key difference lies in the extent of societal corruption, which makes it very common for builders to bribe permit issuers, building inspectors, and other officials, allowing them to dilute concrete, use substandard materials, reduce the quantity of iron bars and

other materials, and violate construction codes in various ways. A study examining over 340 earthquakes in 42 countries between 1975 and 2003 found that, even after accounting for factors such as earthquake frequency, magnitude, proximity of population centers to the epicenter, and economic development levels, higher public sector corruption in a country leads to significantly more earthquake-related deaths. Escaleras et al., "Corruption and Major Earthquakes."

The 1999 earthquake in Turkey, with a magnitude of 7.6, killed more than seventeen thousand people. After the earthquake, the minister of interior stated, "The contractors who built those buildings and those who issued permits committed murder. The builders and bureaucrats were involved in organized crime (Bohlen, 1999)." Escaleras et al., 212.

Twenty-four years later, in 2023, a 7.8-magnitude earthquake claimed over fifty thousand lives in the same country. Although the nation's construction codes were aligned with modern earthquake-engineering standards, "it is common knowledge that many buildings in the areas pummeled [by the earthquake] were built with inferior materials and methods, and often did not comply with government standards." An emergency planning expert remarked, "This is a disaster caused by shoddy construction, not by an earthquake." Bilginsoy and Fraser, "Turkey's Lax Policing of Building Codes Known Before Earthquake."

After the earthquake, the minister of justice echoed a statement made by the minister of interior twenty-four years earlier, declaring: "Those who have been negligent, at fault, and responsible for the destruction following the earthquake will answer to justice." Bilginsoy and Fraser, "Turkey's Lax Policing of Building Codes Known Before Earthquake."

12. Mark Twain, "Corn-Pone Opinions," in *Europe and Elsewhere* (1923; Project Gutenberg, 2022), 399, https://www.gutenberg.org/ebooks/68604.

13. Bisin and Verdier, "Joint Evolution of Culture and Political Institutions."

Bibliography

Acemoglu, Daron, and James A. Robinson. *Why Nations Fail: The Origins of Power, Prosperity, and Poverty*. Crown, 2012.

Adi-Japha, Esther, Jennie Berberich-Artzi, and Afaf Libnawi. "Cognitive Flexibility in Drawings of Bilingual Children." *Child Development* 81, no. 5 (2010): 1356–1366.

Aghion, Philippe, Yann Algan, Pierre Cahuc, and Andrei Shleifer. "Regulation and Distrust." *Quarterly Journal of Economics* 125, no. 3 (August 2010): 1015–1049.

Agüero, Jorge M., and Trinidad Beleche. "Health Shocks and Their Long-Lasting Impact on Health Behaviors: Evidence from the 2009 H1N1 Pandemic in Mexico." *Journal of Health Economics* 54 (2017): 40–55.

Ahmed, Resuf, Paul Brimble, Akhila Kovvuri, Alessandro Saia, and Dean Yang. "Ancient Epics in the Television Age: Mass Media, Identity, and the Rise of Hindu Nationalism in India." NBER Working Paper No. 33417, January 2025. https://www.nber.org/papers/w33417.

Aiello, Leslie C., and Peter Wheeler. "The Expensive-Tissue Hypothesis: The Brain and the Digestive System in Human and Primate Evolution." *Current Anthropology* 36, no. 2 (April 1995): 199–221.

Ajzenman, Nicolás. "The Power of Example: Corruption Spurs Corruption." *American Economic Journal: Applied Economics* 13, no. 2 (April 2021): 230–257.

Ajzenman, Nicolás, Tiago Cavalcanti, and Daniel Da Mata. "More Than Words: Leaders' Speech and Risky Behavior During a Pandemic." *American Economic Journal: Economic Policy* 15, no. 3 (August 2023): 351–371.

Akyol, Pelin, and Naci Mocan. "Education and Consanguineous Marriage." *Journal of Human Capital* 17, no. 1 (2023): 114–171.

Aleshka, Aliaksandr, Volodymyr Ilnytskyi, Vasili Bondar, and Bekir Umerov. "Crimean Tatars: Remembrance of Deportation and the Young Generation." Geschichstwerkstatt Europa, June 1, 2010. https://icatat.wordpress.com/wp-content/uploads/2011/06/hier-zum-download.pdf.

Alesina, Alberto, and Nicola Fuchs-Schündeln. "Good-bye Lenin (or Not?): The Effect of Communism on People's Preferences." *American Economic Review* 97, no. 4 (September 2007): 1507–1528.

Alesina, Alberto, and Paola Giuliano. "The Power of the Family." *Journal of Economic Growth* 15, no. 2 (May 2010): 93–125.

Alesina, Alberto, Paola Giuliano, and Nathan Nunn. "On the Origins of Gender Roles: Women and the Plough." *Quarterly Journal of Economics* 128, no. 2 (May 2013): 469–530.

Alesina, Alberto, Paola Giuliano, and Nathan Nunn. "Traditional Agricultural Practices and the Sex Ratio Today." *PLOS ONE* 13, no. 1 (January 2018): 1–14.

Alesina, Alberto, and Eliana La Ferrara. "Preferences for Redistribution in the Land of Opportunities." *Journal of Public Economics* 89, no. 5–6 (June 2005): 897–931.

Alesina, Alberto, Stefanie Stantcheva, and Edoardo Teso. "Intergenerational Mobility and Preferences for Redistribution." *American Economic Review* 108, no. 2 (February 2018): 521–554.

Algan, Yann, and Pierre Cahuc. "Inherited Trust and Growth." *American Economic Review* 100, no. 5 (December 2010): 2060–2092.

Alladi, Suvarna, Thomas H. Bak, Vasanta Duggirala, et al. "Bilingualism Delays Age at Onset of Dementia, Independent of Education and Immigration Status." *Neurology* 81, no. 22 (2013): 1938–1944.

Almond, Douglas, and Lena Edlund. "Son-Biased Sex Ratios in the 2000 United States Census." *Proceedings of the National Academy of Sciences* 105, no. 15 (April 2008): 5681–5682.

Almond, Douglas, Lena Edlund, and Kevin Milligan. "Son Preference and the Persistence of Culture: Evidence from South and East Asian Immigrants to Canada." *Population and Development Review* 39, no. 1 (March 2013): 75–95.

Ambraseys, Nicholas, and Roger Bilham. "Corruption Kills." *Nature* 469, no. 7329 (2011): 153–155.

Amnesty International. "The Rights of Women Accused of Witchcraft Should Be Protected." Reference: TG AFR 28/2024.5253. March 8, 2024. https://www.amnesty.org/en/wp-content/uploads/2024/03/AFR2878022023ENGLISH.pdf.

Anderson, D. Mark, Benjamin Crost, and Daniel I. Rees. "Do Economic Downturns Fuel Racial Animus?" *Journal of Economic Behavior & Organization* 175 (July 2020): 9–18.

Ang, Desmond. "The Birth of a Nation: Media and Racial Hate." *American Economic Review* 113, no. 6 (June 2023): 1424–1460.

Ang, James B. "Agricultural Legacy and Individualistic Culture." *Journal of Economic Growth* 24 (August 2019): 397–425.

Arrow, Kenneth J. "Gifts and Exchanges." *Philosophy & Public Affairs* 1, no. 4 (1972): 343–362.

Ashraf, Nava, Dean Karlan, and Wesley Yin. "Tying Odysseus to the Mast: Evidence from a Commitment Savings Product in the Philippines." *Quarterly Journal of Economics* 121, no. 2 (May 2006): 635–672.

Bak, Thomas H. "Beyond a Simple 'Yes' and 'No.'" *Cortex* 73 (December 2015): 332–333.

Bak, Thomas H. "The Impact of Bilingualism on Cognitive Ageing and Dementia: Finding a Path Through a Forest of Confounding Variables." *Linguistic Approaches to Bilingualism* 6, no. 1–2 (2016): 205–226.

Banfield, Edward C. *Moral Basis of a Backward Society*. Free Press, 1967.

Bar, Revital, and Asaf Zussman. "Identity and Bias: Insights from Driving Tests." *Economic Journal* 130, no. 625 (January 2020): 1–23.

Barac, Raluca, Ellen Bialystok, Dina C. Castro, and Marta Sanchez. "The Cognitive Development of Young Dual Language Learners: A Critical Review." *Early Childhood Research Quarterly* 29, no. 4 (2014): 699–714.

Baranov, Victoria, Ralph De Haas, and Pauline Grosjean. "Men. Male-Biased Sex Ratios and Masculinity Norms: Evidence from Australia's Colonial Past." *Journal of Economic Growth* 28, no. 3 (April 2023): 339–396.

Barbarino, Alessandro, and Giovanni Mastrobuoni. "The Incapacitation Effect of Incarceration: Evidence from Several Italian Collective Pardons." *American Economic Journal: Economic Policy* 6, no. 1 (2014): 1–37.

Bar-Haim, Yair, Talee Ziv, Dominique Lamy, and Richard M. Hodes. "Nature and Nurture in Own-Race Face Processing." *Psychological Science* 17, no. 2 (February 2006): 159–163.

Barlow, Fiona Kate, Stefania Paolini, Anne Pedersen, et al. "The Contact Caveat: Negative Contact Predicts Increased Prejudice More Than Positive Contact Predicts Reduced Prejudice." *Personality and Social Psychology Bulletin* 38, no. 12 (2012): 1629–1643.

Barro-Lee Dataset. "Education Attainment for Population Aged 25–64, Female Population." GitHub. Accessed April 1, 2024. https://barrolee.github.io/BarroLeeDataSet/BLv3.html.

Bassi, Vittorio, and Imran Rasul. "Persuasion: A Case Study of Papal Influences on Fertility-Related Beliefs and Behavior." *American Economic Journal: Applied Economics* 9, no. 4 (October 2017): 250–302.

Basten, Ulrike, Kirsten Hilger, and Christian J. Fiebach. "Where Smart Brains Are Different: A Quantitative Meta-Analysis of Functional and Structural Brain Imaging Studies on Intelligence." *Intelligence* 51 (2015): 10–27.

Bastian, Adolf. *Die Deutsche Expedition an der Loango-Küste.* Hermann Costenoble, 1874. Practices." *American Economic Review* 111, no. 6 (June 2021): 1880–1917.

Bau, Natalie. 2021. "Can Policy Change Culture? Government Pension Plans and Traditional Kinship Practices." *American Economic Review* 111, no. 6: 1880–1917.

Bazzi, Samuel, Martin Fiszbein, and Mesay Gebresilasse. "Frontier Culture: The Roots and Persistence of 'Rugged Individualism' in the United States." *Econometrica* 88, no. 6 (November 2020): 2329–2368.

BBC News. "Tanzania Arrests 23 over Killing of Seven 'Witches.'" *BBC News*, October 10, 2014. https://www.bbc.com/news/world-africa-29572974.

Becker, Anke. "On the Economic Origins of Concerns over Women's Chastidy." *Review of Economic Studies* 92, no. 4 (2025): 2303–2329.

Becker, Gary S. "Crime and Punishment: An Economic Approach." *Journal of Political Economy* 76, no. 2 (1968): 169–217.

Becker, Sascha O., Katrin Boeckh, Chtista Hainz, and Ludger Woessmann. "The Empire is Dead, Long Live the Empire! Long-Run Persistence of Trust and Corruption in the Bureaucracy." *Economic Journal* 126, no. 590 (February 2016): 40–74.

Becker, Sascha O., Lukas Mergele, and Ludger Woessmann. "The Separation and Reunification of Germany: Rethinking a Natural Experiment Interpretation of the Enduring Effects of Communism." *Journal of Economic Perspectives* 34, no. 2 (Spring 2020): 143–171.

Becker, Sascha O., Markus Nagler, and Ludger Woessmann. "Education and Religious Participation: City-Level Evidence from Germany's Secularization Period 1890–1930." *Journal of Economic Growth* 22, no. 3 (March 2017): 273–311.

Becker, Sascha O., and Luigi Pascali. "Religion, Division of Labor, and Conflict: Anti-Semitism in Germany over 600 Years." *American Economic Review* 109, no. 5 (2019): 1764–1804.

Benabou, Roland, and Efe A. Ok. "Social Mobility and the Demand for Redistribution: The POUM Hypothesis." *Quarterly Journal of Economics* 116, no. 2 (2001): 447–487.

Benabou, Roland, and Jean Tirole. "Laws and Norms." NBER Working Paper No. 17579, November 2011. https://www.nber.org/papers/w17579.

Berger, Joël, and Debra Hevenstone. "Norm Enforcement in the City Revisited: An International Field Experiment of Altruistic Punishment, Norm Maintenance, and Broken Windows." *Rationality and Society* 28, no. 3 (2016): 299–319.

Bernhard, Helen, Ernst Fehr, and Urs Fischbacher. "Group Affiliation and Altruistic Norm Enforcement." *American Economic Review* 96, no. 2 (May 2006): 217–221.

Bezzola, Ladina, Susan Mérillat, Christian Gaser, and Lutz Jäncke. "Training-Induced Neural Plasticity in Golf Novices." *Journal of Neuroscience* 31, no. 35 (2011): 12444–12448.

Bialystok, Ellen. "The Bilingual Adaptation: How Minds Accommodate Experience." *Psychological Bulletin* 143, no. 3 (2017): 233–262.

Bialystok, Ellen. *Where Language Meets Thought: Selected Works of Ellen Bialystok*. Routledge, 2024.

Bialystok, Ellen, Fergus I. M. Craik, and Morris Freedman. "Bilingualism as a Protection Against the Onset of Symptoms of Dementia." *Neuropsychologia* 45, no. 2 (2007): 459–464.

Bialystok, Ellen, Fergus I. M. Craik, Raymond Klein, and Mythili Viswanathan. "Bilingualism, Aging, and Cognitive Control: Evidence from the Simon Task." *Psychology and Aging* 19, no. 2 (2004): 290–303.

Bicchieri, Cristina. *Norms in the Wild: How to Diagnose, Measure, and Change Social Norms*. Oxford University Press, 2017.

Bicchieri, Cristina, and Erte Xiao. "Do the Right Thing: But Only if Others Do So." *Journal of Behavioral Decision Making* 22, no. 2 (April 2009): 191–208.

Bielen, Samantha, Wim Marneffe, and Naci Mocan. "Racial Bias and In-Group Bias in Virtual Reality Courtrooms." *Journal of Law and Economics* 64, no. 2 (May 2021): 269–300.

Bilginsoy, Zeynep, and Suzan Fraser. "Turkey's Lax Policing of Building Codes Known Before Quake." AP News, February 10, 2023. https://apnews.com/article/politics-2023-turkey-syria-earthquake-government-istanbul-fbd6af578a6056569879b5ef6c55d322.

Billig, Michael, and Henri Tajfel. "Social Categorization and Similarity in Intergroup Behaviour." *European Journal of Social Psychology* 3, no. 1 (1973): 27–52.

Bisin, Alberto, and Thierry Verdier. "The Economics of Cultural Transmission and Socialization." In *Handbook of Social Economics*, vol 1A, edited by Jess Benhabib, Alberto Bisin, and Matthew O. Jackson. Elsevier Science, 2011.

Bisin, Alberto, and Thierry Verdier. "On the Joint Evolution of Culture and Political Institutions: Elites and Civil Society." *Journal of Political Economy* 132, no. 5 (2024): 1485–1564.

Björklund, Anders. Mikael Lindahl, and Erik Plug. "The Origins of Intergenerational Associations: Lessons from Swedish Adoption Data." *Quarterly Journal of Economics* 121, no. 3 (August 2006): 999–1028.

Blau, Francine D., Lawrence M. Kahn, Peter Brummund, Jason Cook, and Miriam Larson-Koester. "Is There Still Son Preference in the United States?" *Journal of Population Economics* 33, (January 2020): 709–750.

Blom, Elma, Aylin C. Küntay, Marielle Messer, Josje Verhagen, and Paul Leseman. "The Benefits of Being Bilingual: Working Memory in Bilingual Turkish–Dutch Children." *Journal of Experimental Child Psychology* 128 (2014): 105–119.

Bloom, Paul. *Just Babies: The Origins of Good and Evil*. Crown Publishers, 2013.

Boroditsky, Lera. "Does Language Shape Thought? Mandarin and English Speakers' Conceptions of Time." *Cognitive Psychology* 43, no 1 (August 2001): 1–22.

Boroditsky, Lera, and Alice Gaby. "Remembrances of Times East: Absolute Spatial Representations of Time in an Australian Aboriginal Community." *Psychological Science* 21, no. 11 (November 2010): 1635–1639.

Boroditsky, Lera, and Lauren A. Schmidt. "Sex, Syntax, and Semantics." In *Language in Mind: Advances in the Study of Language and Thought*, edited by Dedre Gentner and Susan Goldin-Meadow. MIT Press, 2003.

Boserup, Ester. *Women's Role in Economic Development*. George Allen and Unwin, 1970.

Bottazzi, Laura, Marco Da Rin, and Thomas Hellman. "The Importance of Trust for Investment: Evidence from Venture Capital." *Review of Financial Studies* 29, no. 9 (September 2016): 2283–2318.

Boyd, Robert. *A Different Kind of Animal: How Culture Transformed Our Species*. Princeton University Press, 2018.

Boyd, Robert, and Peter J. Richerson. *The Origin and Evolution of Cultures*. Oxford University Press, 2005.

Boysen, Sarah T., and Gary G. Berntson. "Responses to Quantity: Perceptual Versus Cognitive Mechanisms in Chimpanzees (*Pan troglodytes*)." *Journal of Experimental Psychology: Animal Behavior Processes* 21, no. 1 (1995): 82–86.

Boysen, S. T., G. G. Berntson, M. B. Hannan, and J. T. Cacioppo. "Quantity-Based Inference and Symbolic Representations in Chimpanzees (*Pan troglodytes*)." *Journal of Experimental Psychology: Animal Behavior Processes* 22, no. 1 (1996): 76–86.

Bratton, William J. "Broken Windows and Quality-of-Life Policing in New York City." *NYPD*, 2015. https://www.nyc.gov/assets/nypd/downloads/pdf/analysis_and_planning/qol.pdf.

Bray, Kerry, Nils Braakmann, and John Wildman. "Austerity, Welfare Cuts and Hate Crime: Evidence from the UK's Age of Austerity." *Journal of Urban Economics* 141 (May 2024): 103439.

Brito, Natalie, and Rachel Barr. "Influence of Bilingualism on Memory Generalization During Infancy." *Developmental Science* 15, no. 6 (2012): 812–816.

Brollo, Fernanda, Katja Maria Kaufmann, and Eliana La Ferrara. "Learning Spillovers in Conditional Welfare Programmes: Evidence from Brazil." *Economic Journal* 130, no. 628 (May 2020): 853–879.

Brown, Heather, and Marjon Van der Pol. "Intergenerational Transfer of Time and Risk Preferences." *Journal of Economic Psychology* 49 (2015): 187–204.

Brown, Meta, John Grigsby, Wilbert Van Der Klaauw, Jaya Wen, and Basit Zafar. "Financial Education and the Debt Behavior of the Young." *Review of Financial Studies* 29, no. 9 (September 2016): 2490–2522.

Brown, Ryan P. *Honor Bound: How a Cultural Ideal Has Shaped the American Psyche.* Oxford University Press, 2016.

B. S., Pooja, and Vasudeva Guddattu. "Understanding the Change in the Prevalence and Factors Influencing the Childhood Stunting Using District-Level Data from NFHS-4 and NFHS-5 in India." *INQUIRY: The Journal of Health Care Organization, Provision, and Financing* 59 (2022): 1–10.

Buonanno, Paolo, and Steven Raphael. "Incarceration and Incapacitation: Evidence from the 2006 Italian Collective Pardon." *American Economic Review* 103, no. 6 (October 2013): 2437–2465.

Burro, Giovanni, Rebecca McDonald, Daniel Read, and Umar Taj. "Patience Decreases with Age for the Poor but Not for the Rich: An International Comparison." *Journal of Economic Behavior & Organization* 193, (January 2022): 596–621.

Burzynska, Agnieszka Z., Irene E. Nagel, Claudia Preuschhof, et al. "Cortical Thickness Is Linked to Executive Functioning in Adulthood and Aging." *Human Brain Mapping* 33, no. 7 (2012): 1607–1620.

Buss, David M. *The Dangerous Passion: Why Jealousy Is as Necessary as Love and Sex.* Free Press, 2000.

Buss, David M., Randy J. Larsen, Drew Westen, and Jennifer Semmelroth. "Sex Differences in Jealousy: Evolution, Physiology, and Psychology." *Psychological Science* 3, no. 4 (July 1992): 251–256.

Calvo, Alejandra, and Ellen Bialystok. "Independent Effects of Bilingualism and Socioeconomic Status on Language Ability and Executive Functioning." *Cognition* 130, no. 3 (2014): 278–288.

Cannonier, Colin, and Naci Mocan. "The Impact of Education on Women's Preferences for Gender Equality: Evidence from Sierra Leone." *Journal of Demographic Economics* 84, no. 1 (March 2018): 3–40.

Cantoni, Davide, Yuyu Chen, David Y. Yang, Noam Yuchtman, and Y. Jane Zhang. "Curriculum and Ideology." *Journal of Political Economy* 125, no. 2 (2017): 338–392.

Cao, Yiming, Benjamin Enke, Armin Falk, Paola Giuliano, and Nathan Nunn. "Herding, Warfare, and a Culture of Honor: Global Evidence." NBER Working Paper No. 29250, September 2021. https://www.nber.org/papers/w29250.

Cappelen, Alexander W., Benjamin Enke, and Bertil Tungodden. "Universalism: Global Evidence." *American Economic Review* 115, no. 1 (2025): 43–76.

Carranza, Eliana. "Soil Endowments, Female Labor Force Participation, and the Demographic Deficit of Women in India." *American Economic Journal: Applied Economics* 6, no. 4 (October 2014): 197–225.

Carrell, Scott E., Mark Hoekstra, and James E. West. "The Impact of College Diversity on Behavior Toward Minorities." *American Economic Journal: Economic Policy* 11, no. 4 (November 2019): 159–182.

Carrell, Scott E., Frederick V. Malmstrom, and James E. West. "Peer Effects in Academic Cheating." *Journal of Human Resources* 43, no. 1 (2008): 173–207.

Castro, Lucio, and Carlos Scartascini. "Tax Compliance and Enforcement in the Pampas: Evidence from a Field Experiment." *Journal of Economic Behavior & Organization* 116 (August 2015): 65–82.

Cattell, Raymond B. *Intelligence: Its Structure, Growth, and Action*. North-Holland, 1987.

Cesur, Resul, Travis Freidman, and Joseph J. Sabia. "War, Traumatic Health Shocks, and Religiosity." *Journal of Economic Behavior & Organization* 179 (2020): 475–502.

Cesur, Resul, and Naci Mocan. "Education, Religion, and Voter Preference in a Muslim Country." *Journal of Population Economics* 31, no. 1 (January 2018): 1–44.

Chabris, Christopher F., David Laibson, Carrie L. Morris, Jonathan P. Schuldt, and Dmitry Taubinsky. "Individual Laboratory-Measured Discount Rates Predict Field Behavior." *Journal of Risk and Uncertainty* 37 (October 2008): 237–269.

Chen, M. Keith. "The Effect of Language on Economic Behavior: Evidence from Savings Rates, Health Behaviors, and Retirement Assets." *American Economic Review* 103, no. 2 (April 2013): 690–731.

Chen, Pin-Yu, Chang-Le Chen, Yung-Chin Hsu, and Wen-Yih I. Tseng. "Fluid Intelligence Is Associated with Cortical Volume and White Matter Tract Integrity Within Multiple-Demand System Across Adult Lifespan." *NeuroImage* 212 (2020): 116576.

Chen, Yan, and Sherry Xin Li. "Group Identity and Social Preferences." *American Economic Review* 99, no. 1 (March 2009): 431–457.

Choi, Yu Yong, Noah A. Shamosh, Sun Hee Cho, et al. "Multiple Bases of Human Intelligence Revealed by Cortical Thickness and Neural Activation." *Journal of Neuroscience* 28, no. 41 (2008): 10323–10329.

Chomsky, Noam. *The Logical Structure of Linguistic Theory*. Plenum Press, 1975.

Chong, Alberto, and Eliana La Ferrara. "Television and Divorce: Evidence from Brazilian Novelas." *Journal of the European Economic Association* 7, no. 2–3 (May 2009): 458–468.

Cialdini, Robert B., Carl A. Kallgren, and Raymond R. Reno. "A Focus Theory of Normative Conduct: A Theoretical Refinement and Reevaluation of the Role of Norms in Human Behavior." In *Advances in Experimental Social Psychology*, vol. 24, edited by Mark P. Zanna. Academic Press, 1991.

Coffey, Diane, Aashish Gupta, Payal Hathi, Nidhi Khurana, Nikhil Srivastav, Sangita Vyas, and Dean Spears. "Open Defecation: Evidence from a New Survey in Rural North India." *Economic and Political Weekly* 49, no. 38 (September 2014): 43–45, 48–55.

Coffey, Diane, and Dean Spears. *Where India Goes: Abandoned Toilets, Stunted Development and the Costs of Caste*. Harper Collins, 2017.

Cohn, Alain, Michel André Maréchal, David Tannenbaum, and Christian Lukas Zünd. "Civic Honesty Around the Globe." *Science* 365, no. 6448 (June 2019): 70–73.

Colom, Roberto, Richard J. Haier, Kevin Head, et al. "Gray Matter Correlates of Fluid, Crystallized, and Spatial Intelligence: Testing the P-FIT Model." *Intelligence* 37, no. 2 (2009): 124–135.

Corbacho, Ana, Daniel W. Gingerich, Virginia Oliveros, and Mauricio Ruiz-Vega. "Corruption as a Self-Fulfilling Prophecy: Evidence from a Survey Experiment in Costa Rica." *American Journal of Political Science* 60, no. 4 (2016): 1077–1092.

Corman, Hope, and Naci Mocan. "Carrots, Sticks, and Broken Windows." *Journal of Law and Economics* 48, no. 1 (April 2005): 235–266.

Corman, Hope, and H. Naci Mocan. "A Time-Series Analysis of Crime, Deterrence, and Drug Abuse in New York City." *American Economic Review* 90, no. 3 (June 2000): 584–604.

Corneo, Giacomo, and Hans Peter Grüner. "Individual Preferences for Political Redistribution." *Journal of Public Economics* 83, no. 1 (January 2002): 83–107.

Costa, Albert, Mireia Hernández, and Núria Sebastián-Gallés. "Bilingualism Aids Conflict Resolution: Evidence from the ANT Task." *Cognition* 106, no. 1 (2008): 59–86.

Couttenier, Mathieu, Veronica Petrencu, Dominic Rohner, and Mathias Thoenig. "The Violent Legacy of Conflict: Evidence on Asylum Seekers, Crime, and Public Policy in Switzerland." *American Economic Review* 109, no. 12 (December 2019): 4378–4425.

Cox, Simon R., Stuart J. Ritchie, Chloe Fawns-Ritchie, Elliot M. Tucker-Drob, and Ian J. Deary. "Structural Brain Imaging Correlates of General Intelligence in UK Biobank." *Intelligence* 76 (2019): 101376.

D'Acunto, Francesco, Pulak Ghosh, and Alberto G. Rossi. "How Costly Are Cultural Biases? Evidence from FinTech." LawFin Working Paper No. 34, February 2023. https://papers.ssrn.com/sol3/papers.cfm?abstract_id=4147353.

Dahl, Gordon B., Andreas Kotsadam, and Dan-Olof Rooth. "Does Integration Change Gender Attitudes? The Effect of Randomly Assigning Women to Traditionally Male Teams." *Quarterly Journal of Economics* 136, no. 2 (2021): 987–1030.

Dal Bó, Ernesto, Pedro Dal Bó, and Jason Snyder. "Political Dynasties." *Review of Economic Studies* 76, no. 1 (January 2009): 115–142.

Davidson, Helen, Amy Hawkins, and Chi Hui Lin. "The Power of Dragon Babies: Could an Auspicious Year Boost China's Ailing Birthrate?" *The Guardian*, February 9, 2024. https://www.theguardian.com/world/2024/feb/10/the-power-of-dragon-babies-could-an-auspicious-year-boost-chinas-ailing-birthrate.

Davis, Lewis S., and Farangis Abdurazokzoda. "Language, Culture and Institutions: Evidence from a New Linguistic Dataset." *Journal of Comparative Economics* 44, no. 3 (August 2016): 541–561.

Deary, Ian J., and Peter G. Caryl. "Neuroscience and Human Intelligence Differences." *Trends in Neurosciences* 20, no. 8 (1997): 365–371.

De Cat, Cecile, Arief Gusnanto, and Ludovica Serratrice. "Identifying a Threshold for the Executive Function Advantage in Bilingual Children." *Studies in Second Language Acquisition* 40, no. 1 (2018): 119–151.

de Kraker, Marlieke E. A., Ermira Tartari, Sara Tomczyk, et al. "Implementation of Hand Hygiene in Health-Care Facilities: Results from the WHO Hand Hygiene Self-Assessment Framework Global Survey 2019." *Lancet Infectious Diseases* 22, no. 6 (2022): 835–844.

de la Croix, David, Matthias Doepke, and Joel Mokyr. "Clans, Guilds, and Markets: Apprenticeship Institutions and Growth in the Preindustrial Economy." *Quarterly Journal of Economics* 133, no. 1 (2018): 1–70.

Della Rosa, Pasquale Anthony, Gerda Videsott, Virginia Maria Borsa, et al. "A Neural Interactive Location for Multilingual Talent." *Cortex* 49, no. 2 (2013): 605–608.

DellaVigna, Stefano, and Ethan Kaplan. "The Fox News Effect: Media Bias and Voting." *Quarterly Journal of Economics* 122, no. 3 (August 2007): 1187–1234.

DeLuca, Vincent, Jason Rothman, and Christos Pliatsikas. "Linguistic Immersion and Structural Effects on the Bilingual Brain: A Longitudinal Study." *Bilingualism: Language and Cognition* 22, no. 5 (2019): 1160–1175.

de V. Cavalcanti, Tiago V., and Jose Tavares. "Assessing the 'Engines of Liberation': Home Appliances and Female Labor Force Participation." *Review of Economics and Statistics* 90, no. 1 (2008): 81–88.

De Waal, Frans. *Good Natured: The Origins of Right and Wrong in Humans and Other Animals*. Harvard University Press, 1996.

Dhont, Kristof, and Alain Van Hiel. "Intergroup Contact Buffers Against the Intergenerational Transmission of Authoritarianism and Racial Prejudice." *Journal of Research in Personality* 46, no. 2 (April 2012): 231–234.

Diamond, Adele. "Executive Functions." *Annual Review of Psychology* 64, no. 1 (2013): 135–168.

Diamond, Jared. *Guns, Germs, and Steel: The Fates of Human Societies*. W. W. Norton, 1999.

Dickerson, Donna L. *The Reconstruction Era: Primary Documents on Events from 1865 to 1877*. Greenwood Press, 2003.

Dinkelman, Taryn. "The Effects of Rural Electrification on Employment: New Evidence from South Africa." *American Economic Review* 101, no. 7 (2011): 3078–3108.

Dinnoo, Shannti. "Why Do Millions of Indians Defecate in the Open?" *BBC News*, June 17, 2014. https://www.bbc.com/news/world-asia-india-27775327.

Di Tella, Rafael, Sebastian Galiant, and Ernesto Schargrodsky. "The Formation of Beliefs: Evidence from the Allocation of Land Titles to Squatters." *Quarterly Journal of Economics* 122, no. 1 (February 2007): 209–241.

Di Tella, Rafael, and Ernesto Schargrodsky. "Do Police Reduce Crime? Estimates Using the Allocation of Police Forces After a Terrorist Attack." *American Economic Review* 94, no. 1 (March 2004): 115–133.

Dohmen, Thomas, Armin Falk, David Huffman, and Uwe Sunde. "The Intergenerational Transmission of Risk and Trust Attitudes." *Review of Economic Studies* 79, no. 2 (April 2012): 645–677.

Draganski, Bogdan, Christian Gaser, Volker Busch, Gerhard Schuierer, Ulrich Bogdahn, and Arne May. "Changes in Grey Matter Induced by Training." *Nature* 427, no. 6972 (2004): 311–312.

Drago, Francesco, Roberto Galbiati, and Pietro Vertova. "The Deterrent Effects of Prison: Evidence from a Natural Experiment." *Journal of Political Economy* 117, no. 2 (April 2009): 257–280.

Draca, Mirko, Stephen Machin, and Robert Witt. "Panic on the Streets of London: Police, Crime, and the July 2005 Terror Attacks." *American Economic Review* 101, no. 5 (August 2011): 2157–2181.

Driemeyer, Joenna, Janina Boyke, Christian Gaser, Christian Büchel, and Arne May. "Changes in Gray Matter Induced by Learning—Revisited." *PLOS ONE* 3, no. 7 (2008): e2669.

Dunham, Yarrow, Andrew Scott Baron, and Susan Carey. "Consequences of 'Minimal' Group Affiliations in Children." *Child Development* 82, no. 3 (2011): 793–811.

Dunn, Thomas, and Douglas Holtz-Eakin. "Financial Capital, Human Capital, and the Transition to Self-Employment: Evidence from Intergenerational Links." *Journal of Labor Economics* 18, no. 2 (2000): 282–305.

Dušek, Libor, and Christian Traxler. "Learning from Law Enforcement." *Journal of the European Economic Association* 20, no. 2 (2022): 739–777.

Edgerton, Robert B. *The Individual in Cultural Adaptation: A Study of Four East African Peoples*. University of California Press, 1971.

Enikolopov, Ruben, Maria Petrova, and Ekaterina Zhuravskaya. "Media and Political Persuasion: Evidence from Russia." *American Economic Review* 101, no. 7 (December 2011): 3253–3285.

Escaleras, Monica, Nejat Anbarci, and Charles A. Register. "Public Sector Corruption and Major Earthquakes: A Potentially Deadly Interaction." *Public Choice* 132 (2007): 209–230.

EVS. "European Values Study 2017: Integrated Dataset (EVS 2017)." GESIS Data Archive, Cologne. ZA7500 Data file Version 5.0.0, May 16, 2022. https://doi.org/10.4232/1.13897.

EVS. "EVS Trend File 1981–2017." GESIS Data Archive, Cologne. ZA7503 Data file Version 3.0.0, December 14, 2022. https://doi.org/10.4232/1.14021.

Falk, Armin, Anke Becker, Thomas Dohmen, Benjamin Enke, David Huffman, and Uwe Sunde. "Global Evidence on Economic Preferences." *Quarterly Journal of Economics* 133, no. 4 (November 2018): 1645–1692.

Falk, Armin, Andreas Kuhn, and Josef Zweimüller. "Unemployment and Right-Wing Extremist Crime." *Scandinavian Journal of Economics* 113, no. 2 (2011): 260–285.

Fausey, Caitlin M., and Lera Boroditsky. "Who Dunnit? Cross-Linguistic Differences in Eye-Witness Memory." *Psychonomic Bulletin & Review* 18 (2011): 150–157.

Fausey, Caitlin M., Bria L. Long, Aya Inamori, and Lera Boroditsky. "Constructing Agency: The Role of Language." *Frontiers in Psychology* 1 (October 2010): 1–11.

FBI. "Crime/Law Enforcement Stats (Uniform Crime Reporting Program)." Accessed April 10, 2024. https://www.fbi.gov/how-we-can-help-you/more-fbi-services-and-information/ucr.

Federico, Giovanni, Emanuelle Reynaud, Jordan Navarro, et al. "The Cortical Thickness of the Area PF of the Left Inferior Parietal Cortex Mediates Technical-Reasoning Skills." *Scientific Reports* 12, no. 1 (2022): 11840.

Fernández, Raquel, Alessandra Fogli, and Claudia Olivetti. "Mothers and Sons: Preference Formation and Female Labor Force Dynamics." *Quarterly Journal of Economics* 119, no. 4 (2004): 1249–1299.

Figlio, David, Paola Giuliano, Umut Özek, and Paola Sapienza. "Long-Term Orientation and Educational Performance." *American Economic Journal: Economic Policy* 11, no. 4 (November 2019): 272–309.

Fish, Jennifer L., and Charles A. Lockwood. "Dietary Constraints on Encephalization in Primates." *American Journal of Physical Anthropology* 120, no. 2 (February 2003): 171–181.

Fisman, Raymond, and Edward Miguel. "Corruption, Norms, and Legal Enforcement: Evidence from Diplomatic Parking Tickets." *Journal of Political Economy* 115, no. 6 (December 2007): 1020–1048.

Fiszbein, Martin, Yeonha Jung, and Dietrich Vollrath. "Agrarian Origins of Individualism and Collectivism." NBER Working Paper No. 29643, July 2023. https://www.nber.org/papers/w29643.

Fouka, Vasiliki, and Alain Schläpfer. "Agricultural Returns to Labour and the Origins of Work Ethics." *Economic Journal* 130, no. 628 (2020): 1081–1113.

Fredriksson, Per G., and Satyendra Kumar Gupta. "Irrigation and Gender Roles." *Journal of Development Economics* 163 (June 2023): 103076.

Funk, Patricia. "Is There an Expressive Function of Law? An Empirical Analysis of Voting Laws with Symbolic Fines." *American Law and Economics Review* 9, no. 1 (March 2007): 135–159.

Gachter, Simon, and Jonathan F. Schulz. "Intrinsic Honesty and the Prevalence of Rule Violations Across Societies." *Nature* 531, no. 7595 (2016): 496–499.

Galor, Oded, and Omer Ozak. "The Agricultural Origins of Time Preference." *American Economic Review* 106, no. 10 (October 2016): 3064–3103.

Garrow, David J. *Protest at Selma: Martin Luther King, Jr., and the Voting Rights Act of 1965*. Yale University Press, 1978.

Gastil, Raymond D. "Homicide and a Regional Culture of Violence." *American Sociological Review* 36, no. 3 (June 1971): 412–427.

Gershman, Boris. "Witchcraft Beliefs as a Cultural Legacy of the Atlantic Slave Trade: Evidence from Two Continents." *European Economic Review* 122 (2020): 103362.

Geruso, Michael, and Dean Spears. "Neighborhood Sanitation and Infant Mortality." *American Economic Journal: Applied Economics* 10, no. 2 (April 2018): 125–162.

Ghosh, Arpita, Heather Flowe, and James Rockey, "Estimating Excess Mortality due to Female Genital Mutilation." *Nature Scientific Reports* 13 (2023): 13328.

Giavazzi, Francesco, Ivan Petkov, and Fabio Schiantarelli. "Culture: Persistence and Evolution." *Journal of Economic Growth* 24 (April 2019): 117–154.

Glock, Charles, and Rodney Stark. *Religion and Society in Tension*. Rand McNally and Company, 1965.

Goette, Lorenz, David Huffman, and Stephan Meier. "The Impact of Group Membership on Cooperation and Norm Enforcement: Evidence Using Random Assignment to Real Social Groups." *American Economic Review* 96, no. 2 (May 2006): 212–216.

Goldin, Claudia, and Lawrence F. Katz. "The Power of the Pill: Oral Contraceptives and Women's Career and Marriage Decisions." *Journal of Political Economy* 110, no. 4 (2002): 730–770.

Goldschmidt, Walter. "Introduction: The Theory of Cultural Adaptation." Introduction to *The Individual in Cultural Adaptation: A Study of Four East African Peoples*, by Robert B. Edgerton. University of California Press, 1971.

Golsteyn, Bart H. H., Hans Grönqvist, and Lena Lindahl. "Adolescent Time Preferences Predict Lifetime Outcomes." *Economic Journal* 124, no. 580 (November 2014): F739–F761.

Gorodnichenko, Yuriy, and Gerard Roland. "Culture, Institutions and Democratization." *Public Choice* 187, no. 1–2 (April 2020): 165–195.

Gorodnichenko, Yuriy, and Gerard Roland. "Culture, Institutions, and the Wealth of Nations." *Review of Economics and Statistics* 99, no. 3 (July 2017): 402–416.

Gorodnichenko, Yuriy, and Gerard Roland. "Which Dimensions of Culture Matter for Long-Run Growth?" *American Economic Review* 101, no. 2 (May 2011): 492–498.

Graham, Jesse, Jonathan Haidt, Sena Koleva, et al. "Moral Foundations Theory: The Pragmatic Validity of Moral Pluralism." In *Advances in Experimental Social Psychology*, vol. 47, edited by Patricia Devine and Ashby Plant. Academic Press, 2013.

Grant, Angela, Nancy A. Dennis, and Ping Li. "Cognitive Control, Cognitive Reserve, and Memory in the Aging Bilingual Brain." *Frontiers in Psychology* 5 (2014): 1401.

Greenberg, Kyle, Matthew Gudgeon, Adam Isen, Corbin L. Miller, and Richard W. Patterson. "Intergenerational Transmission of Occupation: Lessons from the United States Army." NBER Working Paper No. 33009, November 2024. https://www.nber.org/papers/w33009.

Greenwood, Jeremy, Ananth Seshadri, and Mehmet Yorukoglu. "Engines of Liberation." *Review of Economic Studies* 72, no. 1 (2005): 109–133.

Greif, Avner. "Cultural Beliefs and the Organization of Society: A Historical and Theoretical Reflection on Collectivist and Individualist Societies." *Journal of Political Economy* 102, no. 5 (October 1994): 912–950.

Greif, Avner, and Murat Iyigun. "Social Organizations, Violence, and Modern Growth." *American Economic Review* 103, no. 3 (2013): 534–538.

Greif, Avner, Murat Iyigun, and Diego Sasson. "Social Organizations, Risk-Sharing Institutions, and Economic Development." In *Institutions and Comparative Economic Development*, edited by Masahiko Aoki, Timur Kuran, and Gerard Roland. Palgrave Macmillan, 2012.

Grosjean, Pauline. "A History of Violence: The Culture of Honor and Homicide in the US South." *Journal of European Economic Association* 12, no. 5 (October 2014): 1285–1316.

Grosjean, Pauline, and Rose Khattar. "It's Raining Men! Hallelujah? The Long-Run Consequences of Male-Biased Sex Ratios." *Review of Economic Studies* 86, no. 2 (March 2019): 723–754.

Grundy, John G. "The Effects of Bilingualism on Executive Functions: An Updated Quantitative Analysis." *Journal of Cultural Cognitive Science* 4, no. 2 (2020): 177–199.

Guiso, Luigi, Paola Sapienza, and Luigi Zingales. "Cultural Biases in Economic Exchange." *Quarterly Journal of Economics* 124, no. 3 (August 2009): 1095–1131.

Guiso, Luigi, Paola Sapienza, and Luigi Zingales. "Does Culture Affect Economic Outcomes?" *Journal of Economic Perspectives* 20, no. 2 (Spring 2006): 23–48.

Guiso, Luigi, Paola Sapienza, and Luigi Zingales. "Trusting the Stock Market." *Journal of Finance* 63, no. 6 (December 2008): 2557–2600.

Gulino, Giorgio, and Federico Masera. "Contagious Dishonesty: Corruption Scandals and Supermarket Theft." *American Economic Journal: Applied Economics* 15, no. 4 (October 2023): 218–251.

Gupta, Ashish Kumar, and K. G. Santhya. "Proximal and Contextual Correlates of Childhood Stunting in India: A Geo-Spatial Analysis." *PLOS ONE* 15, no. 8 (August 2020): 1–20.

Guzman, Gloria, and Melissa Kollar. "Income in the United States: 2022." United States Census Bureau Report Number P60–279, September 12, 2023. https://www.census.gov/library/publications/2023/demo/p60-279.html.

Hackney, Sheldon. "Southern Violence." *American Historical Review* 74, no. 3 (February 1969): 906–925.

Haerpfer, C., R. Inglehart, A. Moreno, et al., eds. "World Values Survey: Round Seven—Country-Pooled Datafile Version 5.0." JD Systems Institute & WVSA Secretariat, 2022.

Haerpfer, C., R. Inglehart, A. Moreno, et al., eds. "World Values Survey Trend File (1981–2022) Cross-National Data-Set, Data File Version 2.0.0." JD Systems Institute & WVSA Secretariat, 2022. https://doi.org/10.14281/18241.23.

Haidt, Jonathan, and Craig Joseph. "Intuitive Ethics: How Innately Prepared Intuitions Generate Culturally Variable Virtues." *Daedalus* 133, no. 4 (2004): 55–66.

Hamamy, Hanan. "Consanguineous Marriages: Preconception Consultation in Primary Health Care Settings." *Journal of Community Genetics* 3 (2012): 185–192.

Hamamy, Hanan, Stylianos E. Antonarakis, Luigi Luca Cavalli-Sforza, et al. "Consanguineous Marriages, Pearls and Perils: Geneva International Consanguinity Workshop Report." *Genetics in Medicine* 13, no. 9 (May 2011): 841–847.

Hansen, Benjamin. "Punishment and Deterrence: Evidence from Drunk Driving." *American Economic Review* 105, no. 4 (April 2015): 1581–1617.

Hanushek, Eric A., Lavinia Kinne, Philipp Lergetporer, and Ludger Woessmann. "Patience, Risk-Taking, and Human Capital Investment Across Countries." *Economic Journal* 132, no. 646 (August 2022): 2290–2307.

Harmon, Colm, Hessel Oosterbeek, and Ian Walker. "The Returns to Education: Microeconomics." *Journal of Economic Surveys* 17, no. 2 (April 2003): 115–156.

Harris, Gardiner. "Poor Sanitation in India May Afflict Well-Fed Children with Malnutrition." *New York Times*, July 13, 2014. https://www.nytimes.com/2014/07/15/world/asia/poor-sanitation-in-india-may-afflict-well-fed-children-with-malnutrition.html.

Harris, Sam. *The Moral Landscape: How Science Can Determine Human Values*. Free Press, 2010.

Helland, Eric, and Alexander Tabarrok. "Does Three Strikes Deter? A Nonparametric Estimation." *Journal of Human Resources* 42, no. 2 (March 2007): 309–330.

Henrich, Joseph. *The Secret of Our Success: How Culture is Driving Human Evolution, Domesticating Our Species, and Making Us Smarter*. Princeton University Press, 2016.

Henrich, Joseph. *The WEIRDest People in the World: How the West Became Psychologically Peculiar and Particularly Prosperous*. Farrar, Straus and Giroux, 2020.

Herrmann, Benedikt, Christian Thöni, and Simon Gachter. "Antisocial Punishment Across Societies." *Science* 319, no. 5868 (March 2008): 1362–1367.

Hervais-Adelman, Alexis, Barbara Moser-Mercer, Micah M. Murray, and Narly Golestani. "Cortical Thickness Increases After Simultaneous Interpretation Training." *Neuropsychologia* 98 (2017): 212–219.

Hjalmarsson, Randi, and Matthew Lindquist, "The Origins of Intergenerational Associations in Crime: Lessons from Swedish Adoption Data," *Labour Economics* 20 (2013): 68–81.

Hofstede, Geert, Gert Jan Hofstede, and Michael Minkov. *Cultures and Organizations: Software of the Mind: Intercultural Cooperation and Its Importance for Survival*. McGraw Hill, 2010.

Hopkins, William D., Xiang Li, and Neil Roberts. "More Intelligent Chimpanzees (Pan troglodytes) Have Larger Brains and Increased Cortical Thickness." *Intelligence* 74 (2019): 18–24.

Horowitz, Mitch. "The Persecution of Witches, 21st-Century Style." *New York Times*, July 4, 2014. https://www.nytimes.com/2014/07/05/opinion/the-persecution-of-witches-21st-century-style.html.

Hsieh, Chang-Tai, Erik Hurst, Charles I. Jones, and Peter J. Klenow. "The Allocation of Talent and U.S. Economic Growth." *Econometrica* 87, no. 5 (2019): 1439–1474.

Hungerman, Daniel M. "The Effect of Education on Religion: Evidence from Compulsory Schooling Laws." *Journal of Economic Behavior & Organization* 104 (August 2014): 52–63.

Huttunen, Kristina, Martti Kaila, David Macdonald, and Emily Nix. "Punishing Financial Crimes: The Impact of Prison Sentences on Defendants and Their Colleagues." University of Southern California Working Paper, 2024.

Imber, Colin. *The Ottomon Empire, 1300–1650: The Structure of Power*. 2nd ed. Palgrave Macmillan, 2009.

IMDb. "Queen of Katwe." Accessed September 1, 2024. https://www.imdb.com/title/tt4341582/.

İnalcık, Halil. *The Ottomon Empire: The Classical Age, 1300–1600*. Phoenix Press, 2000.

Ingrao, Charles W. *The Habsburg Monarchy, 1618–1815*. 2nd ed. Cambridge University Press, 2000.

Innes, Robert, and Arnab Mitra. "Is Dishonesty Contagious?" *Economic Inquiry* 51, no. 1 (2013): 722–734.

Jacini, Wantuir F. S., Gianna C. Cannonieri, Paula T. Fernandes, Leonardo Bonilha, Fernando Cendes, and Li M. Li. "Can Exercise Shape Your Brain? Cortical Differences Associated with Judo Practice." *Journal of Science and Medicine in Sport* 12, no. 6 (2009): 688–690.

Jayachandran, Seema. "Ten Facts About Son Preference in India." NBER Working Paper No. 31883, November 2023. https://www.nber.org/papers/w31883.

Jayachandran, Seema, and Ilyana Kuziemko. "Why Do Mothers Breastfeed Girls Less than Boys? Evidence and Implications for Child Health in India." *Quarterly Journal of Economics* 126, no. 3 (August 2011): 1485–1538.

Jensen, Robert, and Emily Oster. "The Power of TV: Cable Television and Women's Status in India." *Quarterly Journal of Economics* 124, no. 3 (August 2009): 1057–1094.

Jordan, Jillian J., Katherine McAuliffe, and Felix Warneken. "Development of In-Group Favoritism in Children's Third-Party Punishment of Selfishness." *Psychological and Cognitive Sciences* 111, no. 35 (September 2014): 12710–12715.

Joyce, Theodore J., and Naci H. Mocan. "The Impact of Legalized Abortion on Adolescent Childbearing in New York City." *American Journal of Public Health* 80, no. 3 (1990): 273–278.

Karama, Sherif, Roberto Colom, Wendy Johnson, et al. "Cortical Thickness Correlates of Specific Cognitive Performance Accounted for by the General Factor of Intelligence in Healthy Children Aged 6 to 18." *NeuroImage* 55, no. 4 (2011): 1443–1453.

Kashima, Emiko S., and Yoshihisa Kashima. "Culture and Language: The Case of Cultural Dimensions and Personal Pronoun Use." *Journal of Cross-Cultural Psychology* 29, no. 3 (May 1998): 461–486.

Keenan, Elinor. "Norm-Makers, Norm-Breakers: Uses of Speech by Men and Women in a Malagasy Community." In *Explorations in the Ethnography of Speaking*, edited by Richard Bauman and Joel Sherzer. Cambridge University Press, 1974.

Keizer, Kees, Siegwart Lindenberg, and Linda Steg. "The Importance of Demonstratively Restoring Order." *PLOS ONE* 8, no. 6 (June 2013): e65137.

Keizer, Kees, Siegwart Lindenberg, and Linda Steg. "The Spreading of Disorder." *Science* 322, no. 5908 (December 2008): 1681–1685.

Kelly, David J., Shaoying Liu, Liezhong Ge, et al. "Cross-Race Preferences for Same-Race Faces Extend Beyond the African Versus Caucasian Contrast in 3-Month-Old Infants." *Infancy* 11, no. 1 (December 2007): 87–95.

Kelly, David J., Paul C. Quinn, Alan M. Slater, et al. "Three-Month-Olds, but Not Newborns, Prefer Own-Race Faces." *Developmental Science* 8, no. 6 (November 2005): F31–F36.

Kessler, Daniel, and Steven D. Levitt. "Using Sentence Enhancements to Distinguish Between Deterrence and Incapacitation." *Journal of Law and Economics* 42, no. S1 (April 1999): 343–364.

Keuschnigg, Marc, and Tobias Wolbring. "Disorder, Social Capital, and Norm Violation: Three Field Experiments on the Broken Windows Thesis." *Rationality and Society* 27, no. 1 (2015): 96–126.

Khera, Rohan, Snigdha Jain, Rakesh Lodha, and Sivasubramanian Ramakrishnan. "Gender Bias in Child Care and Child Health: Global Patterns." *Archives of Disease in Childhood* 99, no. 4 (March 2014): 369–374.

Kirby, Kris N., Nancy M. Petry, and Warren K. Bickel. "Heroin Addicts Have Higher Discount Rates for Delayed Rewards than Non-Drug-Using Controls." *Journal of Experimental Psychology: General* 128, no. 1 (March 1999): 78–87.

Klein, Denise, Kelvin Mok, Jen-Kai Chen, and Kate E. Watkins. "Age of Language Learning Shapes Brain Structure: A Cortical Thickness Study of Bilingual and Monolingual Individuals." *Brain and Language* 131 (2014): 20–24.

Klick, Jonathan, and Alexander Tabarrok. "Using Terror Alert Levels to Estimate the Effect of Police on Crime." *Journal of Law and Economics* 48, no. 1 (April 2005): 267–279.

Kovács, Ágnes Melinda, and Jacques Mehler. "Cognitive Gains in 7-Month-Old Bilingual Infants." *Proceedings of the National Academy of Sciences* 106, no. 16 (2009): 6556–6560.

Kuhl, Ulrike, Angela D. Friederici, Frank Emmrich, et al. "Early Cortical Surface Plasticity Relates to Basic Mathematical Learning." *NeuroImage* 204 (2020): 116235.

Kuo, Lily, and Lyric Li. "Could the Year of the Dragon Bring the Baby Boom that Asia Needs? Maybe." *Washington Post*, February 10, 2024. https://www.washingtonpost.com/world/2024/02/10/lunar-year-dragon-babies-china-asia/.

Kuran, Timur. "Behavioral Norms in the Islamic Doctrine of Economics: A Critique." *Journal of Economic Behavior & Organization* 4, no. 4 (December 1983): 353–379.

La Ferrara, Eliana. "Mass Media and Social Change: Can We Use Television to Fight Poverty?" *Journal of the European Economic Association* 14, no. 4 (August 2016): 791–827.

La Ferrara, Eliana, Alberto Chong, and Suzanne Duryea. "Soap Operas and Fertility: Evidence from Brazil." *American Economic Journal: Applied Economics* 4, no. 4 (October 2012): 1–31.

Lakshminarayanan, Subitha, and Ramakrishnan Jayalakshymy. "Diarrheal Diseases Among Children in India: Current Scenario and Future Perspectives." *Journal of Natural Science, Biology and Medicine* 6, no. 1 (January 2015): 24–28.

Lawn, Rebecca. "Tu and Twitter: Is It the End for 'Vous' in French?" *BBC News*, September 7, 2012. https://www.bbc.com/news/magazine-19499771.

Lee, Hangeun, and Kyung Hee Kim. "Can Speaking More Languages Enhance Your Creativity? Relationship Between Bilingualism and Creative Potential Among Korean American Students with Multicultural Link." *Personality and Individual Differences* 50, no. 8 (2011): 1186–1190.

Leeds, Michael, and Hugh Rockoff. "Jim Crow in the Saddle: The Expulsion of African American Jockeys from American Racing." NBER Working Paper No. 28167, December 2020. https://www.nber.org/papers/w28167.

Leikin, Mark, and Esther Tovli. "Bilingualism and Creativity in Early Childhood." *Creativity Research Journal* 26, no. 4 (2014): 411–417.

Le Rossignol, Etienne, and Sara Lowes. "Ancestral Livelihoods and Moral Universalism: Evidence from Transhumant Pastoralist Societies." NBER Working Paper No. 30259, July 2022. http://www.nber.org/papers/w30259.

Levitt, Steven D. "Juvenile Crime and Punishment." *Journal of Political Economy* 106, no. 6 (December 1998): 1156–1185.

Li, Ping, Jennifer Legault, and Kaitlyn A. Litcofsky. "Neuroplasticity as a Function of Second Language Learning: Anatomical Changes in the Human Brain." *Cortex* 58 (2014): 301–324.

Licht, Amir N., Chanan Goldschmidt, and Shalom H. Schwartz. "Culture Rules: The Foundation of the Rule of Law and Other Norms of Governance." *Journal of Comparative Economics* 35, no. 4 (December 2007): 659–688.

Lindquist, Matthew J., Joeri Sol, and Mirjam Van Praag. "Why Do Entrepreneurial Parents Have Entrepreneurial Children?" *Journal of Labor Economics* 33, no. 2 (2015): 269–296.

Lisciandra, Maurizio, and Carlo Migliardo. "An Empirical Study of the Impact of Corruption on Environmental Performance: Evidence from Panel Data." *Environmental and Resource Economics* 68 (2017): 297–318.

Lottier, Stuart. "Distribution of Criminal Offenses in Sectional Regions." *Journal of Criminal Law and Criminology* 29, no. 3 (September/October 1938): 329–344.

Lupu, Noam, and Leonid Peisakhin. "The Legacy of Political Violence Across Generations." *American Journal of Political Science* 61, no. 4 (August 2017): 836–851.

Luttmer, Erzo F. P. "Group Loyalty and the Taste for Redistribution." *Journal of Political Economy* 109, no. 3 (2001): 500–528.

Luttmer, Erzo F. P., and Monica Singhal. "Culture, Context, and the Taste for Redistribution." *American Economic Journal: Economic Policy* 3, no. 1 (February 2011): 157–179.

MacDonald, John M., Jonathan Klick, and Ben Grunwald. "The Effect of Private Police on Crime: Evidence from a Geographic Regression Discontinuity Design." *Journal of the Royal Statistical Society Series A: Statistics in Society* 179, no. 3 (June 2016): 831–846.

Mackie, Gerry. "Ending Footbinding and Infibulation: A Convention Account." *American Sociological Review* 61, no. 6 (December 1996): 999–1017.

MacLaury, Robert E. "From Brightness to Hue: An Explanatory Model of Color-Category Evolution." *Current Anthropology* 33, no. 2 (April 1992): 137–186.

Maguire, Eleanor A., David G. Gadian, Ingrid S. Johnsrude, et al. "Navigation-Related Structural Change in the Hippocampi of Taxi Drivers." *Proceedings of the National Academy of Sciences* 97, no. 8 (2000): 4398–4403.

Mahajan, Neha, and Karen Wynn. "Origins of 'Us' Versus 'Them': Prelinguistic Infants Prefer Similar Others." *Cognition* 124, no. 2 (August 2012): 227–233.

Malinowski, Bronislaw. *Magic, Science and Religion.* Free Press, 1948.

Marble, William, Salma Mousa, and Alexandra A. Siegel. "Can Exposure to Celebrities Reduce Prejudice? The Effect of Mohamed Salah on Islamophobic Behaviors and Attitudes." *American Political Science Review* 115, no. 4 (2021): 1111–1128.

Marian, Viorica. *The Power of Language: How the Codes We Use to Think, Speak, and Live Transform Our Minds*. Dutton, 2023.

Martensson, Johan, Johan Eriksson, Nils Christian Bodammer, et al. "Growth of Language-Related Brain Areas After Foreign Language Learning." *NeuroImage* 63, no. 1 (2012): 240–244.

Martín, Jesús, Pablo Branas-Garza, Antonio M. Espín, Juan F. Gamella, and Benedikt Herrmann. "The Appropriate Response of Spanish Gitanos: Short-Run Orientation Beyond Current Socio-Economic Status." *Evolution and Human Behavior* 40, no. 1 (January 2019): 12–22.

Mazar, Nina, On Amir, and Dan Ariely. "The Dishonesty of Honest People: A Theory of Self-Concept Maintenance." *Journal of Marketing Research* 45, no. 6 (2008): 633–644.

McCloskey, Deirdre Nansen. "Max U Versus Humanomics: A Critique of Neo-Institutionalism." *Journal of Institutional Economics* 12, no. 1 (March 2016): 1–27.

Mechelli, Andrea, Jenny T. Crinion, Uta Noppeney, et al. "Structural Plasticity in the Bilingual Brain." *Nature* 431, no. 7010 (2004): 757–757.

Meier, Stephan, and Charles Sprenger. "Present-Biased Preferences and Credit Card Borrowing." *American Economic Journal: Applied Economics* 2, no. 1 (January 2010): 193–210.

Mello, Steven. "More COPS, Less Crime." *Journal of Public Economics* 172 (April 2019): 174–200.

Menderski, Maggie. "7 Things You Didn't Know about the Trailblazing Black Jockeys at the Kentucky Derby." *Courier Journal*, updated April 23, 2024. https://www.courier-journal.com/story/entertainment/events/kentucky-derby/derby-101/2024/02/02/black-jockeys-dominated-the-kentucky-derby-in-in-the-19th-century/72123291007/.

Michalopoulos, Stelios, and Melanie Meng Xue. "Folklore." *Quarterly Journal of Economics* 136, no. 4 (November 2021): 1993–2046.

Migiro, Katy. "Despite Murderous Attacks, Tanzania's 'Witches' Fight for Land." *Reuters*, March 21, 2017. https://www.reuters.com/article/idUSKBN16S2HT/#:~:text=Tanzanians%27%20belief%20in%20witchcraft%20dates,death%2C%20failed%20harvests%20and%20infertility.

Miguel, Edward. "Poverty and Witch Killing." *Review of Economic Studies* 72, no. 4 (October 2005): 1153–1172.

Miguel, Edward, Sebastián M. Saiegh, and Shanker Satyanath. "Civil War Exposure and Violence." *Economics & Politics* 23, no. 1 (2011): 59–73.

Mocan, Naci. "Taxes and Culture of Leisure: Impact on Labor Supply in Europe." *Journal of Comparative Economics* 47, no. 3 (September 2019): 618–639.

Mocan, Naci. "What Determines Corruption? International Evidence from Microdata." *Economic Inquiry* 46, no. 4 (October 2008): 493–510.

Mocan, Naci, Samantha Bielen, and Wim Marneffe. "Quality of Judicial Institutions, Crimes, Misdemeanors, and Dishonesty." *European Journal of Political Economy* 61 (January 2020): 101815.

Mocan, Naci, and Nur Orak. "Education and Preferences for Desired Traits in Children." NBER Working Paper No. 33135. November 2024. Forthcoming in *Journal of Human Capital.*

Mocan, Naci, and Eric Osborne-Christenson. "In-Group Favoritism and Peer Effects in Wrongful Acquittals: National Basketball Associate Referees as Judges." *Journal of Law and Economics* 67, no. 4 (2024): 731–766.

Mocan, Naci, and Luiza Pogorelova. "Compulsory Schooling Laws and Formation of Beliefs: Education, Religion and Superstition." *Journal of Economic Behavior & Organization* 142 (2017): 509–539.

Mocan, Naci, and Christian Raschke. "Economic Well-Being and Anti-Semitic, Xenophobic, and Racist Attitudes in Germany." *European Journal of Law and Economics* 41 (2016): 1–63.

Mocan, Naci, and Bulent Unel. "Skill-Biased Technological Change, Earnings of Unskilled Workers, and Crime." *Review of Law & Economics* 13, no. 3 (May 2017): 20160017.

Mocan, Naci, and Han Yu. "Can Superstition Create a Self-Fulfilling Prophecy? School Outcomes of Dragon Children in China." *Journal of Human Capital* 14, no. 4 (Winter 2020): 485–534.

Montenegro, Claudio E., and Harry A. Patrinos. "Comparable Estimates of Returns to Schooling Around the World." World Bank Policy Research Working Paper 7020, September 2014.

Morgenroth, Thekla, Michelle K. Ryan, and Kim Peters. "The Motivational Theory of Role Modeling: How Role Models Influence Role Aspirants' Goals." *Review of General Psychology* 19, no. 4 (2015): 465–483.

Moscona, Jacob, Nathan Nunn, and James A. Robinson. "Keeping It in the Family: Lineage Organization and the Scope of Trust in Sub-Saharan Africa." *American Economic Review* 107, no. 5 (May 2017): 565–571.

Mulholland, Michele M., Chet C. Sherwood, Steven J. Schapiro, Mary Ann Raghanti, and William D. Hopkins. "Age- and Cognition-Related Differences in the Gray Matter

Volume of the Chimpanzee Brain (Pan troglodytes): A Voxel-Based Morphometry and Conjunction Analysis." *American Journal of Primatology* 83, no. 11 (2021): e23264.

Mullen, Brian, Rupert Brown, and Colleen Smith. "Ingroup Bias as a Function of Salience, Relevance, and Status: An Integration." *European Journal of Social Psychology* 22, no. 2 (1992): 103–122.

Müller, Charlotte, and Sertan Sanderson. "Witch Hunts: A Global Problem in the 21st Century." *DW*, August 10, 2020. https://www.dw.com/en/witch-hunts-a-global-problem-in-the-21st-century/a-54495289.

National Center for Education Statistics. "Table 318.10. Degrees Conferred by Postsecondary Institutions, by Level of Degree and Sex of Student: Selected Years, 1869–70 Through 2028–29." NCES. Accessed January 6, 2025. https://nces.ed.gov/programs/digest/d18/tables/dt18_318.10.asp.

NCD Risk Factor Collaboration (NCD-RisC). "A Century of Trends in Adult Human Height." *eLife* 5 (2016): e13410. https://doi.org/10.7554/eLife.13410.

Nisbett, Richard E., and Dov Cohen. *Culture of Honor: The Psychology of Violence in the South*. Westview Press, 1996.

North, Douglass C. *Institutions, Institutional Change and Economic Performance*. Cambridge University Press, 1990.

North, Douglass C., and Barry R. Weingast. "Constitutions and Commitment: The Evolution of Institutions Governing Public Choice in Seventeenth-Century England." *Journal of Economic History* 49, no. 4 (1989): 803–832.

Nunn, Nathan, and Raul Sanchez de la Sierra. "Why Being Wrong Can Be Right: Magical Warfare Technologies and the Persistence of False Beliefs." *American Economic Review* 107, no. 5 (May 2017): 582–587.

Nunn, Nathan, and Leonard Wantchekon. "The Slave Trade and the Origins of Mistrust in Africa." *American Economic Review* 101, no. 7 (December 2011): 3221–3252.

OECD. "Average Annual Hours Actually Worked per Worker." OECD Data Explorer. Accessed March 1, 2024. https://stats.oecd.org/index.aspx?DataSetCode=ANHRS.

Oosterbeek, Hessel, Randolph Sloof, and Gijs Van De Kuilen. "Cultural Differences in Ultimatum Game Experiments: Evidence from a Meta-Analysis." *Experimental Economics* 7 (June 2004): 171–188.

Oppenheimer, Mark. "On a Visit to the U.S., a Nigerian Witch-Hunter Explains Herself." *New York Times*, May 21, 2010. https://www.nytimes.com/2010/05/22/us/22beliefs.html.

Orwell, George. *Nineteen Eighty-Four*. Secker & Warburg, 1949.

Owens, Emily G. "More Time, Less Crime? Estimating the Incapacitative Effect of Sentence Enhancements." *Journal of Law and Economics* 52, no. 3 (August 2009): 551–579.

Paap, Kenneth R., Hunter A. Johnson, and Oliver Sawi. "Are Bilingual Advantages Dependent upon Specific Tasks or Specific Bilingual Experiences?" *Journal of Cognitive Psychology* 26, no. 6 (2014): 615–639.

Paap, Kenneth R., Hunter A. Johnson, and Oliver Sawi. "Should the Search for Bilingual Advantages in Executive Functioning Continue?" *Cortex* 74 (2016): 305–314.

Parks, Tim. *Italian Ways: On and Off the Rails from Milan to Palermo.* W. W. Norton & Company, 2013.

Pinker, Steven. *The Language Instinct: How the Mind Creates Language.* Harper Perennial, 1994.

Piot, Charles. "Of Slaves and the Gift: Kabre Sale of Kin During the Era of the Slave Trade." *Journal of African History* 37, no. 1 (1996): 31–49.

Platek, Steven M., and Todd K. Shackelford. "Introduction to Theory and Research on Anti-Cuckoldry Tactics: Overview of Current Volume." In *Female Infidelity and Paternal Uncertainty: Evolutionary Perspectives on Male Anti-Cuckoldry Tactics*, edited by Steven M. Platek and Todd K. Shackelford. Cambridge University Press, 2006.

Pliatsikas, Christos, Lotte Meteyard, João Veríssimo, Vincent DeLuca, Kyle Shattuck, and Michael T. Ullman. "The Effect of Bilingualism on Brain Development from Early Childhood to Young Adulthood." *Brain Structure and Function* 225, no. 7 (2020): 2131–2152.

Porter, Catherine, and Danila Serra. "Gender Differences in the Choice of Major: The Importance of Female Role Models." *American Economic Journal: Applied Economics* 12, no. 3 (July 2020): 226–254.

Querubin, Pablo. "Family and Politics: Dynastic Persistence in the Philippines." *Quarterly Journal of Political Science* 11, no. 2 (2016): 151–181.

Ramakrishnan, Sivasubramanian, Rohan Khera, Snigdha Jain, et al. "Gender Differences in the Utilization of Surgery for Congenital Heart Disease in India." *Heart* 97, no. 23 (November 2011): 1920–1925.

Rao, Guatam. "Familiarity Does Not Breed Contempt: Generosity, Discrimination, and Diversity in Delhi Schools." *American Economic Review* 109, no. 3 (March 2019): 774–809.

Raphael, Steven, and Rudolf Winter-Ebmer. "Identifying the Effect of Unemployment on Crime." *Journal of Law and Economics* 44, no. 1 (April 2001): 259–283.

Ricciardelli, Lina A. "Creativity and Bilingualism." *Journal of Creative Behavior* 26, no. 4 (1992): 242–254.

Richerson, Peter J., and Robert Boyd. *Not by Genes Alone: How Culture Transformed Human Evolution*. University of Chicago Press, 2005.

Riley, Emma. "Role Models in Movies: The Impact of Queen of Katwe on Students' Educational Attainment." *Review of Economics and Statistics* 106, no. 2 (2024): 334–351.

Rincke, Johannes, and Christian Traxler. "Enforcement Spillovers." *Review of Economics and Statistics* 93, no. 4 (November 2011): 1224–1234.

Roos, Dave. "Human Sacrifice: Why the Aztecs Practiced This Gory Ritual." *History*, October 11, 2018. https://www.history.com/news/aztec-human-sacrifice-religion.

Rosati, Alexandra G., Jeffrey R. Stevens, Brian Hare, and Marc D. Hauser. "The Evolutionary Origins of Human Patience: Temporal Preferences in Chimpanzees, Bonobos, and Human Adults." *Current Biology* 17, no. 19 (October 2007): 1663–1668.

Rose, Heather, and Julian R. Betts. "The Effect of High School Courses on Earnings." *Review of Economics and Statistics* 86, no. 2 (May 2004): 497–513.

Rukundo, Solomon. "Witch-Killings and the Law in Uganda." *Journal of Law and Religion* 35, no. 2 (2020): 270–296.

Sachs, Jeffrey D., Andrew D. Mellinger, and John L. Gallup. "The Geography of Poverty and Wealth." *Scientific American* 284, no. 3 (March 2001): 70–75.

Sahgal, Neha, and Aidan Connaughton. "More Americans than People in Other Advanced Economies Say COVID-19 Has Strengthened Religious Faith." Pew Research Center, January 27, 2021. https://www.pewresearch.org/religion/2021/01/27/more-americans-than-people-in-other-advanced-economies-say-covid-19-has-strengthened-religious-faith/#:~:text=A%20Pew%20Research%20Center%20survey,the%20faith%20of%20their%20compatriots.

Schell, Terry L., Samuel Peterson, Brian Garrett Vegetabile, Adam Scherling, Rosanna Smart, and Andrew R. Morral. *State Level Estimates of Household Firearm Ownership*. RAND, 2020.

Schindler, David, and Mark Westcott. "Shocking Racial Attitudes: Black GIs in Europe." *Review of Economic Studies* 88, no. 1 (January 2021): 489–520.

Schonberg, William B., and D. Michael Murphy. "The Relationship Between the Uniqueness of a Given Name and Personality." *Journal of Social Psychology* 93, no. 1 (1974): 147–148.

Schulz, Jonathan F. "Kin Networks and Institutional Development." *Economic Journal* 132, no. 647 (2022): 2578–2613.

Semin, G. R., and Monica Rubini. "Unfolding the Concept of Person by Verbal Abuse." *European Journal of Social Psychology* 20, no. 6 (November/December 1990): 463–474.

Shayo, Moses, and Asaf Zussman. "Judicial Ingroup Bias in the Shadow of Terrorism." *Quarterly Journal of Economics* 126, no. 3 (August 2011): 1447–1484.

Sherif, Muzafer, O. J. Harvey, B. Jack White, William R. Hood, and Carolyn W. Sherif. *Intergroup Conflict and Cooperation: The Robbers Cave Experiment*. Institute of Group Relations, 1961.

Shiller, Robert J., Maxim Boycko, and Vladimir Korobov. "Popular Attitudes Toward Free Markets: The Soviet Union and the United States Compared." *American Economic Review* 81, no. 3 (June 1991): 385–400.

Sieghart, Rudolf. *Die Letzten Jahrzehnte Einer Großmacht: Menschen, Völker, Probleme des Habsburger-Reichs*. Ullstein, 1932.

Sinding Bentzen, Jeanet. "Acts of God? Religiosity and Natural Disasters Across Subnational World Districts." *Economic Journal* 129, no. 622 (2019): 2295–2321.

Sinding Bentzen, Jeanet. "In Crisis, We Pray: Religiosity and the COVID-19 Pandemic." *Journal of Economic Behavior & Organization* 192 (2021): 541–583.

Stevens, Jeffrey R., Elizabeth V. Hallinan, and Marc D. Hauser. "The Ecology and Evolution of Patience in Two New World Monkeys." *Biology Letters* 1, no. 2 (June 2005): 223–226.

Subramanyam, Malavika A., Ichiro Kawachi, Lisa F. Berkman, and S. V. Subramanian. "Socioeconomic Inequalities in Childhood Undernutrition in India: Analyzing Trends Between 1992 and 2005." *PLOS ONE* 5, no. 6 (June 2010): e11392.

Sumner, William Graham. *Folkways: A Study of the Sociological Importance of Usages, Manners, Customs, Mores, and Morals*. Ginn and Company, 1906.

Sunde, Uwe, Thomas Dohmen, Benjamin Enke, Armin Falk, David Huffman, and Gerrit Meyerheim. "Patience and Comparative Development." *Review of Economic Studies* 89, no. 5 (October 2022): 2806–2840.

Sunstein, Cass R. "On the Expressive Function of Law." *University of Pennsylvania Law Review* 144, no. 5 (May 1996): 2021–2053.

Sutter, Matthias, Silvia Angerer, Daniela Glätzle-Rützler, and Philipp Lergetporer. "Language Group Differences in Time Preference: Evidence from Primary School Children in a Bilingual City." *European Economic Review* 106, (July 2018): 21–34.

Tadayon, Ehsan, Alvaro Pascual-Leone, and Emiliano Santarnecchi. "Differential Contribution of Cortical Thickness, Surface Area, and Gyrification to Fluid and Crystallized Intelligence." *Cerebral Cortex* 30, no. 1 (2020): 215–225.

Tajfel, Henri, M. G. Billig, R. P. Bundy, and Claude Flament. "Social Categorization and Intergroup Behaviour." *European Journal of Social Psychology* 1, no. 2 (1971): 149–178.

Talhelm, T., X. Zhang, S. Oishi, et al. "Large-Scale Psychological Differences Within China Explained by Rice Versus Wheat Agriculture." *Science* 344, no. 6184 (May 2014): 603–608.

Tankard, Margaret E., and Elizabeth Levy Paluck. "The Effect of a Supreme Court Decision Regarding Gay Marriage on Social Norms and Personal Attitudes." *Psychological Science* 28, no. 9 (2017): 1334–1344.

Teo, Tracey. "The Kentucky Derby's Forgotten Black Past." *BBC News*, May 4, 2023. https://www.bbc.com/travel/article/20230503-the-kentucky-derbys-forgotten-black-past.

Teso, Edoardo. "The Long-Term Effect of Demographic Shocks on the Evolution of Gender Roles: Evidence from the Transatlantic Slave Trade." *Journal of the European Economic Association* 17, no. 2 (April 2019): 497–534.

Tong, Yunping. "India's Sex Ratio at Birth Begins to Normalize." Pew Research Center, August 23, 2022. https://www.pewresearch.org/religion/2022/08/23/indias-sex-ratio-at-birth-begins-to-normalize/.

Tuchman, Gaye, and Harry Gene Levine. "New York Jews and Chinese Food: The Social Construction of an Ethnic Pattern." *Journal of Contemporary Ethnography* 22, no. 3 (October 1993): 382–407.

Twenge, Jean M., Emodish M. Abebe, and W. Keith Campbell. "Fitting in or Standing Out: Trends in American Parents' Choices for Children's Names, 1880–2007." *Social Psychological and Personality Science* 1, no. 1 (2010): 19–25.

UNICEF. *Addressing Witchcraft in Tanzania: Case Study of a Promising Approach.* UNICEF, April 2021. https://www.unicef.org/esa/media/8961/file/Tanzania-Addressing-Witchcraft-Case-Study-2021.pdf.

UNICEF. "Female Genital Mutilation (FGM)." Last updated March 2024. https://data.unicef.org/topic/child-protection%20/female-genital-mutilation/.

United Nations. *The Sustainable Development Goals Report 2017*. United Nations Publications, 2017. https://unstats.un.org/sdgs/files/report/2017/thesustainabledevelopmentgoalsreport2017.pdf.

United Nations Children's Fund and World Health Organization. *State of the World's Hand Hygiene: A Global Call to Action to Make Hand Hygiene a Priority in Policy and Practice*. UNICEF, 2021. https://www.who.int/publications/i/item/9789240036444.

United Nations Population Fund. "Female Genital Mutilation (FGM) Frequently Asked Questions." Accessed August 26, 2023. https://www.unfpa.org/resources/female-genital-mutilation-fgm-frequently-asked-questions.

United Nations Population Fund. *State of World Population 2020*. UNFPA, June 30, 2020. https://www.unfpa.org/publications/state-world-population-2020.

United States Census Bureau. "Census Bureau Releases New Educational Attainment Data." Last revised February 16, 2023. https://www.census.gov/newsroom/press-releases/2023/educational-attainment-data.html#:~:text=the%20Hispanic%20population.-,From%202012%20to%202022%2C%20the%20percentage%20of%20adults%20age%2025,20.9%25%20for%20the%20Hispanic%20population.

United States Census Bureau. "Historical Reported Voting Rates." Accessed April 19, 2023. https://www.census.gov/data/tables/time-series/demo/voting-and-registration/voting-historical-time-series.html.

UN Women. "FAQs on Female Genital Mutilation." Accessed August 26, 2023. https://www.unwomen.org/en/what-we-do/ending-violence-against-women/faqs/female-genital-mutilation.

Urban, Carly, Maximilian Schmeiser, J. Michael Collins, and Alexandra Brown. "The Effects of High School Personal Financial Education Policies on Financial Behavior." *Economics of Education Review* 78 (October 2020): 101786.

Van Cott, Donna Lee. "A Political Analysis of Legal Pluralism in Bolivia and Colombia." *Journal of Latin American Studies* 32, no. 1 (February 2000): 207–234.

Van Dijk, Marloes, Evelyn H. Kroesbergen, Elma Blom, and Paul P. M. Leseman. "Bilingualism and Creativity: Towards a Situated Cognition Approach." *Journal of Creative Behavior* 53, no. 2 (2019): 178–188.

Varnum, Michael E. W., and Shinobu Kitayama. "What's in a Name? Popular Names Are Less Common on Frontiers." *Psychological Science* 22, no. 2 (2011): 176–183.

Varvarigos, Dimitrios. "Cultural Persistence in Corruption, Economic Growth, and the Environment." *Journal of Economic Dynamics and Control* 147 (2023): 104590.

Vives, Marc-Lluís, Mina Cikara, and Oriel FeldmanHall. "Following Your Group or Your Morals? The In-Group Promotes Immoral Behavior While the Out-Group Buffers Against It." *Social Psychological and Personality Science* 13, no. 1 (2022): 139–149.

Voigtländer, Nico, and Hans-Joachim Voth. "Persecution Perpetuated: The Medieval Origins of Anti-Semitic Violence in Nazi Germany." *Quarterly Journal of Economics* 127, no. 3 (July 2012): 1339–1392.

Vollaard, Ben. "Preventing Crime Through Selective Incapacitation." *Economic Journal* 123, no. 567 (March 2013): 262–284.

Vollaard, Ben, and Daan van Soest. "Punishment to Promote Prosocial Behavior: A Field Experiment." *Journal of Environmental Economics and Management* 124 (March 2024): 102899.

Walker, DeArbea. "Black Jockeys Once Dominated the Kentucky Derby. Why Is It So Rare to See Them Today?" *Yahoo News*, updated May 6, 2022. https://www.yahoo.com/news/black-jockeys-once-dominated-kentucky-225836502.html?guccounter=1

&guce_referrer=aHR0cHM6Ly93d3cuZ29vZ2xlLmNvbS8&guce_referrer_sig=AQAAAB LKiraovKVAMiuX5Oncn7fXhD_rQjVMPurtz6SwhzSYxPlzcXG7ErWkB0sZMAp75FBF-9bJWy5HKL4xPcTQqoORUaZZ38EScIrDNI3Una1Ji6xfN8StOzKgVRjTy0_RWDSpV-ZUapzuAMxjDOsJJAyHvn223tlJuoTkKdtDR8lscj.

Wang, Tianyi. "Media, Pulpit, and Populist Persuasion: Evidence from Father Coughlin." *American Economic Review* 111, no. 9 (September 2021): 3064–3092.

Warren, Donald. *Radio Priest: Charles Coughlin, the Father of Hate Radio.* Free Press, 1996.

Weisburd, Sarit. "Police Presence, Rapid Response Rates, and Crime Prevention." *Review of Economics and Statistics* 103, no. 2 (May 2021): 280–293.

Williams, Brian Glyn. *The Crimean Tatars: From Soviet Genocide to Putin's Conquest.* Oxford University Press, 2016.

Williams, Jhacova. "Historical Lynchings and the Contemporary Voting Behavior of Blacks." *American Economic Journal: Applied Economics* 14, no. 3 (July 2022): 224–253.

Winawer, Jonathan, Nathan Witthoft, Michael C. Frank, Lisa Wu, Alex R. Wade, and Lera Boroditsky. "Russian Blues Reveal Effects of Language on Color Discrimination." *Proceedings of the National Academy of Sciences* 104, no. 19 (May 2017): 7780–7785.

World Bank DataBank. "World Development Indicators (GNI per Capita, Atlas Method [Current US$]; 2018)." World Bank. Accessed July 30, 2024. https://databank.worldbank.org/source/world-development-indicators.

World Bank DataBank. "World Development Indicators (Rule of Law: Percentile Rank; 2022)." World Bank. Accessed July 30, 2024. https://databank.worldbank.org/source/world-development-indicators.

World Bank Group. "The World Bank in DRC: Overview." Accessed April 8, 2024. https://www.worldbank.org/en/country/drc/overview.

World Bank Open Data. "Intentional Homicides (per 100,000 People)." World Bank Group. Accessed May 10, 2023. https://data.worldbank.org/indicator/VC.IHR.PSRC.P5.

World Bank Open Data. "Labor Force Participation Rate, Female (% of Female Population Ages 15–64) (Modeled ILO Estimate)." World Bank Group. Accessed April 25, 2023. https://data.worldbank.org/indicator/SL.TLF.ACTI.FE.ZS.

World Bank Open Data. "Labor Force Participation Rate, Male (% of Male Population Ages 15–64) (Modeled ILO Estimate)." World Bank Group. Accessed April 25, 2023. https://data.worldbank.org/indicator/SL.TLF.ACTI.MA.ZS.

World Bank Open Data. "Mortality Rate, Under-5 (per 1,000 Live Births)—India." World Bank Group. Accessed June 8, 2023. https://data.worldbank.org/indicator/SH.DYN.MORT?locations=IN.

World Health Organization. *Eliminating Female Genital Mutilation: An Interagency Statement—OHCHR, UNAIDS, UNDP, UNECA, UNESCO, UNFPA, UNHCR, UNICEF, UNIFEM, WHO*. World Health Organization, 2008. https://iris.who.int/bitstream/handle/10665/43839/9789241596442_eng.pdf?sequence=1.

World Health Organization and WHO Patient Safety. *WHO Guidelines on Hand Hygiene in Health Care: First Global Patient Safety Challenge Clean Care Is Safer Care*. World Health Organization, 2009. https://www.who.int/publications/i/item/9789241597906.

Yao, Jewelia K., Willa I. Voorhies, Jacob A. Miller, Silvia A. Bunge, and Kevin S. Weiner. "Sulcal Depth in Prefrontal Cortex: A Novel Predictor of Working Memory Performance." *Cerebral Cortex* 33, no. 5 (2023): 1799–1813.

Yuan, Peng, Manuel C. Voelkle, and Naftali Raz. "Fluid Intelligence and Gross Structural Properties of the Cerebral Cortex in Middle-Aged and Older Adults: A Multi-Occasion Longitudinal Study." *NeuroImage* 172 (2018): 21–30.

Zak, Paul J., and Stephen Knack. "Trust and Growth." *Economic Journal* 111, no. 470 (April 2001): 295–321.

Zhou, Mengling, Bing Wang, and Zhongfei Chen. "Has the Anti-Corruption Campaign Decreased Air Pollution in China?" *Energy Economics* 91 (2020): 104878.

Index

Publisher contact:
The MIT Press
Massachusetts Institute of Technology
77 Massachusetts Avenue, Cambridge, MA 02139
mitpress.mit.edu

EU Authorised Representative:
Easy Access System Europe, Mustamäe tee 50,
10621 Tallinn, Estonia
gpsr.requests@easproject.com

Printed by Integrated Books International,
United States of America